10/18 JK

Make College Work for You

Susan Berry Brill de Ramírez

Bradley University

PEARSON

Boston   Columbus   Indianapolis   New York   San Francisco   Upper Saddle River
Amsterdam   Cape Town   Dubai   London   Madrid   Milan   Munich   Paris   Montréal   Toronto
Delhi   Mexico City   São Paulo   Sydney   Hong Kong   Seoul   Singapore   Taipei   Tokyo

Editor in Chief: Jodi McPherson
Acquisitions Editor: Katie Mahan
Development Editor: Claire Hunter
Editorial Assistant: Erin Carreiro
Senior Managing Editor: Karen Wernholm
Executive Marketing Manager: Amy Judd
Marketing Assistant: Megan Zuccarini
Production Project Manager: Mary Sanger
Procurement Specialist: Dennis Para

Image Manager: Rachel Youdelman
Project Manager, Image Rights and Permissions:
   Diahanne Lucas
Design and Project Coordination: Electronic
   Publishing Services Inc., NYC
Composition: Aptara®, Inc.
Cover Design: Tamara Newman
Cover Image: Mark Evans/E+/Getty Images

Image and Text Credits: i–xvii, 1–203: Siimsepp/Fotolia (sand samples); ix: Courtesy of Duane Zehr; xi: Stasique/Fotolia; 5: Mauro Pezzotta/Shutterstock; 6: Wavebreakmedia/Shutterstock; 9: Ilia Torlin/Shutterstock; 11: Pavel L Photo and Video/Shutterstock; 12: Benjamin Haas/Shutterstock; 13: Dmitry Kalinovsky/Shutterstock; 20: Dragoness/Shutterstock; 21: Cosma/Shutterstock; 22: Robert Adrian Hillman/Shutterstock; 23: Sly/Fotolia; 25: Arek_malang/Shutterstock; 28: Anna Furman/Shutterstock; 41, 44: Bikeriderlondon/Shutterstock; 47: Marin Conic/Fotolia; 49: Bikeriderlondon/Shutterstock; 50: Auremar/Shutterstock; 51: Wavebreakmedia/Shutterstock; 55: Shots Studio/Shutterstock; 58: Kentoh/Shutterstock; 63: Dino Osmic/Shutterstock; 64: Ptnphoto/Shutterstock; 65: Racorn/Shutterstock; 68: Ptnphoto/Shutterstock; 69: Istvan Csak/Shutterstock; 72, 77: Merzzie/Shutterstock; 83: Andresr/Shutterstock; 85: Dusit/Shutterstock; 86, 91: iQoncept/Shutterstock; 96: Luna Vandoorne/Shutterstock; 97: Racorn/Shutterstock; 105: Tmcphotos/Shutterstock; 110: Goodluz/Shutterstock; 111: Cartoonresource/Shutterstock; 112: iQoncept/Shutterstock; 117: Ollyy/Shutterstock; 119: Excerpt from the Jacobs essay, pp. 1–12, from *Successful Strategies for Teaching Undergraduate Research* by Marta Deyrup, Beth Bloom. Copyright by Scarecrow Press. Used by permission; 120: Zurijeta/Shutterstock; 121: Ammentorp Photography/Shutterstock; 126: Creativa/Shutterstock; 130: Riccardo Piccinini/Shutterstock; 132: Michaeljung/Shutterstock; 137: Wavebreakmedia/Shutterstock; 141: Pavel Losevsky/Fotolia; 143: Eugene Ivanov/Shutterstock; 144: Michaeljung/Shutterstock; 146: Shots Studio/Shutterstock; 147: Nerthuz/Shutterstock; 153: Merzzie/Shutterstock; 154: Seyomedo/Shutterstock; 157: CandyBox Images/Shutterstock; 162: Monkey Business Images/Shutterstock; 169: Gemenacom/Shutterstock; 170: Sparkstudio/Shutterstock; 174: Wavebreakmedia/Shutterstock; 177, 179: Bikeriderlondon/Shutterstock; 181: Tyler Olson/Shutterstock; 182: Andrey_Popov/Shutterstock; 186: Bikeriderlondon/Shutterstock; 192: Tyler Olson/Shutterstock; 196: Andresr/Shutterstock; 197, 198: Michaeljung/Shutterstock; 198: Pavel Losevsky/Fotolia (pianist); 199: Ptnphoto/Shutterstock.

Library of Congress Cataloging-in-Publication Data

Brill de Ramírez, Susan Berry
Make college work for you / Susan Berry Brill de Ramírez, Bradley University. – 1st ed.
     pages cm
ISBN 0-321-90893-7
1. College student orientation.   2. Study skills.   I. Title.
LB2343.3.B75 2014
378.1'98–dc23

2013045035

10 9 8 7 6 5 4 3 2 1—V003—18   17   16   15   14

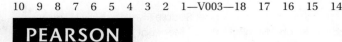

ISBN 10: 0-321-90893-7
ISBN 13: 978-0-321-90893-3

Brief Contents

Contents

3 Academic Skills   61
Commitment, Time Management, Study Habits

4 Strategic Credentialing   81
Majors, Minors, Skill Sets

5 Communication Skills 99
Oral, Written, Digital

6 Campus Activity 128
Clubs, the Arts, Athletics

About the Author

Dr. Susan Berry Brill de Ramírez is Caterpillar Inc. Professor of English at Bradley University. Professor Brill de Ramírez also has an M.B.A. in management and human resource development from the University of Wisconsin–Madison with prior work experience as a research analyst for a management consulting firm and additional training focused on the success of women in the higher education workforce (HERS Summer Institute, MLA workshops). Brill de Ramírez's humanities studies began at St. John's College in Maryland, continued at the University of Wisconsin and the University of Chicago, culminating with nonwestern indigenous studies at the University of New Mexico. As a literature scholar, she is a specialist in the fields of Native American literatures, ecocriticism, folklore, and literary criticism and theory.

Deeply committed to each student's capacity to learn and succeed at the highest of levels, she is a national Councilor for the Arts & Humanities with the Council for Undergraduate Research, a member of the *PMLA* Advisory Committee for the Modern Language Association, and the Book Review Editor for the *CUR Quarterly*. She is an innovator in teaching with extensive experience in college success, undergraduate research, service-learning, ecocomposition, business writing, and digital pedagogies (including using videoconferencing and learning management systems for teaching students in the United States and Middle East and bringing distinguished speakers into virtual classrooms for presentations—from globally distinguished writers and scholars to a Fortune 100 CEO).

A widely published scholar, she is the author of *Wittgenstein and Critical Theory* (1995), *Contemporary American Indian Literatures and the Oral Tradition* (1999), *Native American Life-History Narratives* (2007), and with Evelina Zuni Lucero, co-editor of *Simon J. Ortiz: A Poetic Legacy of Indigenous Continuance* (2009). In her scholarly work, Professor Brill de Ramírez is currently exploring the ecocritical concepts of placefulness and "geographies of belonging" as transformative elements in literary poetics and narrative.

Preface

Humanity may be likened to a tree. This tree has branches, leaves, buds and fruit ... The only real difference that exists between people is that they are at various stages of development. Some are imperfect—these must be brought to perfection. Some are asleep—they must be awakened; some are negligent—they must be roused; but one and all are the children of God. Love them all with your whole heart; no one is a stranger to the other, all are friends.

— *Abdu'l-Bahá, Paris Talks, p. 170 (1995) London, Bahá'í Publishing Trust*

See ye no strangers; rather see all men as friends, for love and unity come hard when you fix your gaze on otherness. And in this new and wondrous age ... we must be at one with every people ... Therefore they are not strangers, but in the family; not aliens, but friends, and to be treated as such.

— *Selections from the Writings of Abdu'l-Bahá, p. 23 (1978) Haifa, Israel: Bahá'í World Centre*

A number of years ago, the news media began to regularly publicize the crisis in education. News stories reported and continue to report college students adrift and unprepared for post-college jobs, colleges unsuccessful in producing critical and creative thinkers with strong communications skills, and American employers recruiting skilled workers from other countries in order to find employees with the needed skills. The PISA (Programme for International Student Assessment) documents had started presenting a clearer picture of the state of global education with stark U.S. statistics. And the current generation of students were being described as needing a stronger work ethic, needing "grit." Around this time, I had an upper-level composition class. Most of the students were excelling; a few were not and accordingly received invitations to meet with me to see how we could turn around their performance.

One young man received such an invitation. As we met in my office, I asked if I could review his records. With his permission, I looked at his low G.P.A.—both overall and even in his major. He said that he was a senior graduating in a few months. I inquired about job interviews, internships, organizational involvement, and leadership experiences. All of his responses were in the negative. When he spoke about college graduation—a time that he should have been looking forward to with excitement, happiness, pride, and a sense of accomplishment—the idea of graduation filled him with dread. He had no clear plans. He did not know what he was going to do; graduation was just a directionless void. I asked if he could put off graduation by a year or two and add to his skill sets, add an extra minor or two, and procure a plum internship or two. But he felt hopeless and resigned to his impending and expected graduation and loans that would need to be paid.

I lost sleep over this one bright student whose potential was being further compromised by a disheartened sense of incapacity. I began to research the published resources for college success to see what would help my students to work harder and to achieve greater success—to "get grit." I wanted to find an inspiring and informational text with concrete advice to help students successfully navigate the trajectory through college and into continued education and professional careers. Having a master's degree in management and human resources and having previously worked as a research analyst for a management consulting firm, I wanted a text that took a behavioral and strategic human resource development approach. I wanted to find such a text for my students, but I also wanted such a text available for every college student. There was no such text available, so I realized that I would have to write it. Thus began the journey forward to produce *Make College Work for You*.

To help remedy the need for such an applied text, *Make College Work for You* is designed to provide current and future college students with a clear pathway forward through college and in life. This book is about each and every student and how students can use their college experiences as catalysts for fulfilling lives rich with meaningful work, rewarding experiences, and wonderful relationships.

Specific areas of strategic decision-making addressed throughout the book:

- Personal health and well-being to provide a better foundation upon which students can achieve their desired goals in college and in life.
- Majors/minors and courses to gain strategic skill sets and important credentials.
- When and how and where to study to yield higher levels of academic success.
- The joy that is part of hard work and engaged learning that, in turn, will renew and reinforce each student's childhood love of discovery.
- The extracurricular activities through participation in clubs, volunteerism, internships, and jobs to gain valuable teamwork and leadership skills.
- Professional networking and mentoring skills for students to practice while they are still in college.
- Oral, written, and digital communication to prepare students for 21st-century jobs.

This book will guide students' progress through college so that they will be better able to develop the needed skills, attitudes, and behaviors to become desired and highly successful employees. And there is no other book that will give your students the complete range of guidance that you will find here.

There are many books that provide extensive guidance for high school students' success in getting into college. There are many books that provide information for college students to make their time in college fun, safe, and active; but the proviso here is that most of these books look at college through the lens of their writers whose college experiences were back in the 20th century. The reality is that students, parents, high school guidance counselors, and college advisors need advice that is relevant for the 21st-century college experiences and the 21st-century workplace.

If, right now, your students are not ready to compete with their hard-working, multilingual math, music, and computer whiz peers in Shanghai, Seoul, and Helsinki, this book will give you the guidance your students need so that by the time they graduate, they will be highly competitive for jobs, graduate and professional schools, and fellowships, and in the workforce, they will be highly valued employees.

If your students follow the advice in this book, fill out the worksheets thoughtfully and thoroughly, and put into action the specific recommendations, this book will help them make the most of college as they learn how to expand and deepen their knowledge base; develop specific and useful skill sets; think critically, creatively, deeply; gain many valuable experiences; discover the joy of learning; and do all of the above strategically, passionately, thoughtfully, enthusiastically, and with relevance for their lives, careers, and service to family, community, and world.

In learning how to navigate their college years in strategic ways to make their college experience as successful as possible, your students will learn how to make strategic choices regarding credentialing and skill sets (e.g., majors, minors, concentrations, classes, workshops) and the various campus organizations (social, service, academic) that they will get involved with. Students will learn the importance of networking while in college, of developing strategic mentors on and off campus, and of using the classroom and study time in effective ways to develop valuable skills and practices for the workplace. And they will learn specific changes they can make to improve their performance in classes, on the job, and in their extracurricular activities.

This textbook is about college, college students, college life, and college success, but perhaps more than anything else, this really is a book about your students, their dreams, and their service to the world. If students play their cards right and "play" the game of college honestly, honorably, with energy and passion, and in smart, deliberative, and strategic ways, they will be well prepared to contribute in big ways to the world, to their country, community, and families: whether that is through their paid jobs and careers or through volunteer service.

Chapter 1, "Daily Habits: Fitness and Wellness," introduces students to a range of successful strategies to make their time in college happier and more fulfilling. Students will discover very specific aspects of their lives that either work well for them or do not, and they will begin to evaluate their lives from a critical and creative standpoint in order to see very concrete changes that they will want to make. In this way, they will see how relatively small changes can effect significant benefits in their everyday lives for their success in college and beyond. The chapter teaches how to take charge of one's overall well-being by (1) learning how to have a victorious attitude, (2) becoming more interested and enthusiastic in life and in different things, (3) discovering ways to nurture one's spirit, (4) learning how to make one's surrounding environment aesthetically pleasing and effectively productive, (5) having fun and learning how to socialize in positive and productive ways, and (6) caring for one's physical well-being. The theme of this chapter relates to three key terms: discipline, balance, and moderation.

Chapter 2, "Class Performance: Preparation and Participation," and **Chapter 3, "Academic Skills: Commitment, Time Management, Study Habits,"** provide the information and tools necessary to improve study habits, increase grades, and make class time much more effective. Students want to make college work for them; they just need to learn what they need to do to make this happen. Most students want top grades and would like their professors to recognize and respect their intelligence and abilities, but most students have simply not learned how to be top students. If implemented effectively, the guidance in these chapters will enable them to dramatically improve their academic performance.

Chapter 4, "Strategic Credentialing: Majors, Minors, Skill Sets," will help your students in their decision-making processes regarding the selection of a major and other areas of skill development. The demands of the 21st century require different skills and abilities, which can often be met through a mix of majors, minors, and concentrations. Gone are the days where one major was sufficient preparation for most post-college careers. Now, more students will decide to double major or add a minor or two. Chapter 4 will help them be strategic about what they want to learn, about what skills they will want to develop, and about what academic experiences they will want to take advantage of while in college. Various worksheets in this and the other chapters will aid students in their strategic decision-making process.

Chapter 5, "Communication Skills: Oral, Written, Digital," delineates specific oral, written, and digital communication skills that are crucial to develop as much as possible while in college. Students' classes in speech communications, composition/ writing, and digital media are among the most important during their undergraduate years. Students should want to work hard in these classes in order to develop their communication skills in preparation for their later careers. All jobs demand skillful communications in one form or another, so it is to your students' benefit to get as much as possible out of each class in which they have opportunities to develop and practice their communications skills.

Chapter 6, "Campus Activity: Clubs, the Arts, Athletics," turns to the many campus organizations with which students can get involved and helps them to understand the importance of active involvement to their developing teamwork, leadership, and problem-solving skills. They will learn why they want to make strategic and balanced decisions regarding which organizations to get involved with and at what level. This and the next two chapters turn more explicitly to the wealth of experiences that are available to college students. College years provide your students with many experiential learning opportunities that are invaluable in preparing them for their post-college years.

Chapter 7, "Off-Campus Endeavors: Internships, Jobs, Volunteerism," addresses the various experiences that students will have off campus in the form of internships, volunteer activities, part-time and full-time jobs, and so on. This chapter provides additional knowledge to help students appreciate and utilize these experiences more fully and effectively as they support their academics and help to prepare them for their careers.

Chapter 8, "Networking and Mentoring: Teamwork, Leadership, Strategic Relationships," introduces students to the world of professional networking and mentoring. College is ideal for beginning to develop professional networks. The first half of the chapter explains the whys and hows to get professional networks started. The chapter then turns to mentoring partnerships, providing guidance to help students find the right mentors for them and their future professional career and to learn the basics in developing and maintaining important mentoring relationships.

The book ends with an **epilogue** that summarizes the importance of achieving a truly outstanding undergraduate education and experience for students.

Remind your students that *they* can really make college work for them . . . as long as they remember that "what counts most is not who you are or where you are but what you do" (Pace, p. 31). It is strongly recommended that students take the worksheets and recommended activities that intersperse the book very seriously. They can do these on their own, with friends, as part of a planning program within their fraternity or sorority, as a structured activity for students in their church, synagogue or other religious organization, as part of your class's series of assignments, or as a required core curriculum for incoming first-year students at your college or university.

As students work their ways through each chapter and as they accomplish the various worksheets and activities, they can mark them off on the "Worksheet for

Success in College" along with the dates that they completed each assignment. [This worksheet could be made available on their course website.] As your students complete more of the book's strategic decision-making exercises, you will begin to see their progress as they learn how to make college work for them.

Instructor Resources

Online Instructor's Manual   This manual provides a framework of ideas and suggestions for activities, journal writing, thought-provoking situations, and online implementation including MyStudentSuccessLab recommendations.

Online PowerPoint® Presentation   A comprehensive set of PowerPoint slides that can be used by instructors for class presentations and also by students for lecture preview or review. The PowerPoint presentation includes summary slides with overview information for each chapter. These slides help students understand and review concepts within each chapter.

Acknowledgements

Many students have inspired this text as they championed their educations and career paths, struggled, and even temporarily met with failure along the way. Each and every one has contributed to the crafting and development of the book. Students who "test drove" earlier draft versions would proclaim, "I haven't been a student like this since seventh grade! It is all your book, Professor Brill de Ramírez."; "In my four years of high school, I *only* studied for a few hours each year during finals, but now I'm taking college seriously. I tell my Mom what I'm doing, and she just cries"; "I always loved music, but I thought that as an engineering major I couldn't do anything else. Now I understand that music can help me be a better engineer, so I just added a minor in music. I am so happy! Thank you, Professor Brill de Ramírez!" These and the other students who have found value in this work have confirmed its importance and spurred me on despite the very real challenges of time and energy. This book is a gift to every student—those I've had in my classes and those who are helped in whatever way possible through my guidance.

My faith in all students and in every person's ability to contribute to the world was instilled early on by my parents, Dr. Robert M. and Dorothy Ann (Retallack) Brill.[*] The quote that begins the Preface speaks to my lifelong belief in the value of every person.

Along the way there have been various guides and networking mentors, both personal and professional who propelled my commitment to education: Tutor Harry Golding at St. John's College, ever-present Professor Alexander B. Chambers at the University of Wisconsin; Professor Heshmat Moayyad at the University of Chicago; Professor Herbert Heneman in the University of Wisconsin's graduate Management and Human Resources programs; Vice President for Academic Affairs and Dean of the Faculty at Trinity University, Michael R. Fischer—previously Dean and Professor of English at the University of New Mexico and my dissertation advisor; Baha'is Jim and Roan (Orloff) Stone in Gallup, New Mexico; Diné (Navajo) artist Chester Kahn and traditional herbalist and healer Annie Kahn; gym owner and weightlifting expert Bob Rosa of the Central Illinois Weightlifting Gym; storyteller and inner-city teacher Miss Juliette

---

[*]I lost both of my parents as a young graduate student, not long after my own undergraduate years. I understand the major tragedies and challenges that can waylay students. If certain people cannot be there as guides, then find others to turn to. It does take a village, only these days our villages are far flung and digital.

Whittaker (the drama teacher who inspired a future comedian, Peorian Richard Pryor); friend and support in the Peoria Bahá'í Faith community over the last twenty plus years Mrs. Caroline Delaney; brilliant contemporary scholars and creative writers Simon J. Ortiz, Leslie Marmon Silko, Evelina Zuni Lucero, Kimberly Blaeser, Gordon Henry, Margaret Noodin Noori; and many remarkable scholars who have actively supported my work through the years: Kate Shanley, David Moore, Richard and June Thomas, Chris Teuton, John Miles Foley, Ellen Arnold, and others too many to name. It has been a great blessing and honor to have known you all. And I would be remiss to not acknowledge the invaluable caffeine provided by the remarkable café 30-30 Coffee and Starbucks in Peoria when a work venue away from home and office was needed.

At my own university there have been many who have supported my professional development. The century-long mission and commitment of Bradley University to educate the whole student has brought to fruition my passion for education and found support in many outstanding colleagues who early on saw the larger needs for student success that this text addresses. Distinguished scholar and professor of management Dr. Larry Weinzimmer encouraged this project from the outset, understanding the value of individual management practices for overall student success in college. It is an honor to have Professor Weinzimmer as the author of the foreword to the book. University President Joanne Glasser also realized early on the importance of this book, and the Office for Teaching Excellence and Faculty Development (now the Center for Teaching Excellence and Learning) provided grant funding for specific stages of the research. My department chair Robert Prescott, departmental secretary Shelly Walker, and graduate assistant Lisa Dooley have supported and contributed to the project in different ways. During the final writing crunch stage, Lisa Dooley stepped up to assist with references, logs, and other needs. And Dr. Dawn Brill Duquès—teacher, education administrator, and lifelong learner—provided a sharp editorial eye from venues as far afield as Turkey and the Ukraine.

I can think of no better publisher for this project than Pearson. Pearson's reach is global; Pearson's growth is visionary; Pearson's commitment to education is stanch and sincere. This book is a pioneering project, shifting the dialogue of college success into a human resource development language and orientation. The needs of students today are paramount, and I am deeply indebted to everyone at Pearson for seeing the value of this work and helping to move this project forward. I have been deeply impressed by Pearson vice presidents Joe Terry and Jodi McPherson (who championed the book early on), acquisitions editor Katie Mahan, executive marketing manager Amy Judd, editorial assistant Erin Carreiro, production project manager Mary Sanger, developmental editor Claire Hunter (who helped manage me and the text through the final stages of writing and through to the production process), and the many other phenomenal people at Pearson commited to the highest caliber of materials for education, learning, and teaching. I am continually humbled by the excellence to which Pearson is dedicated. Thank you all.

For many years, people whom I know who were not academics would ask, "When are you going to write something that we can read?" Here it is. My most heartfelt thanks go to my husband Antonio Ramírez Sánchez Barron and son Jose who have endured my long absences of attention during the processes of research, writing, and revision. I hope that we all have learned through this process as the knowledge and insights in this book guide our own lives and work.

I want this book to be of value in helping college students to grow and develop and make their college years work for them in big ways. Accordingly, I want this text to grow and develop so that it can be of increasing assistance over the years. I welcome suggestions for development and improvement. Please share with me your stories, insights, knowledge, and experience, so that we can all make college work for each other, our communities, our nation, and the world.

Foreword

Make College Work for You

A couple of months ago, I had the inevitable task of dropping my oldest daughter, Kayla, off at college. Although it was difficult for me—more difficult than I would have ever imagined—for her, going off to college was literally the biggest challenge she had ever faced. Not knowing anyone on campus, living away from home for the first time, and trying to figure out how to succeed in a competitive collegiate environment seemed like insurmountable obstacles. But once she learned to navigate these challenges, she realized they were actually incredible opportunities.

As a specialist in management decision making, I have assisted corporations and executives in the tools and methods necessary to improve their companies' and employees' success. As Professor Susan Berry Brill de Ramírez articulates beautifully in *Make College Work for You*, students can learn how to approach their college years in smart and strategic ways with a significant return on that investment. Trying to figure out how to strategically traverse the course is not only about how to succeed in college, but also about how to create a foundation that will benefit you long after you have graduated. So how can you make college work for you? Start by knowing the difference between effectiveness and efficiency.

Think Strategically: The Difference between Effectiveness and Efficiency

In order to be strategic about making decisions in college, you will need to make sure you are effective before ever considering efficiency. Effectiveness focuses on "doing the right things." Efficiency focuses on "doing things right." Strategic decision making ensures that you are doing the right things, such as choosing the right major, joining the right organizations, and getting the right experiences.

- **What is the best major for me?** Let's face it. Trying to decide what you are going to do with the rest of your life is a big deal. I have advised hundreds of students about their majors, their classes, and their careers. Remember that college is a chance to learn and to grow—not only to learn from textbooks, but to also learn about you. Often there is no right or wrong and no one best major for many students. So how do you know what major is right for you? It will be a combination of knowing your interests and passions, leveraging your skills, and being strategic about your opportunities in the marketplace.

- **Which campus activities are right for me?** At most colleges and universities there are literally hundreds of student organizations. Some are professional, some are social, and some are academic. And each organization has different benefits and different levels of commitment. How do you know which ones are best for you—socially, professionally and academically? With so many choices, it is tempting to reach out in too many directions and run the risk of spreading yourself too thin. So how do you strategically choose the right organizations for you when the opportunities seem virtually endless?

■ **The experience paradox.** When you finish college, you will find that most employers require experience; but how can you gain experience until you get your first job? Therein lies the paradox. Internships are a great way to get experience *before* you graduate. Not only do you receive invaluable experience, but you become more employable when you graduate.

Most employers take a very holistic approach when making hiring decisions. Employers today consider many soft-side issues, such as leadership potential, communication skills and the ability to work well in a team environment. Therefore the experiences you have outside of the classroom have become increasingly important. As Professor Brill de Ramírez makes very clear, there are many ways to gain the experience that employers desire, whether that is in internships, part-time jobs, volunteerism, or undergraduate research. You want to follow her advice and guidance in making strategic decisions to ensure your readiness for the job market.

How to Make Intentional Decisions for Success

Where can you go to find the information you need to make the strategic decisions necessary to succeed? Parents? Friends? Facebook? Wouldn't it be great to have a roadmap to guide you through the complexities and obstacles? In *Make College Work for You*, current and prospective students will be guided step by step through this transition so that they can be strategic about the decisions they need to make to maximize their experiences—academically, professionally, and socially. The practical advice in this book will be critically important, not only to your college experience, but also to create a solid foundation for the rest of your life.

In this text, you will gain the tools you need so that you will get the most out of your college experience. Throughout this book, Professor Brill de Ramírez offers both the *how* and *why* for incorporating critical processes into a student's life. You will learn how to strategically choose a major and develop specific skill sets for the workplace. As stated in the text, four years of college prepare you for upwards of forty years of work. Additionally specific tactics are offered regarding how to get the most out of in-class time. As I explain in my book *The Wisdom of Failure*, "Attending to how goals are achieved, rather than the goals themselves, builds strong relationships and solid business acumen" (p. 10). As a college student, you want to attend to how your college, career, and future life goals are achieved. *Make College Work for You* is not only a must read for every student entering college, it is also an important resource for parents, guidance counselors, and college advisors. Professor Brill de Ramírez provides everything you need to know to get the most out of your college experience—and beyond.

Dr. Laurence Weinzimmer

Caterpillar Professor of Business Management and Administration

Introduction
Make the Most of Your College Experience

I will not resist therefore, whatever it is either of divine or human obligement that you lay upon me; but will forthwith set down in writing, as you request me, that voluntary Idea, which hath long in silence presented itself to me, of a better Education, in extent and comprehension far more large, and yet of time far shorter, and of attainment far more certain, than hath been yet in practice.

— *John Milton (1644), Of Education*

Every person who thinks about going to college has hopes and dreams. I want you and every college student to be able to fulfill those hopes and dreams as much as possible. Having taught composition, literature, and seminar-style classes to a diverse and representative population of first-year students for over 25 years, along with advanced classes in my scholarly fields (at Bradley University as a professor and the University of New Mexico as a graduate student), I am convinced that virtually any student who approaches college in a committed and strategic way can make college a great success.

Any student who walks in the door of a community college, four-year college, or university should be able to walk out with a degree, a certificate, or a skill set geared for use in today's workplace. Virtually any student should be able to gain a valuable education that will be of benefit to the world. The book *What the Best College Students Do* (Bain, 2012) surveys a number of exceptionally successful people in diverse fields to learn valuable lessons from them for today's college students. The author Ken Bain affirms the transformative potential of a college education to help you "make better decisions as a juror, citizen, friend, parent, child, student, or in any of the other roles you will play in life" (p. 134). Your job as a college student is to make that happen for you.

As an educator, as a scholar, as a woman and mother, as an American, and as a Bahá'í, I believe deeply in the potential of every person to contribute in big ways to the world. This means that I believe deeply in you and in your potential—both as a student and for your work and life after college. The 20th-century education pioneer Stanwood Cobb was convinced that most people would take their education more seriously when they could see how it would help them to be of greater benefit to the world. In an essay in *The Atlantic Monthly* he wrote, "The writer would state that, in his educational experience . . . there is an immediate and sustained appeal in all [learning] that pertains to human welfare. . . . We like to feel that there is also a spark of altruism in every human breast, and that it responds to the inspiration of human achievement and to the appeal of human needs" (Cobb, 1921, p. 232).

More recently, digital education scholar James Paul Gee (2013) points out the crucial problem for most people in fulfilling their potential: simply not knowing what they need to do and how it will make a difference: "To be agents, people need both opportunities to be an agent and models of effective action. They need to see that taking action can really matter, and they need to see what successful action looks like" (p. 81). You matter, and your learnng matters.

College is a distinctive time in any student's life. It is a time for extensive learning and diverse experiences that are relevant and valuable for you. It is a time for tremendous personal growth. It is a time for meeting new people. It is a time for discovering and planning your future life trajectories → career, family, volunteerism, organizational involvement, and friendships. The opportunities that are available to college students are limitless.

- In your major areas of study, you'll have many opportunities to develop needed skill sets and knowledge for your 21st-century career and work life.
- There will be hands-on opportunities for experiential learning via internships, volunteer activities, class projects, undergraduate research, and on- and off-campus jobs.
- You will be able to expand your horizons with a myriad of concerts and other arts events, lectures, campus organizations, and off-campus opportunities, including study abroad.
- You'll have access to health and fitness facilities where you can learn about nutrition, play basketball, take fitness classes, lift weights, take dance classes, do yoga, run, bike, play golf, participate in martial arts, or swim.
- You will meet people in and out of class: many will become friends (even lifelong friends), many will become important members of your growing professional networks, and some will become mentors for your future career.

And all this is just the beginning. College is a phenomenal time for growth and learning with new and different experiences and many amazing opportunities, including learning about diverse backgrounds, worlds, cultures, and communities. In so many ways, college offers the world to each student.

I want every reader to understand that every college student can make their college education an extraordinary and successful experience. You can fulfill your highest dreams for your desired career and other lifelong activities. *But* to do this, you need to understand the ground rules and you need to play by a 21st-century game plan that will make the most of your college years.

Even if your high school years were not stellar, you can maximize the return on your college investment and propel yourself forward successfully, even within the challenges of tough economic times. Let's take a bit of time here to talk about the realities of the world as it will relate to your career and your college studies.

You can make your college years a great success.

Education, Jobs, and the World Today

It is vitally important that you understand the current and changing educational and employment situations in the world and how they relate to you. Many of the current statistics in the United States about jobs and education are pretty depressing. The last few years have given us a much more accurate, but bleak picture of the state of education in the United States as it has changed over the course of the past several decades:

- Currently over 20 percent of the young people in the United States do not graduate from high school and are, therefore, largely tracked out of the skilled workforce.
- Of those who do graduate, fewer than 30 percent of high school graduates are actually performing at true 12th-grade level. That means that, on average, over 70 percent of high school seniors are not really graduating with the equivalence of complete 12th-grade knowledge and education.
- In many other countries, calculus is considered standard 12th-grade math, yet many U.S. high school graduates have only completed the equivalent of one year of algebra and one year of geometry, and only a small fraction of American high school graduates have completed a year of calculus in high school.

- Elaine Tuttle Hansen, executive director of the Johns Hopkins Center for Talented Youth and former president of Bates College, relates faculty concerns regarding "how unprepared for college-level course work so many incoming students are, even at our highly selective university" (2013, p. A33).

- Around the world, young people are learning English at high levels as their second and third languages while few young Americans have even studied, much less learned to fluency, a foreign language. And many of these young people in different countries are even learning English better that some young Americans.

What does all this mean for you and your future career? I'd like you to think about these facts for a minute. Actually, take a moment to reread them and think about all this for a while. . . . For a long while!

Currently, high school students in China and South Korea and Finland and India are spending longer hours learning one, two, and three foreign languages; perfecting their math and computer skills; and doing this with great respect for their teachers, parents, and other elders. Their respect for their elders means that they listen more consistently, they listen with greater focus, they listen more attentively, and they listen with appreciation—all of which means that they are more likely *to learn more.*

Before even going to college, the majority of American high school graduates are already years behind many of their peers in other countries. Large American corporations recruit in other countries because they say that American college graduates do not have the learning and skills needed for jobs *in* the United States, so young people from other countries are brought here to work.

According to Andreas Schleicher, special advisor on education at the Organisation for Economic Co-operation and Development (OECD), "The U.S. is now the only major economy in the world where the younger generation is not going to be better educated than the older. It's something of great significance because much of today's economic power of the United States rests on a very high degree of adult skills—and that is now at risk" (Coughlan, 2012). Recent news stories in 2013 have pointed out that "one of the biggest threats to the future of the U.S. economy is that more and more of the U.S. workforce lacks the skills needed to fill the jobs being created in the 21st century" (Zeiler, 2013).

If you were a boss at a company in the 21st century and you had to hire new employees, which of the following two candidates would you choose?

1. A friendly young person who has been involved in various extracurriculars; a person who has not really enjoyed studying, but who was able to make the B honor roll in high school and whose college G.P.A. is around 3.0; a student who took two required years of Spanish in high school but no more; a student whose writing skills are not strong and who prefers gaming and Facebook to reading books and who got through high school doing little homework. This college graduate often views parents, teachers, and other superiors as clueless and frustrating; seeks a great job with a high salary; and enjoys part-time jobs as long as there are no "unreasonable" rules that forbid multitasking (e.g., checking FB and texts) on the job. This candidate is likable, but will this millenial perform at the highest levels that the current global workplace now demands?

Or would you rather hire candidate 2?

2. A bright, hardworking young person with excellent English language skills; exceptional math and computer skills; fluency in three languages; top grades all the way through K-12 and in college with two majors and a minor and a steady Dean's List presence; a college degree with high honors; respect for parents, teachers, professors, superiors (and future bosses); expertise in music; membership in honor societies; and the willingness to work hard without expecting an exorbitant salary. This young college graduate enjoys reading and stays current with the news of the day about the United States, his/her family's home country, and the world as a whole, and this graduate worked hard in high school to develop a solid foundational

knowledge of world history, realizing how important that is in understanding the world today. This candidate is friendly, stays physically active and fit, and maintains a daily planner to make sure that there is some downtime most days.

Which of these two job candidates would you choose to hire? Which of these college graduates will help your company excel?

You may read the descriptions of these two college students and think, "OMG! What do I do now?! I don't know any foreign languages, and I was a typical American teen, with different activities, a part-time job, and lots of time with friends. No one really expected me to work hard in high school . . . well, except for the two team sports I played on. My teachers always praised my work and said that I was doing great on the AB honor roll and graduating in the top 30 percent of my class. But now I learn that my B's and even some of my A's in high school may really be the equivalent of C's or OMG even worse in some other countries! What do I do now? I really do want a great job! I love my parents, but I don't want to end up moving back in with them after college because I can't get a job. What do I do now? Is it possible for me to turn things around and become a strong and competitive job candidate? Can I still achieve my career dreams?" Absolutely!

You *can* achieve your dreams, and this book will provide you the road map to do that, but you'll have to roll up your sleeves and get to work! It will be tough, but any accomplishment is the result of effort. You will find it to be extraordinarily fulfilling *and*, believe it or not, fun and often exciting. This is one of the best kept secrets among top students: high achievement is rewarding, and those who work hard and accomplish a great deal while maintaining a sufficiently balanced life are, more often than not, happier than those who achieve at lower levels.

In many ways, this book really is about being happy in college and learning how to achieve lifelong happiness. So, do not despair if you are not fluent in multiple languages and only know English. Do not despair if you were not your class valedictorian. Do not despair if you really like spending time with your friends more than studying. You can make the most of college by learning how to expand and deepen your knowledge base; develop specific and useful skill sets; think critically, creatively, and deeply; gain many valuable experiences; and discover the joy of learning. Do all of this strategically, passionately, thoughtfully, enthusiastically, and with relevance for your life, for your career, and for your service to your family, community, and the world.

Remember the two prospective job candidates described earlier? Here is a third job candidate, the one that I would like you to become:

3. This student is a bright, friendly, and hard-working young person who has been active in various activities; a student whose high school years may not have been exemplary, but who has learned the value of strategic, thoughtful and enthusiastic effort in college. In college, this student has worked hard to develop excellent English language skills (oral, written, and digital), and is graduating with a double major, dean's list presence, two strong internships, and regular work experience. This college student has developed respect for parents, professors, superiors (including future bosses), has had undergraduate research experience with a faculty member and stellar letters of recommendation, a renewed passion about life and the world, and an interest in national and global news. This job candidate is interpersonally engaging, stays physically active and fit, and maintains a daily planner to make sure that there is some downtime most days. This

graduate has combined strong academics with extensive extracurriculars, demonstrating strong teamwork and leadership skills, flexibility and adaptability, and a passion for learning and growth.

Doesn't this job candidate seem even more promising than either of the previous candidates? Wouldn't you like to be this person? This is the job candidate that I know you can become so that you will be well prepared for a happy and fulfilling life, ready to perform at the high levels that today's workplace demands. Even though this candidate may not be fluent in three languages, may not have taken calculus in high school, nor excelled in music, athletics, or academics prior to entering college, with the road map this text provides, you will have the guidance necessary to move your life forward in smart, strategic, and truly wonderful ways.

Approaching College in Smart and Strategic Ways

Phyllis M. Wise, the chancellor of the University of Illinois at Urbana-Champaign, was asked about what undergraduate education should be: "Should we be preparing students for the workforce, or should we be preparing them for lifelong learning? The answer is, 'Yes.'" (Carlson, 2013, p. A26). Wise affirms that an undergraduate education should set students forward on their professional and personal journeys through life: "We must provide students with the tools necessary for gainful employment . . . [and we must] teach students how to learn, how to find information, and how to work collaboratively across disciplines and cultures" (Carlson, 2013, p. A26).

College is about studying. It is about personal growth, maturation, and development. And it is about experiencing, about developing abilities and skills that you will need in the workplace. In the old days, young people would spend years as apprentices to master craftspeople. College is much like an apprenticeship during which you learn and practice many things. If done well, when you go into the workforce, you will be that much more prepared to hit the ground running.

In college you will have many opportunities for work with groups and teams—both in and out of the classroom. If you use these experiences to develop your teamwork skills, you will be that much more valuable as an employee when you serve on a project team or a committee. You will be the team member who spends time preparing for the meetings ahead of time. You will be the team member who comes to meetings with ideas. You will be the team member who listens carefully to everyone else, who makes the effort to appreciate everyone's contributions (even from the weakest team members), who encourages and supports everyone, but who helps to guide the team's work forward in the most effective and productive directions.

This is the type of performance that results when you approach college in smart and strategic ways. Instead of just grumbling one's way through another in-class group assignment, step up to a higher level of performance and approach the group work maturely and with a clear sense of its value . . . not merely for the class assignment grade, but for its value in your own knowledge enrichment and in your teamwork skill development. Higher level group work performance is just one small example of the sort of strategic and executive decision-making skills that you will develop as you read this book and put its material into practice in your own life.

It is important that you understand why you need to approach your college education in *strategic* and *intelligent* ways. It is important for your success in college. It is important for your success after college. It is important in fundamental ways for a well-lived life. And it is important because you and what you will do in life matters.

Preparing for Careers in the 21st Century

The marketplace today is changing very quickly. In the 1990s, globalization meant that American project managers were needed to fly around the country and world to head up project teams and oversee work in different places. The project managers needed to be fluent in English or other European languages because their primary bosses were those in the United States and Europe. And back then, the Americans (and other English-as-a-first-language people) and the Europeans had the best English and other western European language skills.

Now in the 21st century, there are highly skilled employees around the world who can serve as project managers in their own countries and whose English is very strong, even impeccable. And with distance videoconferencing via computers, tablets, and smartphones, employees around the world can easily meet with project team members, managers, executives, and other professionals in other locations without travelling as much. Companies in the United States can work with remote locations much more easily with today's technology. And as the world continues to shrink and become more globalized, increasing numbers of potential employees around the world are being recruited by American companies to come to the United States to work.

Check out the news stories that discuss the current state of unemployment in the United States. Even though there are millions of available jobs across the country, "almost half [of] the 1,361 U.S. employers surveyed in January by ManpowerGroup say they can't find workers to fill positions" (Woellert, 2012). In her recent piece on the U.S. economy, "Why the January 2013 U.S. Jobs Report May Surprise You," Diane Alter (2013) proclaims, "Believe it or not, there are three million jobs going unfilled."

These are indeed stressful economic times on planet earth. Concerns about the job market are taking their toll on students and their families. In Tamar Lewin's (2011) article "Record Level of Stress Found in College Freshmen," Brian Van Brunt, director of counseling at Western Kentucky University and president of the American College Counseling Association is quoted as saying, "More students are arriving on campus with problems, needing support, and today's economic factors are putting a lot of extra stress on college students, as they look at their loans and wonder if there will be a career waiting for them on the other side." This is one of the key concerns that propelled me to write *Make College Work for You*. Your undergraduate and graduate school years can provide you with crucial learning (both academic and experiential) that will position you well for your post-college life and career.

You want to make sure that you are a competitive and successful job candidate, and I want you to be that competitive and successful job candidate. Michael V. Drake, Chancellor of the University of California at Irvine points to his university's "four pillars of excellence" that are a valuable model for any student: "academic excellence, research excellence, leadership excellence, and character excellence" (Carlson, 2013, p. A32). You want to strive for excellence in your academic learning; excellence in your abilities to find, analyze, evaluate, and utilize information and creatively problem solve (the research component); excellence in your experiential learning, which includes significant leadership roles; and excellence in your character development (evidenced personally and in your reference letters and volunteerism). The skills that companies say they need in the 21st century include the following:

- Fluency in multiple languages
- Strong math and computer skills
- Excellent English language fluency
- Knowledge of world history and of the world's diverse cultures
- Strong multicultural communications skills

- Critical, creative, and problem-solving thinking skills
- Knowledge of current events including national and international news
- The ability to work as a key team player on project teams
- A positive attitude and strong work ethic

Upon your graduation from college, you want to convince companies that you are one of their strongest job candidates and very competitive with the employees they are recruiting from China, India, South Korea, and various European countries.

The 21st century is not the 20th century. Our lives are being lived faster. And the game plan is global. Technology and the global economy are driving the greater part of changes all around the world, and the speed of these changes demands that college students today approach their college experiences in a much more strategic way than did earlier generations of college students. The traditional models for high school and college education have much that are still of value, but there are big changes that require different types of choices on the part of college students today.

In many ways, the academic needs of this century are radically different from those of the 20th century. Therefore, it is crucial that you make smart choices that are relevant and valuable for your life and for the world today and the future.

Democracy, Elitism, and the Historical Challenges in American Education

As education developed in the United States over time, colleges and universities evolved toward an increasing higher education divide between long-established liberal arts education foundations that were traditionally intended for the sons and then daughters of the wealthy and elite families of America versus the 20th century's turn toward more applied and pragmatic pre-professional education for all. This divide paralleled secondary school education that was either foundational for future white collar lives or designed otherwise for the "vo-tech" (vocational-technical) high schools of the 20th century that prepared teens for blue collar jobs.

Because of our commitment to democracy and equality in the United States, we like to believe that education is an equal playing field for all young people. But it isn't, and it never has been. As the system moved forward, *where* students went to high school made a big difference in regard to the quality of their education and the probability of *where* they would work or go to college. And *where* they went to college made a huge difference in regard to the quality of their education, *what* internships they would be able to get, and *where* they would be hired after college. So future careers and success have been, to a great extent, predetermined based upon factors such as socioeconomic class, gender, religion, ethnicity, and race.

However, the doors are much wider and opportunities are much greater now than they have ever been. Virtually any student can get a great education at virtually any institution and be well prepared for a great career. Even if your college education is not at Harvard, Yale, or Princeton, if you play your cards right, you can make yourself a very competitive college graduate by, yes, *making college work for you!*

Let's take a minute to look a bit more closely at American educational history and how it relates to you and your college and career success. It is important that you understand that where you are now is largely due to the larger trends in our country: social, educational, and political. The earliest colleges in the United States such as Harvard, Yale, and Princeton were geared toward the sons of the elite founding families. Education emphasized breadth and depth in the liberal arts (literature, science, philosophy, mathematics, and theology). These young men, and later young women, would move in the highest levels of society in business, law, and education. Many would continue in their fathers' (and, later, mothers') occupations. Others would continue their studies further, becoming professors, politicians and statesmen, theologians, lawyers, or doctors.

The 20th century's turn to the great pragmatic legacy of educator and philosopher John Dewey opened up affordable and accessible higher education to the masses along with more applied learning opportunities:

- The sciences expanded into the development of engineering programs.
- Medical education that had focused on the M.D. degree broadened to include formal programs such as nursing and physical therapy.
- The core liberal arts branched out in the development of separate fine arts, communications, and education colleges.
- The traditional liberal arts developed applied tracks upon the foundations of the different disciplines (foreign language studies' shift from literary to language study for interpreters and translators, economics' growth into the various business degrees, the study of English literature to programs in professional writing, sociology's expansion to social work, etc.).

College today represents this history in two intertwined but very different tracks for students:

1. The more applied pre-professional tracks for those learning specific skills for specific careers (engineering, nursing, education, accounting, social work, etc.)
2. The broader liberal arts undergraduate studies programs that emphasize the traditional breadth and depth of a liberal arts education as a foundation with strong analytical, critical and creative thinking, and communication skills

When there is too great a divide between the more applied fields of study and the broader liberal arts, students end up unprepared for the workplace today, in which both forms of education are needed. The applied track is necessary for the specific skill sets (especially in technology-driven areas) that are needed for contemporary jobs, and the liberal arts track is crucial for the critical and creative thinking and humanistic education that deepens one's understanding and broadens one's perspective.

An education today with only pre-professional skills or liberal arts education will handicap college graduates who (1) want to find a job in their preferred career and (2) want to excel in that career with excellent "soft skills" in communications, analysis, and creativity. A narrow pre-professional track teaches skills but without the value of a deeply engaged liberal arts core while a broad liberal arts foundation may underprepare students who graduate without valuable skill sets for their careers after college. Ideally, you want your education to include both.

Currently, many students with majors in more applied tracks (engineering, pre-med, education, etc.) are so overwhelmed with all of their applied learning requirements that their foundational liberal arts education may be shortchanged. Many students try to accomplish their general education liberal arts core as quickly and easily as possible. When the liberal arts foundation of college education is not given its due importance, students will end up with an insufficient breadth and depth of traditional liberal arts learning, leading to undeveloped skills in critical thinking, innovative creativity, and ethical understanding. All too often, students and schools end up giving *short shrift* (little focus or attention) to the liberal arts foundation that has long been the hallmark of American democracy, creativity, and know-how.

Conversely, those students in the broader tracks of the liberal arts, all too often, find themselves adrift with insufficient direction and few practical skills. Many students with majors in English, philosophy, history, foreign language, sociology, communications, and the fine arts graduate without clear career plans and needed skill sets for the workplace.

Both sides of the professional/liberal arts divide are important.

You need a strong liberal arts background with the invaluable critical thinking ability; creativity; and strong foundations in history, philosophy, and literature that employers highly value. You also want clearly defined skill sets and knowledge bases that are part of a well-focused career plan. It is during your college years that you have the best opportunities to achieve an effective balance of the two.

This book is designed in part to help you remedy this problem in two ways:

1. To encourage students who are already focused on a specific career track to broaden and deepen the liberal arts side of their learning, and, thereby, to increase their knowledge base, soft skills, and civic mindedness.

2. To guide liberal arts majors and students who are not in professional tracks to focus and develop specific skill sets, increase their knowledge base, and gain valuable experiential learning (both inside and outside of their majors), and to do all this in strategic ways for their future lives in the workplace.

This balance is vitally important for your career and also for your life. You need to develop both the "hard skills" specific to your areas of study and also the "soft skills" such as critical and creative thinking, problem solving, time management, teamwork, a strong work ethic, and ethical values. You should also build a strong and broad foundation of knowledge across the liberal arts (e.g., literature, sociology, the fine arts) to draw on in the many ways that it will enrich your work and your life, your understanding and what you do.

■ Four Key Factors for Heightened Student Success

Regardless of your career and college plans, there are four key factors or foci that are important to your success in college and beyond. These four areas will center and ground your college life and work and will provide focal points that direct your attention, guide your decision making, and orient your actions toward success, balance, accomplishment, and satisfaction in a life that is well lived.

If you (1) are disciplined and work hard, (2) build on your innate talents and develop key skills, (3) are passionate and in love with what you are doing, and (4) have a deep sense of doing things that will be of benefit to the world, to the country, and to the community, these four foci will orient your college life, your studies, and your life after college in ways that will be rewarding and fulfilling beyond your dreams.

Service: Commitment, Outward Focus, and a Sense of Service

You want to make college work for you, but it is important to remember that what you do in college is not just *about* you but also about what you will be able to offer the world through your work life; through your community service; and through your everyday life with friends, family, and coworkers. College is your time to develop yourself, your skills, your abilities, your knowledge base, your analytic thinking, your creativity, and your empathy and caring—all to prepare you for the myriad ways that you will be of service to others throughout the rest of your life.

Key STEPS for Student Success
- Service
- Talent
- Effort
- Passion

Service
Commitment
Outward focus

Talent
Skill sets
Knowledge

Effort
Discipline
Work ethic

Passion
Enthusiasm
Love of what you are doing

Learning to develop an outward focus while you are in college will make your undergraduate years and your subsequent life and career that much more expansive and rewarding. This is not to say that you should become an ascetic and deny yourself of the pleasures of life. You want a fulfilling life, rich with diverse accomplishments and pleasures; the best way to achieve this is through an outward focus on the world.

Live your life as if it is your gift to the world, your gift to your community, and your gift to those around you. As you live your life with a sense of service (even when that work is paid employment) and live a life of doing for others, of doing things for the forward progress of your community and the world, ironically, your load will be lightened. And your college and post-college life will be that much more rewarding.

In his book *The Nature of College: How a New Understanding of Campus Life Can Change the World*, James J. Farrell (2010) looks at the distinctive roles played by college students in the transformation of their communities and the world: "Students always make history, but now they have the opportunity to make it by design. And all of us have the chance to shape our lives to shape the future of people and the planet. . . . It won't be smooth, but it will be fulfilling" (p. 260). There will always be rough spots, but if you remember to focus outwardly on what you are trying to accomplish, orienting yourself to face the light of service, your shadows will be behind you. Your commitment to others, your developing life of service is what Farrell says is "the promise of our lives, of college culture, and—at its best—a new American Dream" (p. 261).

In 2009 when the president signed into law the Edward M. Kennedy Serve America Act, that act and his words at that event underscored his administration's and our nation's commitment to volunteerism. Your college years provide many opportunities to be of service to others, and this time will help to solidify a strong foundation of service in your life that you will be able to build on and develop throughout your life—thereby always being of service to others and ensuring a satisfying offering of career and life to the world. This topic is explored more closely in Chapter 7: "Off-Campus Endeavors: Internships, Jobs, Volunteerism."

Talent: Innate Abilities, Skill Sets, Proficiency, and Knowledge

Each person is born with a distinctive set of innate talents and strengths. You can look at these as precious gems that lie hidden within you. Your job is to recognize those gems and then unearth them and polish them.

Throughout your life, you want to come to a fuller appreciation of your own strengths and your individual gifts for the world. In order to be of greatest service in the world and your community via your work life, your volunteerism, and your social and family life, you want to build on your innate strengths, talents, and abilities. For example, if you have always been great at mathematics, then you will want to explore ways that you can draw upon your mathematical abilities. If you are a great reader, but always disinclined to science, then you probably do not want to become a scientist. And if you are especially digitally adept—tech savvy—then you would want to explore the many new and developing jobs in tech fields, such as cybersecurity. If you are a person with empathy for others who is a "people person," then you might want to consider the range of human service fields such as psychology, social work, teaching, child care, medicine, and nursing. If you are talented at working with your hands, then various applied fields such as engineering, biology, automotive mechanics, or physical therapy might be good fits for you. And if your natural inclination tends toward hyperactivity, then you probably do not want a 9-to-5 desk job; jobs with a greater diversity of daily tasks (teaching, athletics, food service and the hospitality industry, etc.) would fit you better.

Explore ways to develop your natural abilities to their fullest. Strategic selection of specific majors, minors, concentrations, certificate programs, individual classes, jobs, internships, organizational involvement, and volunteer activities will all help your ability development. This is explored in greater depth in Chapter 4: "Strategic Credentialing: Majors, Minors, Skill Sets." In his great *History of the Peloponnesian War*, Thucydides (2009) records that the greatest successes occur when people map out a clear plan and then work hard to actualize that plan regardless of the barriers along the way: "The bravest are surely those who have the clearest vision of what is before them, glory and danger alike, and yet notwithstanding, go out to meet it."

Effort: Hard Work, Discipline, and a Strong Work Ethic

One of the preeminent scholars of education from the 20th century was UCLA Professor C. Robert Pace, who studied the progress and results of student learning over the course of the undergraduate college years. He developed the College Student Experiences Questionnaire to measure student success in college and to find the primary factors in student success. Pace discovered that student success in college and beyond was largely based on one simple factor: student effort.

This means that the greater part of your success in college is within *your* control. This is really very interesting, isn't it? In other words, even with all the different barriers, challenges, and difficulties that are part of any accomplishment in life, you hold the reins to your college success. By putting out significant effort, by working really hard, and by being sufficiently disciplined to get your work done and done well, you will develop the crucial focal point that Pace found to be key. Pace affirmed that "the amount, scope, and quality of student effort is an indication of the quality of the educational process, and a key to identifying the quality of the educational product" (CSEQ, n.d.). Your college years essentially constitute the apprenticeship preparing you for your post-college career and life, so you want to put out as much effort as possible to make that period as successful as it can be. So work hard. Work really hard, and make much happen.

I want you to make your college years a great success, but there is no way around the fact that college success requires hard work. Angela L. Duckworth and Martin E. P. Seligman studied students to determine factors present in academic success and failure. In their article "Self-Discipline Outdoes IQ in Predicting Academic Performance of Adolescents" (2005), they found that "a major reason for students falling short of their intellectual potential . . . [is students'] failure to exercise self-discipline" in order to organize their time and effort for successful accomplishment. This is especially important today in light of the fact that "all indications are that today's college freshmen are less prepared for college than their predecessors. American College Testing (ACT) Assessment reports that fewer than half of the students who take the ACT are prepared for college" (Nonis & Hudson, 2006, p. 152).

Regardless of the fact that many students are underprepared for college, with the right guidance and commitment to hard work, virtually any student can transform their undergraduate work into a recipe for success, both in college and beyond.

Passion: Enthusiasm, Delight, and a Love for What You Are Doing

If you work hard in college, your work will certainly be much better than if you do not. And if you desire to perform and learn at the highest of levels, you will need to learn to study with a sense of excitement about what you are learning and discovering. Don't worry if thoughts of school and grades and studying tend to make you more nauseated than excited. Don't worry if the very idea of studying fills you more with stress than joy. Don't worry if studying is definitely not what you think of when you imagine joyful activities. You can transform your college experience step by step and day by day into an absolutely wonderful experience, filled with the magic of learning, the magic of discovery, the magic of accomplishment, the magic of volunteerism and service to others, and the magic of friendship and camaraderie and, yes, even teamwork.

Whatever direction you go in life and whatever you do, if you bring passion and enthusiasm to what you do, you will definitely be more successful than if you do your studying and course work as a matter of course or with an attitude of resignation or, even worse, with feelings of resentment and utter boredom. As the 20th-century educator Stanwood Cobb points out, "If we can find no interest in the world around us, it is not the world around us which has ceased to be full of life, full of wonder, full of luster and color and magnificent deeds" (1932, p. 45).

Bain's book *What the Best College Students Do*, mentioned above, reviews the lives of highly successful people in order to see what common factors differentiated them in college from those students whose later lives were not as successful. Bain learned that the most successful students were those who were enthusiastic about their education: "they were simply enthralled with the world, with learning, with the possibilities of reaching new levels of excellence, of finding new ways to understand or do. Their enthusiasm extended to not just one specialized area of study or profession but an array of subjects . . . [They] found the motivation . . . within themselves and took control of their learning" (2012, p. 19). As you throw yourself into your studies, your on-campus college life,

your plans for your future, you will find yourself falling absolutely in love with college and the many ways by which it will propel your life forward in so many wonderful ways.

Henry C. Duquès, former CEO of First Data Corp. and trustee emeritus of George Washington University, affirmed this in a recent interview. He advises students to "Enjoy every single day of your college time. You want to look back with a positive view of college. You should try to make positive memories every day. People are often asked, 'What was the best part of your life?' College can be this for you; it is a time of maturing, learning, meeting new friends. It is an exciting time" (Brill de Ramírez, 2013).

Getting the Most from Your College Experience

As you can see, I want you to have a wonderful life. I want you to have an absolutely wonderful time in college. And I want your college years to be filled with happiness, passion, and delight: academically, vocationally, emotionally, spiritually, and socially.

Caveat: There are so many opportunities in college that it is easy to be very busy without having maximum results. That is why you need to learn the importance of the following:

- Time management and the hours you spend studying (amount)
- The depth and breadth of your studies both in and outside your major and minor fields of study (scope)
- Smart and effective study habits (quality)
- A life that is rich with learning, social activities, volunteerism, a growing social and professional network, a commitment to overall wellness, and a sense of satisfaction in a life well lived (balance)

If this seems like a lot to do and a lot to understand, don't worry. Making the most of your college years is a process that you will gradually develop and fine tune over the course of your time in college. If you are already partway through college, this text will give you the guidance to ensure that you make the most of your remaining time in college.

The main problem that most students have is not being strategic: about what they are doing, about how they are spending their time, and about what and how they are learning. But don't worry if you make some mistakes along the way, if an exam goes awry, or even if a class (or two or more) doesn't go as well as you had hoped it would. Just make sure that you learn to respond strategically—that you learn from those experiences:

1. If you have a class that does not go well, decide to learn from that experience to ensure that your future classes go very well. Ask yourself hard questions about what you could have done differently, and then make a plan for the next term to make sure that you will succeed in all of your classes. Then follow that plan.

2. If you have a group project that does not go smoothly; learn from that experience and decide what you can do differently the next time you have group work to accomplish. Then use those later group work experiences to practice and develop your interpersonal teamwork skills—including contingency management and leadership skills if the group runs into problems along the way.

3. If you run for an office in a student organization but do not get the position, re-evaluate your membership in the organization and see how you can be more productive in that or in another organization. If the doors are closed to you, either you need to change in order to make them open or you need to explore other directions to see where there may be other doors that are already open wide for your higher-level involvement.

The following advice is relevant for all students to follow, but it is pitched especially to first-year college students who may not get this advice elsewhere.

The four most important things to do during your first semester at college:

1. **Put studying FIRST and do well in your classes.** Go through Chapters 2–5 carefully and make sure that you set up a weekly schedule to ensure that you are putting in the hours necessary to excel in your classes.

2. **Look into different student organizations on campus and select two to be involved with right away.** You want to make a difference. You want to make strategic connections. You want to gain experiential and leadership opportunities. And you want to have fun. (chs. 5,6,8)

3. **Go to the career center and attend your first job fair.** Remember that college is to prepare you for your postgraduate life. Find out about internships, part-time jobs, and other opportunities for you. And be strategic and dress professionally when you attend any job fair! (chs. 5,7,8)

4. **Prioritize wellness and fitness.** You need energy for all of the above. (ch. 1)

To optimize your success in college and beyond, a large part of that process is in understanding that college is a laboratory situation for you to develop and practice your learning, studying, communicating, teamwork, networking, and leadership skills—prior to entering the workforce. Take those opportunities seriously.

The process begins by taking Socrates's advice to heart: Know thyself.

■ **Self-assessment.** You need to discover your strengths and weaknesses as well as your interests and abilities. Most of the chapters of this text include self-assessments that will help you in developing your capabilities for success in college and for success in graduate and professional schools and for success in the workforce.

■ **Current affairs.** You also want to understand how the world is changing and how you can best prepare yourself for your life, career, and volunteerism. Your life is lived within the context of the world as it is today and the world as it is progressing. Successful lives continue to grow, learn, and adapt. Be informed and knowledgeable.

■ **College resources.** Finally, you want to learn the various ways that college can help you develop a variety of skill sets, experiences, and opportunities that will position you strategically for your life and work after college. You want to have an absolutely great time in college while you are also approaching it in smart and strategic ways. Learn, experience, mature, and progress.

Over a century ago, Professor Bernard Bosanquet (1901) looked at the Greek philosopher Plato's *Republic* and the role that education played in that imaginary realm. As a philosopher and a former student of the great Socrates, Plato understood deeply the importance of education. Professor Bosanquet reminds us that education is a life-long process and that college is one stage (albeit a foundational one) in that process.

[Plato] means that, in the sense of really doing the best with the human mind, education is a lifelong process and has two inseparable sides.

You cannot complete your studies at twenty three or twenty four and then, leaving study behind, pass on to practice.

The best kind of knowledge, the knowledge of what makes life worth living, cannot be won except by a mind and character trained and matured in the school of life,

and again no good work can be done in the arena of practice unless inspired by the highest spirit of study—the vital enthusiasm for truth and reality. (p.16)

Study and life experience are interwoven parts of a life well lived. What is studied and learned is then applied in actual experience, and, in turn, what is done in applied practice is reflected upon and learned from so that future practice is even better. Developing such high-level critical-thinking skills has always been important, and it is even more important today in our information-driven world.

The associate director of the Technology Enhanced Knowledge Research Institute at Athabasca University, George Siemens, is an expert in the changing dynamics of learning and acquiring and using knowledge in our contemporary digital age. He explains that today, "Learning is a process that occurs within nebulous environments of shifting core elements—not entirely under the control of the individual. . . . New information is continually being acquired. The ability to draw distinctions between important and unimportant information is vital. The ability to recognize when new information alters the landscape based on decisions made yesterday is also critical" (Siemens, 2004).

More recently, in *The Heart of the Matter: Humanities and Social Sciences for a Vibrant, Competitive, and Secure Nation*, the Commission on the Humanities and Social Sciences (2013) asks the question: "Who will lead America into a bright future?" The answer speaks to every current college student. Those who will lead America into a bright future are "Citizens who are educated in the broadest possible sense, so that they can participate in their own governance and engage with the world. An adaptable and creative workforce. . . . We must prepare the next generation to be these future leaders" (p. 2). You will be this future leader. So I want you to roll up your proverbial sleeves and get to work. Show everyone the *mettle* (tough and courageous spirit) that you are made of. Demonstrate your grit and determination, and make your college years an auspicious time far beyond your wildest imaginings and highest aspirations!

1 Daily Habits

Fitness and Wellness

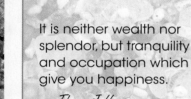

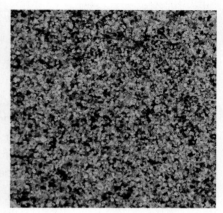

It is neither wealth nor splendor, but tranquility and occupation which give you happiness.

— *Thomas Jefferson*

In this virtuous Voyage of thy Life hull not about like the Ark, without the use of Rudder, Mast, or Sail, and bound for no Port. Let not Disappointment cause Despondency, nor difficulty [cause] despair. . . . [E]xpect rough Seas, Flaws, and contrary Blasts: and 'tis well, if by many cross Tacks and Veerings, you arrive at the Port; for we sleep in lion's Skins in our Progress unto Virtue, and we slide not, but climb unto it.

— *Sir Thomas Browne, Christian Morals, pub. post. 1716*

1. **Wellness:** Achieve health and well-being through discipline, balance, and moderation.

2. **Fit & Fun:** Maintain physical and psychological fitness for wellness and energy.

3. **Grit:** Respond with "grit" and courage to stress and the challenges that you will face.

4. **"Can-Do" Attitude:** Ensure college success by means of a victorious and "can-do" attitude.

College is an incredible time of many invaluable opportunities and life-changing experiences. Whether you are in the 18- to 23-year age range or are a nontraditional student who brings more life experience to the college classroom and campus, in college you will be exposed to many different choices and opportunities that will be of great value to your life and career:

- You will meet new people and develop friendships—some that will last a lifetime.
- You will gain knowledge and skills that will prove invaluable to your future career.
- You will have truly remarkable experiences, both in and out of the classroom.

Regardless of how happy and rewarding your high school years were, you can make your college years even more rewarding. If you have already been out in the workplace, regardless of how fulfilling and enjoyable your jobs have been, you can make your college experience one that is even more gratifying.

College can be an absolutely amazing time for you. But remember that college, like life, is also filled with tests, challenges, and struggles. Along with all the wonderful opportunities that college provides, you should also expect a lot of stress:

- Each term, studying and doing well in your classes will take effort.
- The changes and growth that come with learning and new experiences will, at times, be tough and even painful.
- You will meet many new people and will expand your interpersonal horizons. Living, studying, and working with so many new people is not always easy to do and requires flexibility.

Although the experiences of college, university, and community college life will not always be easy, you can make the process much easier and more successful by remembering and applying this one simple fact: How you take charge of your life during college will determine how well you navigate your way through the stressors of your college years and will prepare you for navigating your way through the stressors of your future jobs, your career, and even your social and family life.

Ken Bain, in his book *What the Best College Students Do* reports that "people who become highly creative and productive" found that they had learned "to acknowledge their failures, even to embrace them, and to explore and learn from them" (2012, p. 100). These people developed strategies to deal with the negatives in life and, in some cases, even found ways to turn those negatives into positives. Bain acknowledges, "That sounds relatively easy, yet for many people it proves enormously difficult" (p. 100).

I have written this text because I am convinced that virtually any college student can learn this lesson and become a "highly creative and productive" person. Perhaps the biggest difference between the most successful students and those who struggle or fail in college is the extent to which they learn how to deal with stress and difficulties. You can learn effective strategies that help. Remember these sayings: "When the going gets tough, the tough get going!" "No pain, no gain!" I know—these mottos do make life sound like a football game, but the concepts have great wisdom. Indeed, the great classical Greek dramatists Sophocles and Aeschylus both tell us that trials and tribulations are an endemic part of life, and that from life experience and suffering comes wisdom and from wisdom comes happiness. The great Austrian philosopher Ludwig Wittgenstein explained that learning and life can be understood as a game, like basketball or chess:

- There are rules to be followed.
- There are abilities and skills to be mastered.
- Success requires effort, time, and practice.

Success in life is all about how well you learn to play the overarching game of life. In college, it is all how well you learn to play the game of college. To do so, as Wittgenstein well understood, there are rules to learn, concepts to understand, and game maneuvers to practice.

You probably have already become proficient at one or more things in life, whether a sport, a musical instrument, gaming, cooking, gardening, camping, or writing. You already understand what it takes to get good at something. Success in college and in life is really this simple: You need to learn the basics, and then you must practice, practice, practice!

Your Health and Well-Being

During your college years, you can maintain your well-being by developing skills in three areas: *discipline, balance,* and *moderation.* These skills will help you to achieve success in college, in your career and jobs, and throughout your life. These skills will promote physical and psychological health now and in the future. In their article "Wellness Factors in First-Year College Students," Janna LaFountaine, Mary Neisen, and Rachelle Larsen (2012) affirm that "developing wellness in college enhances healthy behaviors for a lifetime and enhances success" (p. 62).

Discipline

▶ Develop your capacity to take charge of *what* you do.

In his dialogue *Phaedrus,* the Greek philosopher Plato describes the human soul as a charioteer with a chariot and two horses. The horses are a person's emotions and spirit. The charioteer is a person's mind and intellect, which are used to control and direct the spirited passions of the two horses.

Gaining a healthy control and direction over oneself takes practice, and it is a skill that each person develops throughout life. This means coming up with a schedule, setting parameters, and structuring your days in order to accomplish what is important to do. Develop and practice your executive decision-making by taking charge of your life in college.

Five common activites that people need to control for the sake of their physical well-being are food, sex, alcohol/drugs, physical exercise, and fun/free time. You do want to enjoy life. But you need to hold on to the reins to avoid riding in an out-of-control chariot. This means making smart and strategic choices. To learn how to do this, look for role models—people you know who are disciplined in ways that you would like to be. Spend time with them. Seek them out as valuable mentors (whether they are older or your peers). The most successful people in life—those who are happy with their lives, active in their communities, and healthy with energy to accomplish what they want to accomplish—almost always are those who have learned to successfully discipline themselves. If your life is not as disciplined as you would like, you can change this. Grit and self-control can be learned. Make a plan. Find healthy mentors and a strong support system.

As the thinking charioteer, you want to maintain control of those two spirited horses. There are indeed times when you will want to let the horses run at full speed to reach your goals, but those times should be circumstances that you as the charioteer *choose*. You want to remember to maintain sufficient discipline over yourself and your life so that you will be able to actualize your dreams and goals as much as possible. If this seems daunting to you as a beginning charioteer, then you could find a more experienced charioteer, someone you know with a well-disciplined life who could help you as your coach, mentor, or "college-buddy."

Balance

▶ Develop your capacity to negotiate, evaluate, and prioritize your activities to meet your desired goals.

A great deal has been written recently about the importance of and difficulties in achieving a healthy and satisfying work/life balance for people out in the "real" world. While you are a college student, you will have opportunities to practice achieving a doable school/work/life balance that works for you.

Let's think about this idea of balance for a minute: A physical balance or scale helps to weigh various items in relation to specific weights. To achieve a reasonable and effective balance in your life as a student, you want to weigh or evaluate how you are spending your time. Look at whether your schedule and habits will ensure that your plans, goals, and dreams are being realized. Also look at how your activities are affecting your wellness—your sleep, your peace of mind, and your overall health.

As a student, your studies should be at the top of your priorities, but if you have a job or have important caregiver responsibilities in your family, those are very important too. Your social, fitness, and extracurricular activities are also important. And life and responsibilities change from day to day, so remember to recalibrate your balance when needed. Some days may require additional study time; other days may require more attention to organizational or family involvement.

Approach your time strategically: Think about how you spend your time each day and throughout the week. If you are spending more time socializing than on your academics, that probably needs an adjustment. Decide which of your activities are most important, and then make some strategic choices to place your activities in a healthy balance that makes sense for you. This chapter will provide worksheets that will help you begin to make intentional and strategic choices as you finely hone your life-balance choices.

Moderation

▶ Follow Aristotle's oft-quoted advice of "Moderation in all things" so that no activity gets in the way of others that are also important.

Although there will be times when you need to focus exclusively on one thing—say, a major exam that requires extra studying—you want to take charge of your schedule and daily activities to make sure that you are not giving too much time to any one activity. As a student, your most important job is school; you want to make sure that you are being as successful as possible in your classes. But that doesn't mean that you should spend virtually all of your time studying and not taking care of your overall personal wellness.

Be careful to allot enough time to be successful in your various activities. But also be careful not to allot more time than really makes sense. If you are spending too much time on one class so that your performance in other classes is suffering, review how you are spending your time each day and make the needed adjustments so that you will be successful in all of your classes. If you have a week in which you can't spend time on your academic activities because you are traveling or spending time with family, spend more time studying the week before so that you will not get behind in school.

Moderation also means making smart and strategic choices that will affect your health: food, sex, alcohol/drugs, physical exercise, and free-time activities. If you have a special occasion such as your 21st birthday, you might choose to overindulge, but do this in a smart and strategic way. If you know you will be drinking alcohol, plan to have a designated driver. If you know that you will overeat, watch what you eat the week before. And if you overdo it on occasion, don't beat yourself up about it. Just get up the next day, and make that next day a good day! Look forward and remember that tough periods, mistakes, stress, tribulations, and tests (literally ☺) are part of life.

 ## Physical and Psychological Fitness

College offers many opportunities to support your physical and psychological well-being.

Exercise

At your school's athletic facility, you can lift weights; swim; jog; or play basketball, volleyball, tennis, badminton, racquetball, or squash. There will be individual and team sports that you can participate in and watch, including soccer, football, track and field, basketball, golf, table tennis, and martial arts, among others. There will be classes you

can sign up for, such as aerobics, pilates, Zumba, spinning, and yoga. If the classes or athletic activities you prefer are not widely available at your school, you can explore off-campus opportunities, start your own club on campus, or work out on your own. If you prefer more solitary or reflective ways to get your exercise, then try running, cycling, walking, yoga, or exercising with a workout DVD or online program. Many colleges provide running and walking paths and trails, as well as cycling routes. Find the type of exercise that works for you.

Besides the obvious health benefits, serious physical exercise has recently been connected to higher grades. A *New York Times* article cites research that reports, "On a 4.0 grade scale, students who exercised vigorously seven days a week had G.P.A.'s that were, on average, 0.4 points higher than those who didn't exercise" (Parker-Pope, 2010, paragraph 5). Even though exercising takes time each day, the return on that investment is significant. And research shows that "physically fit individuals do recover more quickly from stressors" (Linden, 2005, p. 70).

Jenny Blake, career development program manager at Google and the author of a popular blog about life after college, is explicit about the importance of exercise: "You have to MAKE time for exercise. No one is going to do it for you, and if you don't carve out and commit, something else will always come up at the last minute or take priority" (Blake, 2011, p. 216). In my own life, I have found that I can fit in exercising either early in the morning or after work and still attend to my other responsibilities. Even when I become extra busy with my work, I make sure that I plan time for exercising almost every day. It helps me to structure and organize my day while also giving me more energy.

Support Services

Your college will also provide a wide range of support services for your overall health, from the medical and health services available on campus to the counseling center and the support at your student affairs office. Residence halls include resident advisors and their assistants, and there will be a police or security service for additional support and security. For dietary wellness, most colleges now offer a range of dietary options in the cafeterias and dining halls, including low-carb, gluten-free, vegetarian, vegan, kosher, and organic foods that you can choose from for your required or preferred diet. And many schools offer weight control programs and personal trainers for physical fitness support.

Become familiar with the various services on your campus and in the community. There will be times when you, your roommates, or others you know will need to take advantage of them. You need to know where to go for safety information, counseling, and medical assistance when the need arises. Of course, the truism that "the best medicine is prevention" is important to remember. Do your best to learn, practice, and improve your wellness choices and behavior. College is a wonderful place to do this because of the many resources available to you.

Extracurricular Activities

Extracurricular activities offer a plethora of opportunities for your free time. You can become involved in clubs and organizations: Fun groups (such as Ultimate Frisbee, ballroom dancing, or scuba), cultural clubs, religious organizations, and service groups. You can participate in and attend arts activities such as musical events, dances, plays, and films—many of which are free to students. There are sports events and lectures on a variety of subjects by many distinguished speakers. Take the opportunity to investigate multiple extracurricular pursuits to see which interest you the most, which will be most beneficial for you to participate in, and which you will want to fit into your schedule.

As you take advantage of these opportunities to expand your social, cultural, and intellectual horizons, your perceptions of yourself will change and develop, usually with significant benefits to your life. Audrey Berman and Shirlee J. Snyder explain, "How you perceive yourself encompasses your interpretation of your environment. This affects how you think, feel, and respond in any situation" (2012, p. 276). So being an active (and healthy) participant in the richness of college life will beneficially affect your thoughts, feelings, and actions. Erin Massoni (2011) reports that "participation in school activities, especially athletics, leads to higher self-esteem and enhanced status among peers, which some argue is deterrent to antiso- cial behavior" (pp. 84–85). This means that your involvement contributes to your overall sense of self and wellness. Because this is so important to college success, extracurriculars are presented much more fully in Chapter 6: "Campus Activity: Clubs, the Arts, Athletics."

Responses to Stress and Challenges

Every person has good and bad days, smooth sailing and rough seas. This is normal, but today it seems as if the bad days are more numerous in people's lives. Sonja Lyubomirsky (2007), author of *The How of Happiness*, documents that "nationally rep- resentative samples of U.S. adults indicate that slightly more than half of us (54 percent) are 'moderately mentally healthy' yet not flourishing—that is, we lack great enthusi- asm for life and are not actively and productively engaged with the world" (p. 14).

If this is the case within the larger population, we should not be surprised to learn that with the added stress of academic life, many college students are also struggling with stress. In 2013, *The Chronicle for Higher Education* reports, "Over the past six years, anxiety in particular appears to have prompted more students to visit counseling centers. . . . The number of college students with severe psy- chological problems continues to increase, while anxiety, depression, and rela- tionship issues most commonly send students to seek help at their campus counseling centers" (Sander, 2013, p. A18). Brian Van Brunt, director of coun- seling at Western Kentucky University and president of the American College Counseling Association states, "More students are arriving on campus with problems, needing support, and today's economic factors are putting a lot of extra stress on college students, as they look at their loans and wonder if there will be a career waiting for them on the other side" (Lewin, 2011).

Think for a minute about the following scenarios and how they could way- lay a student's progress and success.

■ "I have a roommate who watches movies and plays video games when I'm trying to study, and he does that until 3 or 4 in the morning, so I can't even sleep!"

■ "My professor gives these killer exams that I simply cannot pass, and he teaches required classes in my major. Unless I go to another school, I will have to drop my major . . . and I have dreamed about going into that field for most of my life!"

■ "I'm really glad to be in college, but I know I'm spending too much time hanging out with friends [or sleeping, working out, keeping up with my Facebook page, partying, playing video games, being involved with my fraternity/sorority/club, etc.]. My grades are not what I would like them to be, but all my activities are very important to me. I just don't know how to balance them out."

Sleep Takeaway for College Students

Do not underestimate the importance of sleep. It plays a big role in college success (academics, organizational involvement, and personal well-being):

1. Develop a regular sleep schedule that will work for you. Arrange your class schedule, work, and activities so that you can have a regular sleep schedule. And even though some people are morning people and others not, college provides you with time to practice the sleep habits that you expect to have in your chosen career.

2. Make sure that you get enough sleep on a regular basis. Most experts recommend eight hours per night, but you will want to experiment to find the right number for you. Nights with inadequate sleep should be occasional and, ideally, on weekends. And make the all-nighters rare. You want to be awake and alert for each class.

3. You want to make sure that your sleep is restful and uninterrupted. If your roommate stays up late gaming or partying or studying when you want to sleep, or if there is disturbing noise that wakes you up, come up with strategic solutions to resolve the situation. Quantity of sleep hours is important, but you also want to get quality REM sleep.

- "My family responsibilities take a lot of my time. When I'm at school, I really enjoy my classes and want to get involved with campus organizations. But I feel guilty spending more time away from my family, so I just go to class and then come home to study and help out on the home front. I'm not really getting to know any other students very well."

- "My roommate has tons of friends and a great boyfriend, and I wish that were me. I get depressed and eat and gain weight and worry about my future life. And then I can't focus when I try to study. If only I had a boyfriend and could lose weight, I know I'd be happier!"

- "To get through college, I have to work long hours, so it is really hard to find time to study. I've joined two student organizations and am very involved in Greek life on campus, but those activities take time too. My schedule is a mess, and I'm really struggling to maintain even passing grades, much less the grades that I'd like to be getting."

- "In high school and middle school, I didn't have many friends. Now at college, I have a number of friends I party with on the weekends. It's great having friends, but the partying includes drinking and . . . well, you know. I like the socializing, and I want friends, but I'm not happy with my life right now. It just seems so out of control, and I just don't know how to make it better."

- "College is great! I am making the dean's list each semester. I study hard every day. The only breaks I take to relax are playing video games on the weekends. I admit that I am spending too much of my free time on the computer or game station, and I really don't feel all that relaxed. A lot of the other students on campus seem much happier; they seem to know a lot of other students, and they're very involved in various activities. I just go to class, study, and then go home. I'd like to be more active socially and with volunteerism, but I don't see how to get there."

- "Fortunately, I am one of the students who knows exactly what she wants to do. I have my major and career plan all mapped out. Now if I only didn't have to take those general education classes that are not in my field. I know that I can get a high G.P.A. in my major, but I don't want to waste my time on unimportant classes like writing or literature. I know that writing is important, but I don't see how writing essays will help me in my career. Having to take these other classes is a pain and really stresses me out—especially when grades in those classes lower my overall G.P.A."

These scenarios offer glimpses into the everyday conundrums of college life. Remember that throughout your lives, there will be similar challenges and difficulties. But there is good news: In her 2013 book, Lyubomirsky points out that adversity, stress, and tough times can actually be a good thing in a person's life. "Recent research reveals that people who have experienced *some* adversity (for example, several negative events or life-changing moments) are ultimately happier (and less distressed, traumatized, stressed, or impaired) than those who have experienced no adversity at all. Having a history of enduring several devastating moments 'toughens us up' and makes us better prepared to manage later challenges and traumas, big and small" (Lyubomirsky, 2013, p. 3).

Over a half century ago, Hans Selye (1956) explained in his book *The Stress of Life* that stress is simply part of life. It is not possible to avoid stress altogether because it is part of growth and progress. Instead what is needed is the grit and hard work that will keep you moving forward (p. 368). Your college years will provide you with ample opportunities to develop strategies to survive, achieve, and thrive as you surmount the challenges before you. You want to put together a mix of activities, work/study time, and time with friends/family/mentors that will *work for you*. Lyubomirsky (2013) relates, "Researchers have shown that when people behave in ways that fit their personalities, interests, and values, they are more satisfied, more confident, more successful, more engaged in what they are doing, and feel 'right' about it" (p. 12). There will be a lot of trial and error and revision in the process as you learn the tools and strategies that will help you deal with challenges and stress.

Let's look at some specific strategies for dealing with stress and challenges that will make your college time much more successful and happy.

Avoid Problems When Possible

▶ Remember to be strategic and plan ahead!

Learn from your past. If you spent too much time playing video games or watching television during high school, you can simply decide to leave your PlayStation or TV at home when you go to college. If you had problems sharing a room with a sibling, then you might want to request a single room in the dorm. If you missed sharing a room after your older sibling graduated and moved out, then you will want to make sure that you have roommates while you are a college student, even if a single room or apartment is offered to you. And if you've never been able to study well in your bedroom at home, plan ahead and find another place where you will be more successful studying for your college classes (e.g., in the library, at a café, in the student center, or in a study room in your dorm).

Resolve Problems That Have Simple Solutions

▶ Address those problems that can be quickly resolved.

If you discover early on that your roommate situation is just not going to work out, do not let the problem drag on. Speak privately with your resident advisor as soon as possible to see what options you have. It might be possible for you or your roommate to move to another room sooner rather than later.

If your semester workload seems overwhelming with little chance of your making the dean's list or at least a 3.5 G.P.A. for the term, you might consider dropping one class within the first week or two, while you can still switch to another class (one that will be less time consuming). Or you might simply decide to drop one class early enough in the term so that you can focus on your other classes and achieve the success that you want. Your academic advisor at school is there to help. Make an appointment to see what can be done *before* the situation becomes overwhelming.

Perhaps you find that the refrigerator in your dorm room is sabotaging your plan to be healthy and fit in college. You're simply eating more than you need to and not always choosing the best food. If you are in a dorm room and part of the problem is having the refrigerator, you may decide that it is best to simply send the refrigerator home. This alone won't make you eat healthfully, but it will be part of the solution. Often there are simple changes that can be key in helping you along the way.

Address the More Difficult Problems Directly

▶ Deal with the larger and more complicated problems directly, as best you can.

If you are having roommate problems, and you have to wait until the end of the semester to get a different room or roommate, you will need to make contingency plans to ensure a successful semester. You can choose to spend relatively little time in your room. You can study elsewhere. Depending on how extreme the problem is, you may need to meet the problem head-on; for example, if you are not able to resolve critical issues with your roommate directly, you could ask your resident advisor to meet with the two of you to see whether you all can come up with some solutions that will work for everyone. You want your semester and time in college to be successful for both of you. There are always multiple options and solutions; find the one that works for you.

Choose Your Battles

▶ Make strategic choices regarding which problems you need to address.

Some problems are more important to deal with than others. Some problems demand immediate solutions; others can be dealt with down the road. Some problems definitely need to be addressed; other problems may turn out to be relatively insignificant impediments for you. Here are some examples.

- In a café on campus, a friend pays for her food but hides one item from the cashier. She brags that she did not have to pay for one item. You were raised with a higher level of honesty, and her dishonesty makes you uncomfortable. You have to decide whether it is worth getting involved.

- You do well on an exam, but you think that your score on one essay should be higher. If it will not change your solid "A" in the class, you have to decide whether it is a big enough issue to meet with your professor to discuss it.

- Your roommate constantly listens to music that you absolutely do not like. You have to decide whether it is disruptive enough to warrant raising this as an issue of contention.

Whenever a questionable situation arises, you have to decide what action to take. Sometimes the best choice is to see the situation in a different light, to understand the other person empathetically, to minimize those problems that really are not so big, and through such re-evaluation, to choose inaction as a reasonable response. Note that here, inaction is not defeatist but rather a strategic choice regarding a specific case. Remember that your time and energy are valuable; make smart choices where to exert them.

View Some Problems as Positives

▶ Seemingly problematic situations often appear very different when viewed from more optimistic perspectives.

An irritating classmate may turn out to become a close friend or a valuable professional connection down the road. A class and professor that you find impossible may turn out to be those from which you learn the most and with which you find great success. A tough boss makes your job or internship unpleasant, but after you make the effort to appreciate and value this difficult supervisor, you may develop an important mentor who will help you procure a full-time position after you graduate.

Taking Charge of Your Life

Whether you are a traditional-age student or a nontraditional student, during your college years, you have the responsibility to make choices that will make your everyday life easier, healthier, happier, and more successful. When you were younger, the adults in your life were responsible for making decisions and guiding you through difficult times. Now as an adult, you are responsible to step up and take charge to maximize your success, wellness, and overall contentment. With a little effort, you can use your college years to blossom as an individual:

- In the college environment you encounter many different people and can learn how to create your own circle of friends and a beginning network of associates so that you will have a well-rounded and nurturing community of friends and associates.
- Within the intense pace and requirements of academic study at the college level, you can learn how to pace yourself and make healthy choices to maximize your academic success, minimize your stress level, and maximize your overall health.
- In the hectic busyness of contemporary life, you can learn how to intersperse and prioritize joyful moments and satisfying experiences, both academic and recreational, throughout your day.
- Within the academic pressure cooker of studying, writing papers, and taking exams, you can learn how to access resources to maintain a positive and victorious attitude to achieve success and happiness in college.

You need to make strategic choices regarding your time outside of class. This is crucial to your overall college success. Achieving success in life and college is possible, but it requires effort and thought and planning. This can be broken down into two key steps:

1. Select a range of activities that will be conducive to your personal balance, success, and happiness.
2. Create a reasonable schedule to fit those activities into your everyday life in college.

Key to all of this is setting up a doable schedule for yourself and finding ways to stick with that schedule. Success in life and in college is really far less complicated than many realize. What all this is about is discipline, structure, organization, and focus.

Take charge of your college years so that you will find them more rewarding. Happy and fulfilling college years are the best preparation for happy and fulfilling lives later on. Use your college years to practice the very skills and habits that will carry you forward throughout your life. Your undergraduate years are the foundation for your post-college life, so you want to make the most of college, and you really do want to *make college work for you.*

As you know, college is about gaining the skills and knowledge that you will need in the workplace, *but* the skills and knowledge that you want to gain during your time in college are not limited to what is taught in your classes. The undergraduate experience offers a rounded and holistic education that prepares you for life after college: this means education for your chosen career path, but it also means a broad education that leads to a more intentional, purposeful, meaningful, fulfilled, *and* happy life.

During your years of schooling from kindergarten to 12th grade, the adults around you provided many opportunities for helping you and your peers develop into well-rounded persons. Coaches and scout leaders spent innumerable hours helping develop your discipline, physical fitness, and athletic and outdoors skills. Teachers and parents assisted with various after-school clubs and other activities to expand your interests and abilities. Leaders in various educational, religious, and service organizations guided you in volunteerism and community service. Now that you are in college, you need to seek out such opportunities and make them happen for yourself.

- If you want to be a competitive college athlete, you have the responsibility to practice your chosen sport seriously.

- If you want to be physically active but not on a college team, consider participating in the competitive or noncompetitive athletic activities available at your college—whether this is jogging or weightlifting on your own; participating in Zumba, yoga, or BodyPump classes; or playing intramural sports with other students.

- If you were active on your high school newspaper and enjoyed that work, you will want to explore similar possibilities in college.

- If you were very involved in the Spanish club in high school, it would be wise to consider studying abroad in Spanish-speaking countries.

- If you have played music for years and have enjoyed that, you might want to seek out opportunities to continue playing music while in college (e.g., band, orchestra, chorale, quartets, a jazz or rock band, or continued music lessons or classes).

It is important to have an active and balanced life. College is not only about studying and career planning. Embellish your life with activities you enjoy and others that are new to you. Remember to incorporate the arts and music in your life. A full and rich college life contributes in big ways to college success.

Having a Victorious Attitude

To be successful in college and in your future life, it is important to have a "can do" attitude. Every person has strengths and interests and abilities that can be developed. Explore and capitalize on those to achieve success in college and beyond. Even when situations do not go as you would like, look around and focus more deeply on what is working well in your life. Bring a positive orientation and "can do" attitude to your studies, job, family, and organizations.

In the text *How Learning Works: Seven Research-Based Principles for Smart Teaching*, Ambrose, Bridges, DiPietro, Lovett, and Norman (2010) emphasize the extent to which the successful process of learning is primarily contingent upon learner attitude and effort: "Learning is not something done *to* students, but rather something students themselves do" (p. 3). Citing the research of Pascarella and Terenzini (2005), they affirm the difficulties that students face in "managing their own learning" (Ambrose et al., 2010, p. 191). College success for any student depends on the student's ability to take charge of the overall college experience with a positive and victorious attitude committed to success regardless of the impediments along the way. Expect impediments. But do not let those impediments waylay your progress.

Twentieth century educator Dr. Stanwood Cobb (1932) explained, "If we could realize [the value of having a positive attitude], if we could put our energy not into complaints against life and the bitter sense of deprivation but into the overcoming of obstacles, we should make the path to success straight and clear. We have enough to do without wasting our thoughts in envy of others and the creation of excuses for our own lack of triumph. . . . The negative attitude never leads anywhere except to stagnation. It is only by cheerfulness and courage that the individual can progress to higher goals of living" (pp. 160–161).

Noting the great achievements of two of ancient Rome's most renowned philosophers, the emperor Marcus Aurelius and the slave Epictetus (Greek for "acquired"), Cobb points out that much of Rome's philosophical greatness came from two men with completely different life circumstances, and yet both left remarkable legacies to posterity. It is not so surprising to learn of a famous Roman emperor who also became a great philosopher, but it is remarkable to read of Epictetus, born a slave and who lived in poverty his entire life, and yet who, impassioned with learning and teaching, became a great philosopher of equal and famed status to Marcus Aurelius.

The point that Cobb is making is that each person has to make choices. You can choose to make college work for you. "Suppose our lot is low. Suppose, even, that we suffer from more disadvantages than the majority of our fellows. We can still enjoy the opportunities we have. We can master our circumstances and live victoriously, [but] we must ourselves have more faith in ourselves than anyone else has in us. . . . All of us can make the most of ourselves, and it is this which is the real victory" (Cobb, pp. 161, 163).

Here is a lesson I learned in graduate business school: In one graduate class, we were taught that no matter what we would try to accomplish in the workplace, there would always be some kinds of barriers, impediments, and challenges to trip us up. We were told to face those impediments head on, and if they could not be easily removed or resolved, then we would have to accept those problems, but not necessarily give up on our plans. The professor advised us to look at other variables and to focus on what was in our control. By making changes with other variables, we just might be able to make our desired plan a reality.

Let's look at a few hypothetical examples to give you an idea about how this would work in the real world:

- If your first choice for college or a class is not available, then simply look for another option that might eventually prove to be an even better choice.
- If you are having difficulty majoring in a particular field, consider minoring in that field and picking a different major where you will find greater success.
- If one friendship or relationship is not working out, seek others.

Look at yourself, at your college and future plans, and at the various aspects of your everyday life with *a positive and hopeful attitude*. Whatever is negative in your life can be overcome by the positives that you bring into your life. Ultimately through practice you will gain "unwavering faith in [your] abilities, a consciousness of [your] inner power to achieve, the vivid realization of success to come" (Cobb, p. 161). Cobb continues, explaining that faith in yourself and vision toward your goals "are the essential factors in the dynamics of a career" and in a person's successful accomplishment of their dreams (p. 161).

Let's look at some of the positives that already exist in your life today.

Victorious Attitude Worksheets

Worksheet A. Start by listing ten individuals you know who are almost always positive influences in your life, who are your biggest cheerleaders, and who really want you to succeed in college and in life:

1. _____
2. _____
3. _____
4. _____
5. _____
6. _____
7. _____
8. _____
9. _____
10. _____

Now look over your list and select five of these people who are your biggest cheerleaders/guides/mentors. Look at the qualities that these positive people manifest. Think of the various qualities that make them great friends, coworkers, or family members. Are they understanding and caring? Are they giving and generous with their time and good deeds? Are they honest and trustworthy? Are they reliable? And are your relationships with them balanced and healthy—not suffocating or otherwise dysfunctional or codependent?

Worksheet B. Choose five of the people from the above list who are really exemplary friends, relatives, and coworkers. After writing their names, add a sentence for each that describes one situation that demonstrates their positive effect on you in a big way. Then note what specific quality or virtue they demonstrated. For example, you might write, "My coworker, John Doe, came through and backed me up at work when another employee had spread a lie about me. John demonstrated courage, faithfulness, and truthfulness."

1. _____
   _____
2. _____
   _____
3. _____
   _____
4. _____
   _____
5. _____
   _____

Reread what you have written. How fortunate you are to have the support of these people. During college and throughout the rest of your life, you will want to include more such positive people. This does not mean that you avoid those who are struggling or are more negative; in fact, you want to be a positive influence to help others. But surround yourself with more positive than negative people. If you feel that friends, relatives, and coworkers are bringing you down, then you need balance. How else will you be able to build and perpetuate your "can-do" attitude?

Worksheet C. Now turn to some moments and accomplishments of which you are especially proud. Every person has those special moments when he or she rose to the occasion and demonstrated the highest levels of self-discipline, self-mastery, selflessness, and self-exertion. This worksheet will list a number of these moments in your life. As you think of those times when you possessed a victorious attitude and the capacity to achieve, you will see what is needed to succeed in college and throughout life. And you will begin to see your own strength of will and effort that you will want to nurture and grow as you move forward in accomplishing your goals. Here are some possible examples:

- One day you were really tired, and all that you wanted was to just go home and rest. But on your way home, you saw an old woman struggling with her bags, so you crossed the street and offered her your help, which she greatly appreciated. Here you demonstrated compassion, kindness, and sacrifice.

- At school your friends were making fun of a particularly naïve and gullible boy. You looked at them and said, "Enough is enough. He doesn't deserve this. I don't want to hear anyone making fun of him again!" And to your surprise, they all stopped ridiculing him—both at that moment *and* thereafter. Here you demonstrated courage, kindness, and justice.

- You won a major competition or succeeded in completing a major accomplishment after many weeks and months (and perhaps even years) of preparation. It was not the medal or trophy or rank that you received that was important; rather it was your committed training for the event and the focus and effort that you displayed in order to succeed. Here you demonstrated discipline, confidence, and excellence.

List five things that you've done of which you are really proud and that demonstrate your victorious attitude. At the end of each description, note the qualities or virtues that you demonstrated.

1. _____
   _____
   _____
2. _____
   _____
   _____

3. _____
   _____
   _____
   _____

4. _____
   _____
   _____

5. _____
   _____
   _____

These examples demonstrate the special qualities that you possess and that will be invaluable to you and others as you move forward through college and life. Remember that there will always be struggles in life, but what holds most people back from achieving the success they desire is not hard times but the lack of a positive attitude—the very attitude that you demonstrated in each of your examples.

Worksheet D. Review your five examples and list the different qualities/virtues that you demonstrated (e.g., patience, empathy, bravery, faithfulness, self-sacrifice, caring, etc.):

   _____
   _____
   _____
   _____
   _____

Worksheet E. To get a clear view of the areas of your life that you want to improve, rate your own levels of satisfaction. On a scale of 1 to 10 (with 10 the highest), how would you rate your satisfaction and happiness with the following areas?

_____ Academics (major, grades, learning, studying)

_____ Extracurriculars (organizational involvement on campus)

_____ Career planning (major, skill set development, career center visits, job fairs)

_____ Service and volunteerism (on campus, off campus, individually, with groups)

_____ Job or internship (company or organization, your performance, boss)

_____ Physical fitness (exercising, sleep, diet)

_____ Emotional and spiritual wellness (downtime, yoga, prayer, meditation, faith)

_____ Fun (time with friends, enjoyment during studying and on the job, free time)

_____ Friends and colleagues (socially, on the job, in organizations)

_____ Family (immediate, extended)

Any areas on this list that you rated below an "8" are areas that you want to give extra attention. This checklist gives you a good idea of the areas that are currently strongest in your life as well as the areas in need of improvement. Most important is to be pleased with what is working and going well in your life right now. Second, you want to have a positive "can do" attitude that you can and will do good things in your life and in the world. You cannot solve all the world's problems, but you can move yourself forward and, thereby, position yourself to achieve even more.

Learning from Your Worksheets. Look back at your completed worksheets and what they tell you about your ability to succeed:

- You have gained a clear sense of the people around you who have positive, supportive, and encouraging attitudes.

- You have considered the importance of ensuring that the majority of those in your inner circle are positive, supportive, and encouraging friends, relations, and coworkers.

- You have taken the time to review moments in your life when you have demonstrated a victorious attitude and when you have overcome your weaknesses and accomplished things of which you are especially proud.

- You have seen that the best way to accomplish goals is by practicing positive behaviors in your everyday life.

So look forward. Remember your past victories and accomplishments. Feel good about what you have achieved. Do not dwell on past mistakes or failures. Instead, look forward, work hard, and succeed.

2 Class Performance

Preparation and Participation

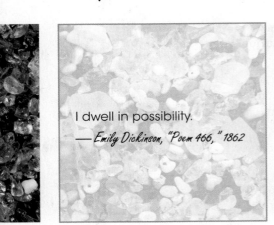

I dwell in possibility.

— *Emily Dickinson, "Poem 466," 1862*

We never know how high we are
Till we are called to rise;
And then, if we are true to plan,
Our statures touch the skies—

The Heroism we recite
Would be a daily thing,
Did not ourselves the Cubits warp
For fear to be a King—

— *Emily Dickinson, "Poem 1197," 1870*

Being busy does not always mean real work. The object of all
work is production or accomplishment and to either of these
ends there must be forethought, system, planning, intelligence,
and honest purpose, as well as perspiration. Seeming to do is
not doing.

— *Thomas A. Edison*

learning outcomes

1. **Attendance and Participation:** Maintain smart and strategic class attendance and participation.

2. **Focused Reading:** Craft thorough and substantive notes from required and recommended readings.

3. **Homework:** Accomplish homework with high levels of success through engaged and interactive out-of-class reading and assignments.

4. **Interaction with Instructors:** Achieve strategic benefits from respectful interactions and intensive learning opportunities with faculty.

5. **Note Taking in Class:** Take smart and strategic notes from class.

6. **Additional Learning Opportunities:** Be attentive to other possible learning opportunities.

How you perform in the classroom is one of the most important factors for your success in college and beyond. Your classroom performance is on-the-job training for how you will perform in the workplace: in meetings, on project teams, in seminars. Think about those times in class when you have seen students put their heads down on the desk when they are tired. Can you imagine doing this in a meeting at work? That behavior will decidedly *not* get you raises and promotions in the workplace! That behavior will also *not* get you the respect of your professors! You want to practice smart, focused, and engaged classroom behaviors.

It is important to understand that intelligent, focused, and mature classroom performance will strategically prepare you for success in the workplace. Remember that you want to make your in-class time work for you.

Over my three decades of teaching, I have seen far too many students go to their classes and view the classroom setting as an appropriate venue for passive activity. Even if your head is not resting on the desk, just sitting in class disengaged will not give you the valuable return on your college investment that you desire and deserve.

- Sitting in class bored and daydreaming is definitely not strategic!
- Spending most of your time on Facebook, texting friends, checking email, shopping, and surfing the Web are clearly not strategic uses of your in-class time!
- Simply showing up to get counted for attendance and then just waiting for class to end so you can get on with your day are decidedly not strategic!

If you think that going to class is unimportant and/or optional, you are neither approaching nor understanding the value of in-class learning and the life-long significance of your classroom behavior and performance!

The McGraw Center for Teaching and Learning at Princeton University provides additional insights into active class participation. The center's webpage "Understanding and Overcoming Procrastination" makes explicit the connection between how you perform in the classroom and the extent to which you get your work done well and on time:

> [K]ey to overcoming procrastination is to stay actively engaged in your classes. If you are passive in class you're probably not "getting into" the course and its topics, and that weakens your motivation. What's more, if you are passive you are probably not making as much sense out of the course and course materials as you could. (McGraw Center for Teaching and Learning, 2012)

So when you take your in-class performance seriously and ratchet it up to higher levels, there will be a payoff in your out-of-class studying and work as well.

Unfortunately, far too many students do not approach their in-class work in smart and strategic ways. According to recent research, far too many students who attend class are actually paying relatively little focused attention on the classwork during the class session. Instead they are texting friends, reading and chatting on Facebook, and simply not paying attention in class. In a recent article in *The Chronicle for Higher Education*, Berrett (2013) reports observations of particular classrooms in the United States in which "few [students] followed directions, took notes, or brought their textbooks to class. 'Many students often asked repeatedly how to do assignments even though the instructors explained several times'" (p. A6).

Distracted students compromise the quality of their learning. Wei, Wang, and Klausner (2012) studied the effect of texting during class, reporting in the *Communication Education* journal that text messaging during class adversely affects cognitive learning: "self-regulated students are less likely to text during class and are more likely to sustain their attention to classroom learning, which, in turn, facilitates cognitive learning . . . i.e., grade-oriented academic performance and experience-oriented cognitive learning" (p. 185).

You want to go to class in a timely fashion. You want to go to class with a positive attitude. And you want to perform with focus and effort during the class session. *When* you go to class, *how* you go to class, and *what* you do while you are in class matter. This includes your performance in physical classroom settings and in digital learning sessions, both synchronous and asynchronous.

Your performance in class contributes not only to the grades you will achieve and how well you learn the course material, but also to the development of invaluable performance skills that will help you hit the ground running when you're ready for the workplace. You want to be one of the employees who performs at the highest levels in meetings, on project teams, in training seminars—arriving well prepared, engaged, and ready to participate actively.

The following guidance holds true for any of your classes: regardless of whether a class takes place in a traditional classroom, off campus during a class outing, within a synchronous (live) distance learning class session, or during your individualized distance-learning sessions online. Regardless of the format of any class, there are certain parameters and insights that hold true for smart and successful performance.

Remember that you are spending money and time on your education. You want that investment of money and time to pay off with the highest possible returns on that investment. It's just like the stock market. You are investing money, time, and effort. The return on that investment is your degree, academic credentials, valuable experiences, learning, increased knowledge, and bolstered skill sets. By being strategic as a student, you can substantially increase the value of your investment. There are just a few rules for you to follow to make your class attendance and participation work for you. If you follow these rules, you will maximize the return on your investment of time in class.

1. Go to every class, except in the case of a serious illness, religious observance, or funeral.
2. During class time, follow/track the instructor and stay focused on the course work to make your in-class time *work for you.*
3. During class, take notes that are extensive, yet strategically focused.
4. Pay attention to the course syllabus and do *all* of the assigned readings *before* going to class.
5. Do *all* of the assigned exercises, problems, papers, and projects. *Do them well* and get them in *on time.*
6. Pay special attention to any intensive learning opportunities that may be required or optional (e.g., project teams, undergraduate research or creative production, service learning, related out-of-class lectures and other events, etc.).
7. Utilize faculty office hours in strategic and smart ways.

If you take these seven rules seriously and apply them to your course work, your academic productivity will be significantly higher. Remember that you should want to gain knowledge. You should want to increase your skill sets. You should want to develop your abilities to become a more valuable job applicant, employee, or graduate student. Your dreams and hopes for your life are deeply important, and you *can* succeed, but that requires effort, disciplined effort, commitment, and passion. Also note that such behavior will impress the other students who will view you more positively. You never know how this may be of benefit for you or for others down the road. One day, you may be applying for a job or recommending a young person for an internship and one of the decision makers just may be someone who was in one of your classes.

Class Attendance

Go to every class—except, of course, in the case of a serious illness, religious observance, or funeral. You simply must attend class regularly and learn as much as you can in each class session. After all, you are a college student. Being a student is what being in college is all about, so attending your classes in smart and strategic ways is really your #1 job right now. Class attendance is important for a number of reasons, including the following.

Academic Learning

▶ The majority of your academic learning occurs through your attendance and participation in class.

Your instructors know a great deal more than you about the classes they teach, and they are sharing their knowledge with you in class. By being present and attentive, you will learn that much more from the material being presented. You do not want to miss out on these crucial learning opportunities. If you ever have trouble staying focused and interested in class, meet with your professor or advisor for help. Note that other students are focused and engaged. Learn and practice effective in-class performance.

Additional and Auxiliary Material

▶ Some class sessions will include important additional and/or auxiliary material that is neither in your textbooks nor in other class material.

You need to be in class and paying attention to take advantage of these learning opportunities. Sometimes, a professor will realize that some difficult material can be best understood through additional explanations or examples, so those are provided in class to help the students learn the material that much more successfully. Other times, instructors will include peripheral information or anecdotal stories that may seem unrelated, but for students who are paying close attention, these auxiliary detours are understood to be integrally connected to the course material. Often the additional information presented in class is key to exam questions, problem sets, and heightened development in essays.

Practice for High-Level Job Performance

▶ Your attendance and attention in class are directly relevant to and preparation for high-level job performance.

In the workplace, being present, timely, and ready to perform communicates to your coworkers and bosses that you respect and value your job, your work, and the organization for which you work. Being there is important. Being on time is important. And being there effectively with a positive attitude and active participation is important. Use your responsible class attendance as practice for later high-level performance on the job.

Professorial Respect

▶ Your class attendance affects how your professors perceive you.

Attending class every day *and arriving on time or early* communicates that you perceive and appreciate the importance of the class. How you attend class demonstrates your respect for the class, your classmates, and your professor. This is important. After all, who is it who evaluates and grades your work? Be present—in body and mind.

Professional Networking

▶ Being in class is key for your strategic networking in class.

Arriving early to class gives you the opportunity to get to know the other students who also arrive early. Many of these are strong students whom you will want to add to your developing academic and professional network. And should you ever miss a class and need notes, or should you want to work on an assignment with another student or study together for an exam, you will have gotten to know students in the class who will be strategic connections for such collaborative activities.

Missed Classes

As noted above, the acceptable reasons for missing class are religious holy day observances, significant health issues, a funeral in the immediate family, or some other approved and prearranged excused absence.

Do not miss class due to minor health issues such as a headache or a hangover or a cold. Many of your professors show up to teach with migraines and colds to make sure that their students do not fall behind in the needed course work. So can you. This is one area where you show your grit and toughness. If you have a headache, take a pain reliever or tough it out. If you have a hangover (whose choice was it in the first place?), take a pain reliever, have some herbal tea or coffee, and get to class. And if you have a minor cold, go to class, but sit away from the other students to avoid infecting them. Of course, if you are seriously sick, stay home or go to your school's health center; but make sure that you take care of your class obligations:

- Get class notes from another student who will spend the time to review them with you to make sure that you understand the notes and what you missed in class.
- Contact your professor about your absence and ask about any in-class work that you may need to make up.
- Keep up with all assignments and readings so that when you go back to class you have not fallen behind.

For virtually any student, there will be times and days when you will need to miss class for legitimate reasons, which also include significant scheduling conflicts at school (e.g., a required athletic event in which you are competing, a speech team event, or a required academic event that conflicts with a class time). Whenever possible, let your professor know *ahead of time* that you will be absent. Even if you are sick, in most cases, you will know that before class time starts. There are steps to take prior to the missed class session and after you have missed class (and are catching up with work and returning to class).

Prior to the Missed Class

- Review the syllabus for each class and understand the specified absence and make-up work policies for the class.
- Throughout the term, keep up with all of the assigned work on the syllabus. Try to stay a bit ahead of the readings and assignments so that you have a bit of a buffer should you get ill or otherwise need to miss a class. In other words, do not leave your assignments to the last minute.
- In each of your classes, get the contact information for several top students whom you have observed taking thorough notes during class. These are the students you will want to meet with to get missed notes.
- For an anticipated absence, send an email to your professor to explain, to affirm your commitment to the class, and to schedule an immediate office hour meeting to catch up on the missed work.

After the Missed Class

- Contact a responsible student in the class for the class session notes. Arrange a time and place to meet to get the notes and to go over them together. Be courteous and appreciative. Most students like to schedule such meetings at a student center, library, or café; plan to buy your classmate a beverage in gratitude.
- Based on the arrangements you have worked out with your instructor, turn in any work that is due upon your return to class.
- Once you return to class, thank your professor for any accommodations that were arranged due to your needed absence.

Remember that you want your professor to perceive you as a responsible student. Think about this for a minute. If your professor knows that you are an especially diligent and responsible student, and then one day you accidentally sleep in and miss an exam, your professor *might* let you take the test anyway.

Let me share a personal story about the value of attending class and demonstrating your responsibility to your professors. As an undergraduate, I had one class in which a major midterm exam was scheduled when I had religious observance in the Bahá'í Faith. I contacted the professor ahead of time in writing, explaining the reason for the absence and politely requesting a different time to take the exam. Not wanting him to think that I might use the day off as an excuse to have additional time to study, which wouldn't be fair to the other students taking the exam at the scheduled time, I made it clear that I would be willing to take the exam early. He agreed, and I took the exam the day before. When I thanked him during the next class session, he mentioned that, as a Christian, there were important days during which he too would not want to take an exam! He also said that he was impressed to have a student schedule an exam ahead of time due to an absence. The absence provided an opportunity to communicate to my professor my commitment to the class. In this way, he got to know me better, and he later became an important mentor and a strong reference for me.

The same principles of attendance and preparedness also apply to your work in the real world. In the real world, if you have a meeting, you will be expected to have the courtesy and responsibility to let the others know ahead of time if you are unable to attend the meeting. In some cases, your work absence may mean that the meeting needs to be rescheduled. If you do not inform others of your *necessary* absences or tardinesses, you are demonstrating that you do not take the meeting nor the others' time seriously. Don't expect promotions and raises and strong letters of recommendation if you have such absences or tardinesses that reflect a lack of respect for others' time, the meetings, and the work involved.

Every semester you will have a different schedule with different classes that meet on different days in different classrooms and sometimes in different buildings. By the end of your undergraduate years, if you have attended your classes consistently, reliably, and intentionally, you will have developed a habit that will be invaluable for the rest of your life. So, go to class conscientiously and purposefully as you lay down a foundation for mature and smart workplace responsibility and courtesy.

Before finishing up this section, it is important that you take stock of your past history regarding absences and tardiness. Please list five examples from your own life when you missed or were late to a class, job, organization meeting, family gathering, or other event. Briefly describe the event, whether you were absent or tardy, and why that happened.

1. _____
   _____
2. _____
   _____
3. _____
   _____
4. _____
   _____
5. _____
   _____

Look over the five examples to see any patterns that emerge. Are there common reasons that led to your missing or being late to events? For example, do you have trouble getting to things in the morning? The solution may be as simple as getting to bed earlier. It may also be that you really need a class schedule and future career that permits a daily schedule that starts later in the day. Regardless of the reasons for your absences, take stock of your performance as depicted above to see where you can improve.

Preparation for Class: Assigned Readings

For the vast majority of your courses, there are assigned readings for particular class sessions. It is crucial that you do *all* of the required readings for each class *ahead of time*. When you walk into class or log on to an online synchronous class session, you want to make sure that you are fully prepared to work with the assigned material at the highest level of engagement.

In the technologically driven culture of the 21st century, people are spending more of their time on social media, videos and movies, gaming, and nonacademic websites. Technology has opened up the world to any person who is digitally connected, and this is wonderful—a tremendous benefit that is fusing the world into a smaller and smaller global community with all of its challenges, dysfunctions, and beauty. But, yes, there is always the "but." A major downside to technology is that people tend to be reading in bits and bytes rather than longer articles, chapters, and books. Longer written works explore historical events, individual lives, societal changes, market trends, educational needs, health care advances, and artistic accomplishments in greater detail *and* depth.

This level of development and the added time that you spend with a longer reading help you to engage with it more deeply, thereby deepening and expanding your knowledge and understanding in important ways. This is one of the hallmarks of college education: achieving comprehensive and deep understanding about many different areas of study. But this is now a great challenge for many students. According to a recent story in *The Chronicle for Higher Education,* students report that they do not enjoy doing assigned readings for class and that they try to avoid required reading as much as possible (Berrett, 2013). Students are reading fewer long texts on their own, and even when assigned during the academic year, students spend very little time doing reading for class. Indeed much of the time that students report doing reading for homework is actually being spent multitasking so that even that reading is not done well with students retaining little of what they have read.

A study presented at the annual meeting of the American Educational Research Association documents that "students spent nearly 21 hours reading each week: 8.9 hours on the Internet [mainly social media, such as Facebook and Twitter], 7.7 hours on academic reading, and 4.2 hours on extracurricular reading" (p. A6). Dan Berrett cites other research that looks more broadly at teenagers and younger adults and that presents even more extreme results: "Other studies have painted an alarming picture of students' reading habits. . . . Americans between the ages of 15 and 34 are spending on average, about one hour per week reading" (2013, p. A6).

Many students arrive at college with limited reading habits, mainly reading shorter texts (e.g., social media) and not developing their abilities to read longer texts. Therefore, it is not at all surprising that "students said in interviews that reading textbooks was 'tedious' and 'time-consuming'" (Berrett, 2013, p. A6).

Suppose that you are a student who does not like reading longer texts. There really is only one way to change this so that your comfort level with reading longer texts goes up. Do you know what the answer is to this? It really is *practice, practice, practice.* Think about it this way. If you are beginning to learn a sport or to play a musical instrument, at the beginning, you are not going to be ready to compete in the Olympics or play at Carnegie Hall. If you can only stay focused for 10 or 15 minutes when you read, then do that, but do it *well.* Then do something else for a while, and then do another 15-minute stint of focused reading. The next day, move up to 20-minute periods of focused reading. Little by little, you will develop your reading "muscles" and your reading stamina. Most college students can significantly improve their reading within just one month's effort. But to do so, you have to make the effort and practice.

It is important to do all of the readings and *to do the readings well,* even if the textbook may be boring to you or even poorly written and confusing. When you are in the workplace, if you have a manual to study that you find boring or poorly written, are you going to tell your boss that you won't/can't do the work or end up doing it poorly because of missing key points in the manual? Your responsibility will be to do the reading completely and well. And if there is any missing or erroneous information, your job is to figure that out early on and then track down the needed information so that you can complete your job well and on time. So take advantage of the many opportunities in college to develop your reading comprehension, analysis, and interpretation skills. Here are some additional reasons why this is important.

Respect

▶ When you do the readings completely and well, you communicate to your professor your strong work ethic and self-respect, your respect for the class, and your respect for your professor.

Remember who will be grading your work and your performance in your classes. The best ways to show your respect for your professors, instructors, and teaching assistants are by being a diligent and top student in their classes, by being engaged and interested in the course material, and by being appreciative of faculty expertise.

You may wonder about larger classes where your professors may not get to know you personally. Even if your work is computer graded and your professor doesn't know who you are, your commitments of time and effort in doing the course readings thoroughly and timely are important practice for your career and work life. The extent to which you do your homework seriously and thoroughly is the extent to which you will demonstrate your work ethic and your respect for your future coworkers, supervisors, management, and yourself in the pride of work well done. And remember that the heightened learning that comes from your performance as a serious student in all of your classes will benefit you in many different ways throughout your life.

Distinction

▶ When you do the readings completely and well, you will stand out among your fellow students who have not yet fully developed their reading muscles.

Remember the statistics cited previously about the extent to which most people are reading less on a daily basis? When you do all of the assigned readings for your classes and show up to class being one of the most prepared and engaged students, you will distinguish yourself among your peers. You will come to be seen as a leader in your classes. Your performance in class will be distinguished for your preparation, thoughtfulness, and interest.

Say that you show up to class unprepared. As you listen to the other students' ideas about the readings you didn't read, you come up with an interesting idea of your own that you share with the class: "Based on the comments made by Jack and Jill, one logical implication is XYZ." This is good, because it demonstrates your engaged and intelligent interest in the discussion at hand.

Instead, let's say that you come to class prepared, having done the readings with focus (understanding), effort (annotating, highlighting, and taking notes), and interest (jotting down some of your own thoughts in response to specific passages). As you listen to the other students' comments, you realize that their ideas do not take into account a key point from the assigned readings. You raise your hand and provide your contribution to the discussion: "The comments made by Jack and Jill are very interesting. Jack says X, while Jill adds Y. If we take into account Brill de Ramírez's explanation in the chapter 'Class Performance: Preparation and Participation,' in which she states W, we can reasonably conclude Z."

When your intelligent ideas and questions are built on the foundation of course material, (1) your ideas and questions are grounded in facts and information, (2) your ideas and questions demonstrate your currency in the course material, (3) your ideas and questions contribute in heightened ways to the learning of each person in the class, and (4) your memory and understanding of the readings are strengthened and solidified as you think about the readings and reference that information from the readings in your group and class contributions (whether oral, written, or digital).

As you step up to high levels of performance in class, in person, and online, you will be one of the students that the other students seek out in group work because you will be seen as one of the students who demonstrates interest in the material, actively listens to other students' contributions, offers smart and informed thoughts, and asks intelligent questions. Accordingly, you will be perceived as a key member of the class and a desired person with whom to work in pairs, groups, and teams.

By being a diligent student, you will get to know your peers in class—especially those who are also top students in class. Many of your fellow top students will be people you will want to have in your developing professional network—students with whom you will want to meet outside of class for study sessions, students with whom you will want to network together as you seek prestigious internships and jobs, and students with whom you will want to stay in contact after college as part of your postgraduate professional network. And you will be someone they will seek out in turn.

Finally, when you have given proper attention to the readings, you will enter the classroom or online discussion forum as one of the most prepared students. This is exactly the sort of training you want for your career so that when you have meetings at your place of employment, you will distinguish yourself through your high level of preparation, having read and reviewed thoroughly all relevant material for the meeting.

Time Management

▶ When you do the readings completely and ahead of time, you are learning how to make strategic and efficient use of your out-of-class learning time.

You can optimize your learning and skill development in college to increase the return on your college investment for your future. You want to maximize your learning from the assigned readings *before* you walk into the class setting. Prioritize your time and do the assigned readings *before* class. Staying on target with the readings keeps you on point throughout the term so that you do not fall behind. In this way, you will be able to strategically plan your time studying for exams and writing papers and doing projects because you will not end up playing catch-up with your daily course work.

Some students are slow readers. In my own family, there are individuals with dyslexia who have struggled to become strong readers. If you are not yet an expeditious reader, you might want to take a tip from top students who are slow readers. Many of these students get their textbooks several weeks before the term begins and do much of their readings ahead of time. Such contingency preparations help to build in the time needed during the semester to ensure successful learning and course work.

By doing the readings ahead of time, you will be able to proactively ask your instructor for help if there is anything in the readings you do not understand. Answering such questions and providing help are the primary purposes for faculty office hours; stop in.

By staying on top of the readings, you also are in a good position to consider aspects of the course material for possible further exploration and study. Regardless of whether the course is in your major (or minor) field of study, if you put forth significant effort, your learning of the course material will be accordingly heightened. Such heightened learning will spark topics for research projects or developed essays on exams or in term papers. Other topics may be explored further in intensive research opportunities during for-credit summer study, in formal research guided by your professor, in discussions with faculty, or in student seminar and study sessions—all valuable intensive learning opportunities to develop your knowledge and skill sets . . . and that can translate into valuable line items on your résumé.

Performance

▶ When you do the readings completely and well, you are that much more prepared to perform at the highest levels during class time.

If there is in-class group work, you will be highly prepared if you have read the assigned material thoroughly. If you work with other highly prepared students, your collaborative work will raise all of your learning and thinking to even higher levels. And if, unfortunately, you end up in a weak group working with underprepared students, you will be able to carry the load and still produce a quality product. I know that this situation is frustrating for the student or students carrying the load for others, but remember in this situation that you are learning the most from the exercise or project and are also gaining invaluable teamwork and leadership skills.

If the class is structured as a lecture, you will understand what is presented in the lecture that much more fully. Many students sit in class struggling to know what to write down from class lectures and discussions. If you have read the assigned readings and even taken notes from the readings for your personal reference and study, then you will be better able to decide what information in class is new, what is not in the course texts, and what is important to get into your in-class notes. Some of the class lecture will be information that is also in your textbooks. If there is repetition, think about whether the repetition of information during class time is emphasizing important facts to learn and remember. You want to be an active note taker in class. Do not sit in class like a bump on a log. Make sure that your presence in class is strategic and purposeful. You want to be there and be prepared. You do not want to be a student who wastes valuable learning time in class skimming through the textbook or other course materials simply because of not doing all of the assigned reading.

Quizzes, Papers, and Exams

▶ When you do the readings completely and well, by underlining, highlighting, and otherwise annotating your readings, you will be better prepared for quizzes, essays, tests, term papers, and major exams.

Often, students think that just passively reading the text is enough. To the contrary, engaged and involved reading practices are important for learning, memory, and practice.

When you highlight, underline, annotate with comments in the margins, take notes, or otherwise actively respond in writing to what you are reading, you use your brain differently. When you (1) think about the reading, (2) evaluate what you consider important to highlight or write down, and (3) craft responsive thoughts and questions that annotate the reading, these processes result in a much deeper and higher level engagement with the material. Even if you do not return to what you have written down or highlighted, these actions alone will help you to understand and remember the material better than would be the case if you did not do all this.

Underlining, highlighting, and otherwise annotating your textbooks creates a marked-up text that will help you to find passages, quotations, and other information that you will need to use in your out-of-class papers, take-home exams, and homework assignments. You don't want to waste time trying to find something in your textbooks or readings. By having a well-annotated set of readings and notes, your time will be used much more strategically in studying the material rather than trying to find it!

When you have tests, quizzes, and exams to study for, your annotated texts and reading notes will prove to be invaluable aids. If you take extensive notes from your readings, when you need to study for an exam, you will not need to read the textbook all over again. You have reading notes to study from. Many of the best students review their pages of notes and then take notes from their extensive reading summary notes. You may take eight pages of reading notes and later condense that into one or two pages of notes. This process will give you a manageable set of notes to study that summarizes all that you have read. At the end of this chapter there will be an exercise that will help teach you how to do this—utlizing the material in this chapter as your base for strategic note taking.

When you are well prepared for tests and quizzes (including pop quizzes), your performance will be solid, and your stress level regarding those quizzes or exams will be significantly lessened. This counts for a lot. Increased effort directed strategically and scheduled reasonably can end up lowering your stress about school, and this in turn contributes to better performance.

Preparation for Class: Homework Assignments

Let's take some time to see why it is important for you to do all of your assigned homework. You want to pay strategic attention to the amount of time and effort that you devote to each class and to each assignment, even the little assignments.

Practice

▶ Your performance on each assignment gives you crucial practice for your later performance on exams, large assignments, projects, and term papers.

The extent to which you perform well on your small work largely determines the quality of your work on the bigger assignments, so take the little assignments and exercises seriously.

If you are assigned 15 homework problems that are to be turned in for grading, I recommend that you consider doing 10 to 15 additional practice problems. The extra practice will help you learn the material better and make you faster. Putting out this additional study time will actually give you more time later when it is critical: on your exams and large assignments, projects, and term papers. By doing the additional practice problems, you will be able to handle the easy questions on your exams that much more quickly, which, in turn, will buy you extra time for the tougher questions and problems that will need more time and thought.

Note that your homework and in-class work is often directly relevant for larger assignments or exams. Often questions on quizzes reappear on exams. Often the work on smaller assignments can be integrated into larger projects and papers. So do not blow off the small work. Hold your head high and aim for excellence in all you do.

Networking

▶ When you put out highly focused and committed effort on your assignments, you will become one of the top students in your classes.

If you are one of the students who is highly prepared, other top students will want to work with you in class and for out-of-class projects and study sessions. This is strategic networking. Chapter 8: "Networking and Mentoring: Teamwork, Leadership, Strategic Relationships," will go into this in greater depth, but for now, it is important that you understand that your in-class performance is key to networking in college.

Time Management

▶ Doing your out-of-class work consistently throughout your classes develops your time-management skills in big ways.

It is important to accept that unforeseen problems will occur from time to time during your college years. You want to build in a time buffer that will ensure that you turn your assignments in on time even when the unexpected occurs. It is smart to work with early deadlines. If a paper is due on Tuesday, work with a Sunday deadline: If your printer runs out of ink when you try to print on Sunday, you have time to deal with that and get your paper in on time; or if the school course website is down on Tuesday, you will have already successfully submitted your paper on the prior day.

  Time-Management Example from Business Travelers

Many people who travel for work are cognizant of the importance of strong time-management skills. Accordingly, many of them prefer to travel with longer time in airports between flights. Why is this? The longer layovers of 3+ hours build in contingency planning. That way, if the first flight is late, it provides enough of a buffer to make the second flight. Equally important is the fact that the longer layover also provides a comfortable and relatively stress-free time period during which to work in an airport lounge, business center, or restaurant.

Use your college years to practice comparable contingency preparations, especially when big assignments, projects, and exams are concerned. *Never* leave things to the last minute. Use your college classes and extracurricular activities as practice as you develop your strong time-management skills.

In-Class Performance

When you are in class, you want to demonstrate mature and focused attention toward your in-class learning activities (e.g., listening attentively to a lecture and taking notes, working on problem sets with deliberation, participating actively in group work, and asking and answering questions intelligently and with interest). Remember that you want your professor and the other students to walk out of each class perceiving *you* as a diligent, responsible, intelligent, and impressive student.

Think about it this way: What if your professor in one class is engaged in a research project and is able to use two additional undergraduate students on the research team, wouldn't you want to be one of the first students your professor would think of to contact to join the project? And you may not even be majoring in that professor's field! Even as the instructor for a general education or core curriculum class, because of your top performance, your professor extends to you the opportunity to develop some really impressive skill sets by being involved in an exciting project—and gaining a strategic résumé line item.

What if one of the other students in one of your classes learns about a really amazing (and paid!) internship opportunity for the coming summer, wouldn't you want to be one of the first people she thinks of as another possible intern with that company? Even though you are not close friends, she thinks of you because you have impressed her so much with your performance in class.

You can do this. If you are showing up for every class on time, being exceptionally well prepared for each class, and working hard on all of your assignments, including the small ones, now all that is needed to do exceptionally well in your classes is to stay focused on the class work consistently throughout the class sessions.

Coming Prepared

▶ Make sure that you have the needed textbooks, notebooks, laptop, calculator, tablet computer, or other mobile device with you in class.

You want to be well prepared, so bring the tools you need to class. If you have multiple classes on certain days and your textbooks and digital devices are too much to carry in your backpack, then you simply have to be creative and figure it out. You could move to a digital format for a number of your textbooks, carrying them with you on your tablet, laptop, or e-reader. You could also invest in a rolling backpack or briefcase to

carry your print texts and other course materials. Better to err on the side of having more than you need than missing needed materials.

Being Alert

▶ Stay alert so you can pay serious attention in class.

Figure out what works for you to stay focused in each of your classes. For some students, having a beverage in class helps. But beware of sugar! You don't want to end up sleepy with a sugar crash in the middle of a class. Also beware of the dopamine effects from foods like turkey and milk. For many, a granola bar, trail mix, or some nuts do the trick for in-class alertness. Try getting up early to exercise in the morning to increase your energy and decrease your restlessness. Each person is different, but you need to figure out what you need to do to be highly focused in class. If you absolutely cannot stay awake in class, then you need to excuse yourself and rest elsewhere. Do not use class time as nap time.

Listening

▶ Listen attentively and appreciatively to your instructor and take careful notes based upon what he or she says.

Your instructor knows a great deal more than you about the course material. Listen to your instructor appreciatively and with an aim to learn so that when you walk out of each class, you will know more than you did when you came in. Even if the professor lectures on the material that you have already read and diligently taken notes on, as the professor goes over that material, you will have new thoughts and questions based on your prior understanding from the readings and homework. Put those ideas and questions in your class notes and bring them up in class or with your professor during office hours. In this way, your learning will be increased and heightened, and you will communicate to your professor and the other students that you are a committed student.

Multitasking

▶ Beware of multitasking during class; do multitask but only in ways that are directly relevant to the course work for that specific class.

Multitask in ways that are strategically helpful for you in your class. Do not multitask activities that are unrelated to your class. Do not shift to check your Facebook, Twitter, or email accounts, unless that is for directly related class work. Resist opening up online documents and other materials unrelated to your class. Studies document that class time is being seriously damaged due to students' lack of discipline and online habits. A *Chronicle for Higher Education* article reports that "more than 40 percent of the time [that students] spend reading is on social media, and that reading often is done during class" (Berrett, 2013, p. A6). It is your responsibility to ensure that your time in class is focused and on point.

Remember to stay focused on the course at hand. This also means not taking out any textbooks, notebooks, or work for any *other* class—even if you have a big exam in another class during the very next period! Do not open up materials unrelated to your class. If you finish your in-class work ahead of other students, use your additional class time for study that is directly related to the class. You could use those moments to look over your work for that class, read ahead in the course text, or jot down a question to raise in class or with the professor after class or during office hours.

In the same way, when you have a meeting on the job, you want to be focused on the meeting's agenda, not doing unrelated work. You want to help move forward the team's work as much as possible.

Participating

► Ask and answer questions in class.

You want to do this in smart and prepared ways. It is often helpful to jot down your ideas and questions on paper, digitally, or in your class notes document before raising your hand and sharing them in class. Writing down your ideas, questions, and answers before raising your hand in class or before sharing them in your group helps you to frame them better. Then you are able to share them with greater focus and brevity. (Here, too, this is excellent practice for the workplace when you work on project teams and have meetings.) Also, your highly focused and strategic ideas, insights, questions, and answers may point the way to promising lines of further inquiry and research—for your own assigned papers and projects and possibly also for collaborative work with your professor.

Do not sit passively and silently in class. If you are a quiet person, make an effort to be an active participant in class. Even if this is hard at first, like most behaviors, as you practice this more and more, it will become easier. Use group activities to practice sharing your ideas and contributing actively; then later try speaking in your larger classes.

For online class sessions that are synchronous in chat form without video, be an active *and* present participant with your professor and other students. It is neither smart nor strategic to log on as present and then go do other things. It is obvious to your professor which students are actively participating and which students are logged on but really M.I.A. Stay focused, read everyone's comments and questions, respond thoughtfully, and contribute at least once every five minutes to communicate to your professor and your fellow students that you are focused on the study session and are an active participant.

Giving Space for Others' Participation

► Do not take up too much of the class time with your own comments, thoughts, and questions.

You want to be an active participant in class, but be careful not to over-participate. Some people in your classes will not participate unless there is some silent space during which they can raise their hands or otherwise contribute. As a team player in class and in meetings, you want to insure and value the participation of your fellow students and team members. Some people will participate, but they need some silent space during which they will raise their hands or otherwise contribute; others participate more quickly and readily. The best classes and meetings are those where everyone feels comfortable contributing and, in turn, values the contributions of the others.

Whether it is in classwide discussions or in group work, be gracious and inviting of others' contributions. Do feel free to share your thoughts; you want to be actively engaged, but you also want to be a team player. Remember to give space for others' contributions.

Respecting Your Classmates

► Listen attentively, respectfully, and appreciatively to your fellow students.

Make an effort to appreciate and learn from each student's contributions in class. When the other students ask questions or share their thoughts, try to understand what they are saying. Even if it seems patently wrong or foolish, take a few moments to mull over what they have said and try to find some value in that. Sometimes a statement that is dead

wrong or absolutely off topic may be just the comment that sparks your thoughts in a new direction that then open up relevant and new insights for the discussion. And if you can build on someone else's idea or query, give them credit in class: "Jane's point about X is really interesting. While I'm not completely convinced that it would happen, if it is a legitimate concern, then wouldn't Y follow from that?"

Do not judge your fellow students negatively. Some students may have really good ideas or questions, but a learning or speech difficulty means that their ideas do not come out as clearly as they would like. Other students may jump in precipitously with ideas that are not fully thought out, perhaps unrelated to the discussion, or altogether incorrect. Regardless of the quality of a student's contribution, respond respectfully. Eye rolling, negative looks, and sighs are not acceptable. You never know whether the student may just be having a bad day, a bad week, or even a bad semester or term.

Respecting Your Instructor

▶ Value your instructors' knowledge and experience and their efforts to share that learning and information with you and your fellow classmates.

Give your professor courteous attention, and appreciate his or her efforts to share knowledge and information with you and your classmates. If you think that something the professor has said or put on the board may be incorrect, point out the information and ask the professor to clarify it, but do this in a respectful way, not confrontationally or critically. Have empathy for your professor, and remember that your professor is working hard to help you and the other students gain a valuable education.

These class performance guidelines are designed to give you practice for the mature and focused attention and deliberative effort that will help to distinguish you as an impressive student now. And in your career, such higher level performance will distinguish you in the workplace as a focused, respectful, and diligent employee. So use your in-class time strategically to develop and practice your interpersonal listening, thinking, and speaking/contributing skills.

 Takeaways from the Above Guidelines

These practices demonstrate your self-respect and dignity.
These practices demonstrate your respect for the classroom setting and its learning environment.
These practices demonstrate your respect for your professor, instructor, and teaching assistant.
These practices demonstrate your respect for your fellow students.
These practices will contribute to your learning and skill development in big ways.
These practices will contribute to the overall learning environment of the classroom.

Class Notes

Part of smart and strategic in-class performance involves the information document that you compile from class lectures and discussions. Taking notes in class is a skill that most students need to learn and practice more consistently and more thoroughly. In a recent freshman composition class, I spent 30 minutes of the first class period of the semester going over the parameters for the class and presenting key points and facts—all useful for the course throughout the term and directly useful for the students' essays due the following week. All but one of the students were first-semester college students. Only one student pulled out a notebook, sheet of paper, tablet, or other digital device to take down notes from that class period. However, at the end of class, when I gave the students their reading assignments for the next class, almost every student pulled out a planner to write those down. This demonstrates that otherwise bright and prepared beginning college students, although prepared to record their assignments, nevertheless need to learn how to be effective listeners and note takers in class.

It is really very simple: when you are in class, take notes. If your professor is lecturing, take down what strikes you as important. And pay attention to make sure that you write down whatever the professor lectures about that is not in the assigned readings. If you have followed the earlier guidance regarding coming to class having completed the assigned readings and done that well, then you will be that much more prepared to make strategic decisions regarding what and what not to write down.

Notes from Lectures

▶ Take notes when the professor, lecturer, T.A., or guest speaker is talking.

Take extensive notes. These people know a great deal more than you about the subject. Trust that they will be giving you information that is important for you to know, learn from, and use in your assignments and tests. And you never know how much of the information may be useful later in life. Write down as much as possible. Later when you read over your notes, you will decide which parts of your notes you want to highlight or otherwise annotate for review.

Notes from Q&A and Discussions

▶ Take notes when your fellow students are speaking.

Whether your classmates are asking a question, answering a question, or otherwise sharing their thoughts, write down the main ideas that you see as potentially valuable to your course work and your learning. Some questions and off-the-cuff comments may be directly valuable to your studying or other work for the class, so pay close attention to your peers' contributions. Doing so contributes to your learning, and it communicates to your peers that you value their contributions and that they matter. Even such a simple act can mean a great deal to someone else.

Notes from Audiovisual Material

▶ Take notes when there is a film, short video, or other multimedia used in class.

Based on your readings in the text, your alert attention in class, and your extensive note taking throughout the term, you can use your

strategic decision making to determine what to write down and what not to write down about a film, video, or other multimedia event presented in class. As usual, it is better to err on the side of writing down too much rather than not enough.

Notes from Group Activities

▶ Take notes when you are doing group work.

Even when your group is instructed to have one note taker to record your group's thoughts to share with the class as a whole, it is smart to also include the ideas from your group discussion in your own class notes. Sometimes another student's contribution will be the catalyst for your own ideas later on as you work on an essay, an exam, or a term paper. And as noted previously, writing down others' thoughts and questions communicates to them that you value their contributions.

As you begin to pay greater attention to the importance of note taking for your assigned readings and in-class lectures, discussions, and group work, you will become a more accomplished note taker. Over time, you will learn how to decide what is important to include in your notes, and you will develop your own structure and format for your notes. Nowadays, notes are more often taken in digital form, but some situations will necessitate handwritten notes. If the latter is the case, take the time to transfer your handwritten notes into digital form for clarity, organization, and later use.

Faculty Office Hours

You can make faculty office hours *work for you*. Every month, go to your instructors' office hours at least once. If you want to do better in class, ask for their advice about how to proceed, how to improve, and how to excel. And if you are already doing very well in class, still go to office hours to talk with your professors about the course material, your ideas, and how you might be able to develop your work into potential undergraduate research or creative projects. Plan your office hours meetings ahead of time. Bring your ideas and questions (brainstormed and written down in advance of your visit). Pay close attention to what your instructor says, be appreciative, and take notes about what is said! Here are a few additional tips to make even more strategic use of your office hours visits.

Career Guidance

▶ Ask your professors for career guidance.

Remember that your professors are experts in their respective fields. Some professors do interdisciplinary work and have more than one specialization. Your professors will have some very good suggestions for you about majors, minors, concentrations, careers, graduate study, and job prospects.

Experiential Learning Opportunities

▶ Ask your professors how and where to gain experiential learning opportunities.

These opportunities are important in balancing out your academic learning. It is crucial that you gain significant and valuable experiential apprenticeships such as internships, work study, independent study, research assistantships, undergraduate research, service learning, and other applied learning opportunities. Your professors will be able to assist you in finding these or at least pointing you toward others who can help you.

Additional Readings

▶ Ask your professors to suggest additional reading that might be of interest and value to you.

Your professors have devoted their lives to their love of learning. Your professors know a great deal. Take advantage of their knowledge and seek valuable suggestions from them that will benefit you in their classes, in your other classes, in the workplace, and throughout your life. Utilize your professors in support of your continued learning.

Faculty Research and Scholarly/Creative Interests

▶ Ask your professors about their research and scholarly/creative interests.

Remember that your relationships with your faculty are two-way. Be courteous, not self-centered in your interactions with faculty. College is not all about you. You do want to learn as much as you can while you are a college student. You want to increase your knowledge and skill sets, and much of that development comes from your professors. When you ask your professors about their research and scholarly interests, you (1) show your interest in learning, (2) demonstrate your respect for your instructor's expert knowledge, (3) show interest in your instructor's current scholarly and/or creative pursuits, and (4) learn more. All of this is important for a range of reasons that will be explored in the "Intensive Learning Opportunities" section. Also, instead of asking specifically about your instructors' research, you might want to phrase it in a way that asks about their "research and scholarly interests." If your instructors are not currently doing research, this enables them to talk about their current scholarly interests. If a professor works in an arts area, ask about her or his "current creative interests in the field."

Group Visits to Office Hours

▶ Go to office hours with some other students.

By being in a group, you can make office hours an extension of your class time. You can raise questions and talk about related, but somewhat off-topic, materials that would be out of place in the classroom. Or you can raise current topics in class for an impromptu review session. Every so often, get together with a few of your peers from class for a special office hours visit.

Intensive Learning Opportunities

Pay special attention to any intensive learning opportunities that may be required or optional (e.g., project teams, undergraduate research or creative production, service learning, related out-of-class lectures and other events, etc.).

Project Teams and In-Class Group Work

You should expect that you will have many opportunities to work in groups throughout your college years. Group work presents one of the most difficult aspects of undergraduate study. Even so, it provides you with invaluable opportunities to develop and practice some of the most important skills for the workplace: interpersonal communications, individual integrity, teamwork, initiative, personal work ethic, and leadership.

All students have the challenging experience of working in groups. Everyone knows the problems that occur when team members do not pull their weight. Unfortunately, you will not always be in groups in which every student is fully prepared, fully engaged, and fully participative. Do not dwell on the people who are not fully contributing to your group's success. Instead, focus on making your group's work highly successful and

Be a leader and solid team member when you work in groups.

ensuring that your own participation is at the highest level. To do so, here are a few helpful suggestions.

- **Listen to each student's contributions.** Even if students are saying things that make little sense, such that you can tell they are not well prepared (or not even prepared at all!), still listen. They might have some ideas that are of value to the group anyway. If a student is wholly unprepared, you could ask them to take a few minutes to quietly review one page of the text (even if you know it will be their first reading). In this way, that student can contribute, even if not at a high level.

- **As a strong group member, do be careful not to take over the group and do too much.** Remember to make space for everyone to contribute as best she or he can. Feel free to ask your group members how they would like to contribute.

- **Encourage your fellow group members to play to your group's strengths.** Consult together about each other's ideas. Build on them. You want your group to produce the best work possible. If someone suggests a really good idea, before it gets lost, tell your group what you see as strong in that idea. And if someone suggests a pretty weak idea, see how you can build on it and move the group forward with a better developed idea.

- **If your group needs to present some work to the class as a whole, encourage your teammates to select the ideas, answers, and examples that are the most impressive for presentation.** You want your group (and you) to look good! You want to show the class and your professor that your group's work is on task, insightful, thorough, creative, and innovative. Do not buckle under to a student who insists on his or her pet idea for presentation. Encourage your teammates to select what will make your team look best to the rest of the class and to your professor. And make smart choices regarding *who* and *how* to present your work to the class so your team's presentation is highly professional—in content and presentation. Even with solid material, you want to ensure that it is presented well. Consult with your team members regarding the best individuals to present and the best style, structure, and manner of your group's presentation.

- **If you end up in a group in which you are convinced that you are the only or one of the few well-prepared students, then carry much or all of the load for your group, do that *very* well, and be gracious to your group mates.** Who knows why any student is unprepared for a class? Each student has his or her own story about what happened and about what is going on in his or her life. If you need to carry your whole team, do it with dignity. Do it with class. And you will be able to be proud of your quality work and performance.

- **Be a leader in your group.** Make your ideas clear to your teammates. Find ways in which the others can contribute. Even if they are underprepared for the task at hand, they just might be able to suggest possible ideas that *you* can connect to the actual material that was supposed to have been read and studied ahead of time. Under-prepared team members will happen in the workplace as well. Group assignments in college will be good practice for dealing with such situations after college.

- **Be proud of your work in each of your groups.** Do not be bitter about times when you have to carry the load. Even if other students end up receiving a grade they do not deserve, you know that in receiving a top grade, you have earned it. You also know that you are developing valuable skill sets and gaining the learning that the other students are missing out on.

Undergraduate Research or Creative Production

Among the most rewarding experiences that students report from their undergraduate years are the opportunities to work closely with faculty on research and creative projects. Whether you are a biology major working in a lab with one of your professors, a creative writing major revising a new creative piece with your professor's guidance, a business major working intensively on a study of business ethics for your senior project, or a music major preparing for your senior recital, students report that such intensive undergraduate research and creative productions are exciting and rewarding! It is here that students see the fruition of their hard work, the results of their study and practice.

Much of your undergraduate research and creative production will be required of you in your classes as term papers, lab work, and class projects. You want to take all of these very seriously and do your best. You want your papers, lab work, and projects to be so strong that they can be considered for competitions, presentation in student research exhibitions, revision for presentation at professional conferences or juried creative competitions, or simply kept in your developing professional portfolio as exemplary models of your work.

- **In student research colloquia and expositions in your department, college, or university, you can present your research in poster, video, and paper presentations.** Throughout your work life, you will need to articulate your work to peers, bosses, and those who report to you. In your student research colloquia and expositions, you have the opportunity to (1) practice your professional communications skills, (2) share your in-depth research and creative production with others, and (3) learn how to translate work in your field so that it is accessible to people working in other disciplines.

- **At professional conferences and workshops, you can present your research or creative work.** Your professors, instructors, and graduate teaching assistants can provide you with information about undergraduate conferences relevant for your field and specific project. Depending on your work, you may also be directed to consider higher level regional, national, and international conferences for presentation on your own or in collaboration with your professor. Many colleges and universities provide funding to assist undergraduates to attend such events, along with their faculty who oversaw the project.

- **For displays of student-produced creative work, there are music performances, dramatic productions, poetry/prose readings, gallery art shows, and other expositions that you can consider.** Your professors and fellow students

will be able to guide you toward the appropriate venues for your creative work. In most cases, there will be opportunities to present your work at your own college or university. Speak with your professors and fellow students to learn about other opportunities outside your institution.

■ **Even more competitive opportunities for your undergraduate research and creative production can be found in professional publications and juried presentations.** Talk with your professors to learn about scholarly journals, creative writing journals and magazines, and competitive juried presentations of art and music that might work for your research or creative product.

For more information on undergraduate research and creative production, you can go to the website of the Council for Undergraduate Research: www.cur.org. In Chapter 8: "Networking and Mentoring: Teamwork, Leadership, Strategic Relationships," additional information regarding undergraduate research opportunities will be discussed. If you are fortunate enough to be able to participate in such work, you will have the opportunity to increase your learning, develop new skill sets, and practice your learning in the experiential and applied manner that employers greatly value.

Feel free to meet with your professors to talk about opportunities to conduct research with them. Most professors are engaged in active research and creative production, and they appreciate interested undergraduate research assistants who can help with research and creative work. When you assist a faculty member in her or his work, this is experiential learning that students find especially exciting and rewarding and that will be valuable on your résumé or professional vita.

If you have observed the rules presented earlier in this chapter, demonstrating mature and focused attention toward your learning activities, your professor will perceive you as a diligent, responsible, intelligent, and impressive student. That image may result in opportunities with your professors.

In one class I taught, I had a student with absolutely terrible writing skills. I was concerned how well the student would do in the class, but she worked really hard and did much better than I expected. The next semester, that student signed up for another class with me. Even though I was worried that she would not succeed in the second course, she ended up working so hard and improving so much that her course grade rose to a solid A by the end of the term! She made so much progress that she would be one of the first students that I would invite onto a research project team.

You want to be such a student—one of the first students that your professors will think of when they have such special learning opportunities to extend to strong students. In this way, you will gain valuable experiential learning, hands-on practice, and a significant and strategic résumé line item.

Service-Learning Opportunities

Service learning involves volunteer activities that relate to your course work. The volunteer activities serve as hands-on practice that you then incorporate into your class study—either as part of a larger project or as experiential learning that you write about in an essay or term paper. In some cases, your volunteer service draws directly upon the skills that you are learning in your classes. In such activities, you will see concrete uses of your learning as it relates to actions in the world that address social, environmental, and economic problems.

Feel free to ask your professor or department chair in your major or minor for possible relevant service activities. Your professor may recommend specific activities that relate directly to your class assignments. If service learning is required in one of your classes, then you will be participating in such experiential learning activities as part of your class; take advantage of this opportunity, perhaps spending more than the required hours volunteering. This can turn into a significant activity that you can emphasize to prospective employers. If service learning is not required in your classes, there may be other faculty members who are actively involved in service learning who would be happy to help you further your learning in this direction; department chairs can usually give you this information.

Your college or university will have an office of student affairs that can point you in the right direction to find service-learning opportunities—either classes that incorporate service-learning into the curriculum or volunteer opportunities that you can relate to your course work as part of a project or paper. Think about the projects and term papers that you will be assigned and think about any ways that you could incorporate service activities as central parts of the project or paper. If you are not involved in an undergraduate research project, you can discuss your firsthand experiences in class papers and assignments for heightened experiential learning and later talking points for future employers. Definitely include them on your résumé.

Lectures and Other Events Related to Your Classes

Explore the range of out-of-class learning experiences that will benefit your course work and your overall learning as a college student. On most college campuses, there are arts events and lectures, workshops and conferences, colloquia, and demonstrations. Many of these are on campus; many more are off campus in the surrounding area and further afield. Even more of these are accessible digitally via websites, online videos, recorded lectures (audio and video), and interactive events. Some of these will be announced and recommended by your professors; others you will need to seek out. Each week, you should check the postings of events on campus. Most department, college, and university websites include this information, usually with daily updates. Many events are still chalked on campus walkways and put up on bulletin boards. Also, individuals whom you are adding to your professional network may inform you of particular events. Remember to add these people to your Facebook, LinkedIn, and other social networking sites.

This chapter, "Class Performance: Preparation and Participation," has provided you with key information and guidance to make your class sessions work for you. Remember that you want your college years to provide you with the training and knowledge that you will need to excel in the workplace and to be a success in your chosen field. You also want to gain as much knowledge as possible for your future role as an active and participatory member of your community, nation, and world.

The more well educated and experienced you are, the more you will be able to contribute to the well-being and restoration of the world as an effective community member, citizen of your nation, and 21st-century citizen of the world. Each person who can contribute in important and valuable ways is vitally needed. And your in-class learning combines the academic learning of course material, in-class experiential practice for in-session work (e.g., meetings and project team work), and additional opportunities for disciplined focus, rigorous thought, and applied practice.

Assigned Reading Note-Taking Exercise

The following note-taking experience will give you a model for strong and strategic note taking in your classes so you will know how to make note taking work for you. Then all that is needed to become an experienced and astute note taker is to practice. As you take notes from each assigned reading and during class, your note taking will become increasingly easier, more strategic, and more effective over time.

Review this entire chapter and, if you haven't already done so, highlight, underline, or otherwise mark important points. Even if they are already in bold or a large-type font,

you need to mark them yourself. As you do this, include any thoughts and questions that you might have in relation to any of the topics, and write down your thoughts in the margins or in note form.

Worksheet A. Now that you have thoroughly annotated the reading, write down all the key points, explanations, arguments, and examples in the chapter that you see as especially important. You want your notes to be complete and strategic. Think about what is really important. You want your notes to include all of the key elements of the reading. Please list here the key points and examples in the chapter:

1. _____
   _____

2. _____
   _____

3. _____
   _____

4. _____
   _____

5. _____
   _____

6. _____
   _____

7. _____
   _____

8. _____
   _____

9. _____
   _____

10. _____
    _____

11. _____

12. _____

13. _____

14. _____

15. _____

16. _____

17. _____

18. _____

19. _____

20. _____

21. _____

22. _____

23. _____

24. _____

25. _____

26. _____

27. _____

28. _____

29. _____

30. _____

Worksheet B. Review the notes you just listed. Now you are to study those notes and condense the chapter's main ideas as delineated in your notes down to 10 key ideas. In this way, you are making strategic decisions regarding what are the most important ideas from the longer list. This is an important critical-thinking decision-making activity.

1. _____
   _____

2. _____
   _____

3. _____
   _____

4. _____
   _____

5. _____
   _____

6. _____
   _____

7. _____
   _____

8. _____
   _____

9. _____
   _____

10. _____
    _____

This much shorter list provides the type of abbreviated and summarized set of notes that you would use to study just prior to a test or exam. Each point in this shorter set of notes points back to more information on the prior sheet, which connects back to the more extensive and involved material in the readings. This is exactly the sort of condensing exercise that you want to do in relation to your regular class assignments. This is also the sort of activity that you want to engage in when you prepare for meetings in the workplace.

3 Academic Skills

Commitment, Time Management, Study Habits

I have had my dream—like others—
and it has come to nothing, so that
I remain now carelessly
with feet planted on the ground
and look up at the sky—
feeling my clothes about me,
the weight of my body in my shoes,
the rim of my hat, air passing in and out
at my nose—and decide to dream no more.

— *William Carlos Williams (1921), "Thursday," Sour Grapes*

Every great dream begins
with a dreamer. Always
remember, you have
within you the strength,
the patience, and the
passion to reach for the
stars to change the world.

— *Harriet Tubman (1820–1913)*

Failure is simply the
opportunity to begin
again, this time more
intelligently.

— *Henry Ford*

The average person puts only 25% of his energy and ability
into his work. The world takes off its hat to those who put in
more than 50% of their capacity, and stands on its head for
those few and far between souls who devote 100%.

— *Andrew Carnegie*

1. **Learning and Skills:** Gain the high-level learning and skills that are reflected in a strong G.P.A. and that will be useful in life and career.

2. **Class Performance:** Develop a consistently high-caliber performance in classes in order to earn higher grades.

3. **Time Management:** Practice simple yet powerful time-management strategies in order to accomplish more . . . better.

4. **Commitment:** Intensify your commitment to each class to produce improved performance and greater satisfaction.

5. **Personal Study and Learning Styles:** Strategically build upon individual study and learning styles for heightened success.

Virtually any student can achieve top grades. Even though many will argue that you should not focus on your grades, the truth of the matter is that grades are really important—not just for getting the high G.P.A., but because of what that number represents. If you have a good G.P.A., that shows that you do good work. An *exceptional* G.P.A. shows that you do *exceptional* work.

> "You say that a high G.P.A. is important, but is it really all that important? I'm doing okay in most of my classes. I get mainly B's and a few A's and C's, so that I have a good 3.2 G.P.A. Why should I want to get higher grades and a higher G.P.A.?"

> "Some classes are boring, not in my major, and taught by professors I don't get. But I do really well in the classes I like in my major. Those classes will show companies that I can do top work for them. Isn't this enough? I shouldn't have to work hard in classes that are not in my major."

> "I am very involved on campus. If I study more, I'd have to take time away from the organizations and clubs I'm involved with, and social time with friends is important too. You've already said that a well-rounded college experience is important! Do I really need to study more?"

These are all great questions and comments that get to the heart of the issue. Grades may well be the most sensitive and stressful topic for college students. Most important is for you not to stress about grades. Productive stress keeps you on your toes, but you do not want stress to become debilitating.

My husband's uncle Pepe would remind us, "No te preocupes." ("Don't worry." "Don't let yourself be preoccupied.") When he would say this to me, he would playfully anglicize the Spanish into "Don't precupe," which, of course, doesn't really mean anything. But combining the reminder not to stress out along with his made up and playful "Spanglish" would bring a smile to whoever was stressing out about whatever. The reminder plus the humor would help the person to relax. Sometimes just such playful, caring, and wise advice can relieve a bit of one's daily stress. As Chapter 1 emphasizes, there are many ways to eliminate, reduce, or even avoid stress, and some of these ways are as simple as Tio Pepe's playful advice.

Insofar as grades are concerned, instead of stressing, you should just do the work, put in the hours, do your best, and then feel good about that, *even when the grade you receive may be bit lower than you want.* If you work really hard and in smart ways, you *will* do very well. You *will* get higher grades. And if a grade here or there is a bit lower, that will not matter in the long run because overall you will still have an impressive G.P.A.

In this chapter, you will learn first why high grades are so valued by graduate schools, professional schools, and employers. And you will learn some simple strategies that will help you make exceptional grades.

High Grades

- Students with high G.P.A.s are encouraged to include that number on their résumés.
- If your overall G.P.A. is not great, but your G.P.A. in your major or in a specific skill set area is higher and pretty good, list that on your résumé.
- Employers and graduate and professional schools want to see high G.P.A. scores, but they also expect to see other *evidence* that demonstrates what a high G.P.A. is supposed to show.
- Some students achieve a high G.P.A. in their major, but it is important to do well in all of your classes, including those not in your major.

Time-Management Skills

- To get a high G.P.A. that reflects substantive effort and learning, you need to put in the hours that the top students are spending studying.
- There is absolutely nothing wrong with graduating in 4.5 or 5 years—especially if you are doing this strategically and in ways that make sense, such as picking up an additional major, minor or other academic credential, internship, or other first-hand experience.
- In organizing your time to get a high G.P.A., you are learning and practicing invaluable time-management skills of great value in the workplace. And as you restructure your time from semester to semester, you are practicing adaptive time-management skills that an increasingly dynamic workplace demands.

Commitment and Increased Satisfaction

- Students with the highest G.P.A.s bring the same drive and commitment to excellence

in their general education and core classes as they do to the classes in their major fields of study.

- Top students perceive both short-term and long-term benefits in the learning they gain from each of their classes.
- There is enjoyment in the act of discovering new things and in developing new skills. Top students strive to find areas of interest in every class.

Personalized Study and Learning Styles

- Effective study habits need to be adapted individually for and differentially to each student.
- Even though students will differ in their preferred and successful study and learning modes, there is no substitute for doing the hard work, putting in the time, and demonstrating the necessary discipline for academic success.
- Beware the distractive dangers of multitasking. Evaluate when that works for you and more importantly when it does not work for you. Ensure that your studying is effective.

Let's start with a look at why your G.P.A. is important. It is far more than just a number.

The Learning and Skills Your G.P.A. Represents

Grades are important to students for a number of reasons. First of all, the grades a student receives in each class will average together into the all-important grade point average. Grade point average is taken seriously by potential employers, and it is taken *very* seriously by graduate programs, professional schools (medical, business, law), and other postgraduate programs.

Résumés

When students are looking for employment, their G.P.A. is one of the first line items on their résumés—that is, if it is a strong G.P.A. Say that you work for a company and you are hiring someone for a position and you have two very promising candidates right out of college. What if both have similar majors and experiences and they both come from comparable universities and programs? One job applicant has a 3.75 G.P.A. and graduated with honors. The other has a 3.15 G.P.A. or (worse) no G.P.A. even listed on the résumé. Which job candidate would you hire?

Students with average or low G.P.A.s are advised to leave their G.P.A.s off their résumés because a résumé is supposed to present a person's strengths and achievements, not their weaknesses. But be aware that the absence of a G.P.A. on a résumé communicates to potential employers that your academic work may very well have been substandard.

If your overall G.P.A. is not great, consider including a more specific high G.P.A.

- If your G.P.A. in your major is strong, list that, but be prepared to answer questions about the difference between your major G.P.A. and your overall G.P.A.

■ If your freshman and sophomore years were not great, but you really turned around your performance during your junior and senior years, then you can list your overall G.P.A. from just those years (e.g., "G.P.A. 3.75 junior/senior yrs."). If a potential employer asks about that, it provides you with a great talking point about your academic turn-around, your now disciplined and *high-level* academic and extracurricular performance, and how that will translate into the highest caliber of work on the job.

■ Look over your course grades and see whether you have top grades in a grouping of classes that center around a specific skill set. For example, if you did very well in your philosophy and literature courses, demonstrating your analytical and critical thinking skills, highlight those grades. You could include several line items on your résumé that showcase your strong skill sets:

Concentrated Course Work in Strategic Skill Sets

Communications Skills: Freshman Composition, Speech Communications, Business Writing, Argument and Debate, and Web Page Design. G.P.A.—4.0

Analytical and Critical Thinking Skills: Introduction to Philosophy, Logic, Existentialism, Early American Literature, Shakespeare I, Chaucer, Milton, Emily Dickinson. G.P.A.—3.7

Multicultural and Globalization Literacy: African American Literature, Women and Culture, Native American Literatures, Asian Religions, Western Civilization. G.P.A.—3.85

Students with high G.P.A.s should include that number on their résumés.

G.P.A. Grounds—Evidence of What You Have Done and Learned

The real value of a high G.P.A. is what it represents: namely your learning and accomplishments. Employers and graduate and professional schools do not value a high G.P.A. simply because it is a higher score. They value a high G.P.A. because it demonstrates discipline, a strong work ethic, learning at a high level, respect for your professors, strong time-management skills, responsibility, and intelligence.

■ Your strong work ethic: "This job candidate will be a hard worker."

■ Your discipline: "This job candidate will follow through."

■ Your time-management skills: "This job candidate will get the job done on time."

■ Your responsibility: "This job candidate will do what he is asked to do and will take responsibility for his actions."

■ Your respect for your professors: "This job candidate will respect and listen to bosses, other superiors, and other legitimate authorities."

■ Your education: "This job candidate has the needed education and skills for the job."

■ Your engaged learning: "This job candidate is committed to being highly informed, even when that means changing course on a project. She will continue to learn after college."

■ And your intelligence: "This job candidate has strong critical and creative thinking skills and will find solutions for problems."

Your G.P.A. needs to be backed up by evidence. Your letters of recommendation; project reports; papers;

portfolios of your work, extra classes, academic credentials (e.g., majors, minors, concentrations, certificates, etc.); extracurricular organizational involvement; leadership roles; collaborative research with a faculty member; conference presentations; tutoring other students; academic honors and awards; and other distinguishing academic accomplishments from your college time—all this presents your evidence.

■ Better Class Performance to Improve Grades

Doing well in your major classes shows how well you have done in the field in which you have strengths and interests. It is important to do very well in your chosen field—after all, this demonstrates your competency and skills for the job. But it is also important for you to do well in your other classes outside your major, even in your general education and core curriculum classes.

If you do very well in a class that is in a field that you have struggled with previously, a high grade shows that you can and will accomplish at a high level even when the work is difficult. This is important to employers. When you are in the workplace, you will not always be doing work that plays to your strengths. If you plan to succeed at a high level in life, you need to learn early on to strive to succeed even when the work is difficult. Many of your college classes will give you the opportunity to practice and demonstrate this important work ethic.

If you do very well in a class that is in a field that you are not interested in at all, this high grade shows that you can and will accomplish at a high level even when you are not very interested in the topic of study. This also means a great deal to employers. When you are in the workplace, you will not always be doing work that you enjoy. If you want to succeed at a high level in life, you want to practice in your college classes working hard and succeeding even when the work is not the most interesting to you.

- Remember that you want to get a *great* education that will prepare you for a lifetime of fulfilling contributions in the world.

    You want to be of service in your community.

- Remember that you want to be a *very* competitive job candidate.

    You want to get a job.

- Remember that you want to be a *very* competitive applicant to graduate or professional school.

    You want to get into graduate or professional school, and you want to get into your desired graduate or professional school.

- Remember that you want to perform at the *highest* levels when you are in the workforce.

    You want to excel at work, maintain job security, and get promotions and raises.

- Remember that you want to perform at the *highest* levels in graduate and professional school.

    You want to excel in graduate or professional school and receive awards for your work.

You might be asking, "OK, but *how* do I get great grades in all of my classes?" The good news is that it is not all that hard to learn how to become a top student. There are many books that will give you suggestions for improving your studying, your productivity in your classes, and overall G.P.A. These guides will provide helpful recommendations about whether to keep daily lists, study with other students, take practice tests, review previous exams, take hard classes, avoid certain instructors, read all of the assigned readings, and so on. You'll also find suggestions about shrewd time management and even how to get good grades by spending less time studying.

If you really want to make college work for you, there really is one central element to college success, and that is . . . TIME.

Smart and Strategic Use of Your Time

There is no way around it. To get a high G.P.A. that reflects your substantive effort and learning, you need to put in the hours that the top students are spending studying.

Many students think that those who are on the honor roll and dean's lists, who are members of prestigious academic societies (e.g., Phi Beta Kappa or Phi Kappa Phi), who are conducting undergraduate research projects and presenting their work with faculty and at conferences, and who have the highest G.P.A.s are the ultimate nerds and geeks who are somehow different from all of the other students. Well, they *are* different from the other students who are not studying as much. Top students are more motivated, disciplined, and committed. But it is important for you to understand that any person can become a more motivated, disciplined, and committed student. People are not born this way. These are learned behaviors.

The simplest way for you to accomplish the higher grades achieved by the honor roll and dean's list students is by reassessing how you are spending your time. Top students are spending *a lot of time* on their studies, on their future plans, and on significant extracurricular activities. If you want top grades, then you too need to spend your time in smart and intentional ways.

Most students can get through their courses by putting in the minimum time necessary, but if you do this, you will neither be thinking nor acting strategically regarding how you want to *make college work for you.* To do well, you want to spend an average of two to three hours of study time each week for each credit hour you are taking. For the average full-time load of 15 credit hours, that means 30 to 45 hours of studying each week. If you have 18 credit hours, then you will need to find 36 to 54 hours of time to study each week. It is best to not overload your time with more credit hours than you can truly succeed with.

> "But I need to take extra credits so that I can graduate in four years without having to take out more loans. And I work 20 or 30 hours each week to pay for school. AND having a double-major requires that I take additional classes, so I really need to take the 18 credits each term. What with working and taking 18 hours of credits, I can't study 36 hours, much less 54 hours, each week for my classes!"

Time Spent in College

Yes, if you're working part-time to pay for school, studying 30-plus hours a week is a challenge, but that does not mean it is impossible. Even though the academic system was originally set up for wealthy young people several centuries ago for whom school was a full-time activity, if you need to work during the school year and have additional time constraints than may have been the case for students of a bygone era, you will need to figure out how to ensure that you are putting in the hours necessary to take college seriously and strategically and to make the most of your college years. If doing better in your classes means taking fewer credits each semester, then you need to figure out how to make that possible. You just need to make a plan that will work best for you. Be flexible, and consider these options:

- Begin your college career at a two-year college and then transfer to a four-year college or university to finish up, thereby giving yourself an economic buffer to be able to take additional courses or credits.

- Take one semester or one year off from your four-year college to attend a community college where you can take the additional lower-level courses you need for your second major or minor or to pick up an applied skill set and credentialing that the community college offers.

- Take five or more years to graduate so you can get the learning and skills from a double major or major and minor or other such configurations.

- Take five or more years to graduate so you can study abroad, run for political office, or develop a new and valuable skill set before graduation.

- Take five or more years to graduate to allow yourself time to focus on community service work or other nonprofit work.

- Take more time to graduate with your undergraduate degree so that you can focus on your high-level performance at your part-time or full-time job.

- Take more time to graduate in order to lighten your course load each semester to provide greater attention to each class and ensure top grades.

- Transfer to a college that is less expensive in order to afford to take additional credits, gain additional learning and credentialing, and be more involved experientially on and off campus. (As a bonus, when you transfer, the new school reports your G.P.A. only based on your grades at that school. If your prior course work was not as successful as you would like, this provides a fresh G.P.A. start at your new school.)

- Take summer classes for added course work undergraduate research, and other educational and experiential opportunities.

- Intersperse your degree with a number of select classes from an accredited online university or MOOC (massive open online class)—thereby gaining an added certification or other credential.

Strong time management that includes planned, intentional time will lead to heightened academic and experiential success in college. Remember to take your time in college to do your best, to spend more effective hours when you study, and to organize your time to include extracurricular activities. Do not rush through college. After all, you do want to get as much out of your college years as possible.

Take your time. Rushing through may gain a degree more quickly, but just getting the credential is not what is most important. It is what you have learned and accomplished that are most important. If you rush through your studying and let your time in college slip through your fingers with time that was insufficiently focused or even wasted, then your degree will mean much less. It is better to graduate strongly in five years or more than it is to graduate in four years with overloaded semesters, a lower G.P.A. than you want, few extracurricular activities, little leadership experience, and minimal learning.

If you make strategic decisions regarding classes and majors and organizational involvement and volunteer activities, you can make a degree on the five-year plan look very impressive to prospective employers and to graduate and professional schools.

If you are graduating on the five- or six-year plan because you are working to pay for your meals in restaurants, because you spent too much time partying, because of classes that you dropped or had to retake, because you changed your major too late to graduate on time, or because your boyfriend or girlfriend broke up with you and you couldn't focus on school, well, these things happen. But they will not make your college years look very strategic to employers and graduate schools. Instead, your five- or six-year plan will look more like a failed four-year plan. Life happens, so this is where contingency planning is essential. Review your overall package and see where you can make the most effective choices now so that by the time you graduate your résumé and grades will reflect your strategic planning, effort, and best work.

Time-Management Skills

To excel in any field or activity requires the requisite number of practice hours. As a student, it means spending the hours that are necessary to do required and even recommended readings, spending time taking and studying notes, doing homework and extra practice problems, writing and revising paper drafts, taking practice tests, and working on projects. Chickering and Gamson emphasize that time management is one of the key elements to success in college. They assert that "time plus energy equals learning. There is no substitute for time on task. Learning to use one's time well is critical for students and professionals alike. Students need help in learning effective time management" (1987, n.p.).

The good news is that you can learn how to improve your time-management skills. As Kelci Lynn Lucier points out in her short piece "Learn to Manage Your Time in College," "Time management isn't a skill you pick up right away. It takes—ironically—time to learn and time to master" (2011, n.p.). As you practice better time management by setting up clear and doable daily and weekly schedules for your study time, extracurricular activity time, work and family time, and personal and downtime, you will see a heightened return on your effort through higher productivity, greater success and happiness, and lower stress levels.

In a *Chicago Tribune* interview, Diana Scharf Hunt, author of the book *Studying Smart: Time Management for College Students,* explains that "one of the top four reasons for dropping out, other than the economic and personal reasons and not being able to make it academically, is the inability to get organized" (Maes, 1986, n.p.). So simply by working out a clear plan for your daily and weekly work, you can address two of these four potential challenges to college success: organization and academics. And as you develop your time management skills, you will find the time for studying.

If the specified number of study hours for the number of credits you are taking or planning to take seems impossible to you, then you will need to decide the level at which you want to succeed in college. It might mean dropping a class in order to excel in the others. It might mean becoming less active in a campus organization or two. It might mean working more in the summer in order to work less or not at all during the school year. But to excel in your learning requires effort and hours. There are no shortcuts. Let's break this down into some simple numbers for your time studying.

Credit Hours	×	Hours of Study per Credit	=	Study Hours per Week
18		2–3		36–54
17		2–3		34–51
16		2–3		32–48
15		2–3		30–45
14		2–3		28–42
13		2–3		26–39
12		2–3		24–36
11		2–3		22–33
10		2–3		20–30
9		2–3		18–27
8		2–3		16–24
7		2–3		14–21
6		2–3		12–18
5		2–3		10–15
4		2–3		8–12
3		2–3		6–9

In their *College Teaching* journal article "Cell Phones, Text Messaging, and Facebook: Competing Time Demands of Today's College Students," Drumheller, Hanson, Mallard, Mckee, and Schlegel (2010) affirm the fact that most college students are simply not spending enough time studying to learn the material in their course at sufficiently high levels.

> Nearly two-thirds (62%) of students surveyed by the Pew Research Project reported studying for classes no more than seven hours per week, while only 14% reported studying 12 or more hours per week. Students focus more on updating their Facebook status than downloading their homework assignments, which profoundly impacts their collegiate experience (p. 24).

Note that hours spent studying does not include time hanging out with friends in the library for an hour or two during which little actual studying is accomplished.

Research conducted by Nonis and Hudson (2006) and published in the *Journal of Education for Business* supports the findings regarding the crucial role played by focused and effective study time:

> Students with high ability who also spend more time studying are the ones who are most likely to excel in college as indicated by their GPA. It should be clearly communicated to [students] that their abilities, motivation, and behavior work in tandem to influence their academic performance. If students are lacking in even one of these areas, their performances will be significantly lower. . . . The results of this study show the impact of ability on academic performance to be much higher for students who spend more time studying than for those who spend less (p. 157).

Some who have not yet learned how to be top students who are studying smart and studying hard might think, "What's the point of spending more time and putting out more effort and studying more if my grades will only improve a little and

I still won't be learning things relevant to my future career? Why do I need to get an "A" in my general education classes? They're not in my major." These are all great questions! They really get to the heart of studying and grades: which is learning. Remember that it is not the number that is important. You want to get the greatest return on your college investment in terms of increased knowledge, developed skill sets, rediscovered joy in learning, and heightened creative and critical thinking abilities.

In today's competitive global economy and workplace, by prioritizing your studying, you will make yourself one of the most viable candidates for competitive internships and jobs. You just need to put in the hours necessary to succeed in every class. Although the total number of study hours may seem impossible in light of your other time commitments, most people can find ways to better organize their time, reduce periods of wasted time, and increase time allotted for strategic and focused studying.

Heightened Commitment and Increased Satisfaction

As you reorganize your daily and weekly schedules to accommodate more studying more effectively, you will find that your increased studying leads to actual enjoyment of not only the results but also the process. When people really work hard to accomplish something, more often than not, they discover that there is a joy involved in hard work and successful effort. This means that as you study more, you will find increasing joy and rewarding pleasure in the process of learning and in your heightened accomplishments. Of course, the flip side of all this is that if you put out only a modicum of effort with little success, more often than not the work will seem pointless because you are neither engaged nor achieving substantive success. This then becomes a self-fulfilling prophecy in that a lack of interest in particular classes and studying leads to less productive efforts, which in turn, lead to diminished interest and, inevitably, poorer academic results. What is crucial for any student to understand is that any student can achieve a positive process that leads to success and happiness. As students study more, they find more success and happiness, and as they obtain greater success and pleasure, they study even harder. You just need to decide which of these two trajectories you want to choose for your own academic career.

Also note that students with the highest G.P.A.s bring the same drive and commitment to excellence in their general education and core classes as they do to the classes in their major fields of study. I have heard hundreds of students proclaim that their general education classes and other classes outside their majors are less important than their major courses. This lack of interest in classes outside the major is one of the main reasons that so many students have a higher G.P.A. in their majors than their overall G.P.A.

And yet if you really work hard in every class and really do your best in every class, you will be surprised to find that you can make virtually any class *work for you*. This means that you may even begin to find value in your general education classes! After all, there is valuable learning that occurs in *every* class you take. While you are in school, it is impossible to know exactly which classes and which information and which skills will serve you best throughout your life. So, do not let valuable learning opportunities slip through your fingers.

You may have a class that is not in your major field, but as you work hard and begin to excel in that class, you might discover that you are really talented in that area. You might even decide to add that field as a second major or as a minor. Or one

You should want to do very well in every one of your classes.

particular class that is not in your major may offer valuable skills not directly available in your major:

- A philosophy class in which you learn the processes of ethical reasoning and how to approach different ethical problems
- An argumentative writing class in which you learn logical argumentation and advanced writing skills
- A statistics class in which you learn how to read, understand, and evaluate statistics, graphical analysis, and various types of charts
- An economics class in which you learn how to understand economics data presented by governments, corporations, or your local school district
- A literature class in which you learn critical and evaluative processes for discerning key underlying elements in stories, events, and situations

Perhaps now you're asking, "In the chapter on picking a major, you write that I should play to my strengths, pick a major in an area that I am good at and that I like. Now you're saying that I should put a lot of effort into classes that I am lousy at and that I have no interest in. So which is it?!" The answer is short and sweet: both. Students should play to their strengths in their primary fields of study, and they should work hard to excel in *every* class.

You are absolutely right that it is wise to select majors and minors that fit with your abilities. You're going to spend a lot of time on them. You definitely want to build on and develop those abilities as you progress in your chosen fields of study and in your career. A key word here is *develop* because in any job, there will be responsibilities that play to your strengths as well as other responsibilities that do not. As a college student, you want to strengthen crucial areas of learning and skill development in which you may be weaker. Some of these areas could be especially useful later on.

This is why class success is important in all of your classes, including those in which you have little interest and lesser aptitude. And such an achievement demonstrates your discipline and capacity for hard work and achieving success even when it is hard. These are the classes in which you have the ability to stand out and really impress a professor. When you work really hard in these classes, your achievement is much more impressive than doing well in classes that you like and are easy for you. And if you ask your professor for a letter of reference, he or she will be able to write enthusiastically about your ability to excel regardless of the challenge or difficulty of the task. This is exactly the sort of letter of reference you want to have in your portfolio when you are looking for jobs.

A news story from 2011 helps illustrate this: First Lady Michelle Obama said that she requires her girls, who are very athletic, to participate in two sports: one that they like and one that they don't like as much. She picks the second sport for them. When asked why, Mrs. Obama explained that, in life, we often have to do things that are important but that we do not want to do (at work, at home, in social and volunteer organizations, etc.). She said that it was important for her girls to learn to do their best even when the task is not a favorite. She explained that in learning this lesson as children, they will be better prepared to work hard throughout their lives, no matter what they would be asked to do (Kantor, 2012).

There is enjoyment in the act of discovering new things and in developing new skills. As a child, you were excited

when you learned something new. You need to rediscover that joy. If you can regain the joy of learning while you are in college, that will translate into successful performance in college and in your chosen career and work life. I can promise you that the extent to which you learn to live your life within a culture of discovery, learning, and growth is the extent to which your life will be that much more rewarding and fulfilling.

There is one other secret that top students know regarding undesired classes: Many classes that might otherwise seem boring can actually become very interesting and even fun once the student puts out more effort to learn the material. And many classes that might otherwise seem useless may actually prove to be especially useful in unforeseen ways.

Personalized Study and Learning Styles

There are many ways to study better. There are as many tips and strategies as there are students, classes, assignments, and professors. Each student is different. Each of you will find different ways of studying that *work for you*. There is no one answer to how to study that will fit every student— except the requirement of putting in sufficient focused hours. Each student and each course is unique. Professors teach differently and give different types of assignments and grade those assignments differently. And this is all okay. These differences will help you in important ways for your future careers and work:

> *Effective study habits need to be adapted individually for and differentially to each student.*

- You will develop your own personal ways of working effectively and strategically.
- You will develop flexibility in applying your work methods to different situations.
- You will have many different opportunities in your different classes to practice both.

This is why taking different types of classes with different types of assignments, different pedagogies, and different professors is a very good thing! This is also why it is good to take some classes that are relatively easy for you and other classes that are more of a challenge. This will help you learn how to respond to different challenges throughout life and in the workplace.

Successful adaptability will help you learn how to vary your studying to fit the needs of different classes and professors. This experience is invaluable for your internship, volunteer, fieldwork, and work experiences as an undergraduate because you will be that much more prepared to evaluate different situations and successfully fit your responses to the needs of each situation.

These are skills that are crucial for your success in college. Entwistle, Thompson, and Wilson (2004) cite research that documents that the most successful students approached their studying in smart and strategic ways; they "organized their studying and time allocations, worked during free periods, decided on priorities and tried to improve their study techniques" (p. 386). In their research published in the journal *Perspectives on Psychological Science*, Crede and Kuncel (2008) confirmed the extent to which students' smart and strategic studying was productive of greater academic success and higher grades: "Study skills, study attitudes, study habits, and study motivation exhibited strong and robust relationships with academic performance in college" (p. 439). You want to make smart, intentional, and strategic choices regarding where, when, and how you study.

Where to Study

Some students do really well studying in their dorm rooms, apartments, and homes. Other students find that there are too many distractions in their living space and need to hole themselves up in the library or a study hall. Some students do best in a Starbucks with their drink of choice, preferred tunes, and the surrounding activity of the café.

Think about those study sessions when you have been able to focus at the highest of levels, being focused intently on your studies. What were the surrounding circumstances when you were able to achieve this?

Worksheet A. Please list five different places where you have studied really well, bringing an intensity of focus to your work and being able to work intently for an extended period of time:

1. _____
2. _____
3. _____
4. _____
5. _____

Now look over the five places that you have listed where you have studied successfully. What are the common denominators among these places? Think about each place you've listed. You need to get a good idea about the *types of places* where you study effectively. What do these places have in common?

It is important to understand the spaces in which you work most effectively. This knowledge will also be important in your future work life. You may find that you work best when you can tune out everything else, but you end up in a job where you are working in a cubicle surrounded by lots of office noise. Then you know to keep your headphones and music handy so that, when necessary, you can tune others out in order to focus intently on what you need to get done.

Worksheet B. For each place in your list in Worksheet A, please describe four to five aspects that you feel contribute to your comfort level there and to your successful studying (e.g., silence of a library or the general bustling activity of a café, good indoor or outdoor lighting, being away from friends or with friends, available coffee and food or no accessible food nearby, comfortable seating such as a couch or a more rigid desk and chair, etc.).

1. _____
_____
_____
_____

2. _____
_____
_____
_____

3. _____
_____
_____
_____

4. _____

_____

_____

_____

5. _____

_____

_____

_____

Worksheet C. Use the factors in Worksheet B to describe the types of environments that are reflected in your successful study locations. For example, when I work most effectively, I like to have headphones with music to tune out all other sounds and possible auditory interruptions. I prefer to have a clean, well-it, and attractive space, especially with artwork on the walls or a beautiful outdoor scene. Food distracts me, but I like to have coffee or some other beverage. And I want to have the materials needed readily available. For highly successful work sessions, I need to have an environment that is (1) a clean, well-it, and attractive space, (2) the availability of a beverage, (3) the capability to eliminate auditory distractions, (4) needed materials readily available, including a wide table or desk if needed, and (5) a surrounding environment that will help restore my focus when needed (e.g., being surrounded with others studying and working seriously or a beautiful nature scene). Locales that work for me include Starbucks and other cafés, hotel rooms with a view, my office and living room, library rooms where beverages are allowed, and outdoor venues in nature. Describe your effective venues.

1. _____
2. _____
3. _____
4. _____
5. _____

You now have a clear list of the various aspects of study places that work for you. Remember what your common denominators are for highly focused and effective studying; these will be relevant factors for you to consider for your career and workplace success in the future.

Strategically recreate these sorts of spaces so that your studying and future work life are highly effective. Remember that you want a strong return on your investment of time, and making sure that your study/work venue will be successful for you is smart, intentional, and strategic.

What to Listen To

Some students wear headsets and listen to music to shut out the surrounding activity and noise. Some swear that classical music helps studying more than other types of music (some believe that Baroque music is especially effective). Some students like to have the background noise of the main room of a library or the activity in a Starbucks, Barnes and Noble café, independent café, or other public venue when they study. Many prefer the silence of library study rooms.

Worksheet D. Based on the five places where you study well listed in Worksheet A, please take a moment to describe the different sounds around you when you are most effective in your studying and work (e.g., total silence or sound, certain types of music or no music, surrounding conversations, the sounds of nature outside or recorded, everyday sounds at home, etc.):

1. _____
_____
_____

2. _____
_____
_____

3. _____
_____
_____

4. _____
_____

5. _____
_____
_____

Utilize the listening power of your surrounding environment so that it works for you and helps you to focus most intently on your studying and work. This can make a huge effect on the extent to which you can maintain your focus while you are studying.

There may be places that work for you most of the time for effective studying, but there are occasional distractions. If the venue fits, but the distractions are somewhat, well, distractive, consider earplugs or headphones with the type of music or other sounds that heighten your focus and productivity.

When to Study

Some students are very efficient in their use of time and will find a nearby place to study during an hour between classes. Some students like to study early in the morning, waking by dawn. Most students like to sleep in and do most of their studying later in the day and at night. You need to think about when you study most efficiently. Perhaps this is due to your personal biorhythms. Perhaps this is due to habit and when you have studied or had free time growing up. Regardless, you need to have a clear view regarding when you study most effectively and with the greatest sustained focus.

Worksheet E. Please list four or five times over the course of your life when you have been very effective in your studying and work (e.g., morning, afternoon, or night, anytime between classes, late at night, before dawn, before or after meals, right after classes are done for the day, etc.). Think of actual examples, whether at your community college, college, or university, in high school, or even as an elementary or junior high student. Think of specific times when you did your homework really effectively, and list five such times (e.g., one afternoon in a hotel restaurant looking out at the ocean and drinking coffee; or in the early morning beginning prior to dawn almost any day).

1. _____
2. _____

3. _____

4. _____

5. _____

Worksheet F. Now you need to think about your weekly schedule (current or future) as a college student. Based on the number of credit hours you have or will have, you need to map out a schedule that will provide at the very least two hours of study for every credit hour that you have each week. If you have 15 credit hours, then you need to schedule at least 30 hours of study time for each week to ensure a high level of success in terms of grades and learning.

For each day of the week, please list the times and the number of hours you can study. Remember that the total needs to equal at least double the hours that you are in class each week and, ideally, with some extra hours built in for heightened results and contingency planning.

Monday _____

Tuesday _____

Wednesday _____

Thursday _____

Friday _____

Saturday _____

Sunday _____

Total number of prospective study hours for the average week = _____

Okay, now you have a clear idea about where and when you have studied best over the years. Now you want to take advantage of this knowledge and put it into practice in your current and future determinations regarding where and when to study as you map out a new schedule that will work for you and maximize the return on your study times. The rest of this chapter turns to a few best tips for what to do during those study periods to make them even more successful. Some of these will be tailored just for you. Others will be tried and true study tips of direct value for every student.

How to Begin an Effective Study Session

Beginnings are important. How you begin an essay sets the stage and provides the crucial focus for the paper as a whole. How you begin a project often determines the progress your team will make over the course of the project. How you begin a study session is also important. Once you arrive in your study venue, there are some additional factors that you need to take into account.

First, you need to begin your study session when you

are not exhausted. The best situation is to have a regular schedule with sufficient sleep so that you will be awake and with energy during your study sessions. Daily exercise also helps to increase your energy levels. And if you are tired, eat something with sugar and something with protein to avoid the dreaded sugar crash. Fruit and nuts are a great combination! So are mocha lattes!

Begin your study sessions during the times when you have plenty of energy. Play to your strengths. If you are a morning person, make time in the mornings to study, even if that means getting up two hours earlier than usual and going to bed two hours earlier. If you are a night person, schedule your evening hours for studying; you can hang out with friends on the weekends or during the days.

Go to a place where you know you will study effectively. Refer to Worksheet C to recall that the right environment for studying is very important. Make smart and strategic choices regarding where you study, where you do your reading, where you do your homework.

Once you have honed in on the place and surrounding environment where you study effectively, design your work space in a way that maximizes your efficiency. If you need to refer to the Internet, to print notes from class, and to read class books, make sure that you have a big enough table for you to spread out. You want to have what you need at your fingertips. You need to spend your study time focused on the project and homework problems and test preparation; you don't want to interrupt your study session having to look for the materials you need. Do that ahead of time. And make your workspace effective and efficient. As you do this, you will be developing a key to success for your future work life.

Feng shui notwithstanding, there is much to be said regarding the value of a neat, clean, and attractive work space. If your desk is cluttered, either tidy it up or find a different place to work. Cluttered, messy, or dirty spaces are not conducive to the highest levels of creativity and productivity. Aesthetically pleasing and stimulating places contribute in big ways to creative thinking powers. Remember the inspiring and invigorating value of artwork, attractive interior design, and outdoor scenes.

Begin in a way that helps you shift gears from everyday activities and into a state of focused study. For some people, headphones and music help to make that shift. For some, beginning with prayer or meditation, reading scripture, reading a favorite poem or quotation, sitting a certain way, facing a window with a beautiful nature scene, or just getting out a favorite pen or photo helps to reorient attention into a state of focused study. Whatever works for you, it is important to do whatever is necessary to refocus away from your daily activities and into a state of focused study. Think about what works for you to achieve this.

Worksheet G. Please list five different things that you do that help you shift into a state of focused study (e.g., turning off your cell phone, saying a prayer, putting on your "intense study" music, logging out of Facebook and Twitter, reading a special meditative passage, using a computer without your games on it, having coffee or other beverages handy, or sitting away from others):

1. _____
   _____
   _____

2. _____
   _____
   _____

3. _____
   _____
   _____

4. _____

_____

_____

5. _____

_____

_____

 ## Multitasking

According to a 2006 poll in the *Los Angeles Times,* 53 percent of 12- to 17-year-olds (now college aged) say they multitask when studying; young adults 18 to 24 also reported multitasking when studying, although at only a 25 percent rate (Gaither, 2006). Many students reported that they texted friends; spent time on Facebook; and watched television, movies, or videos while studying. They also reported that much of the study time was unfocused and less effective than they would like.

As you develop and finely hone your studying routine, work out a system that works best for you for getting your work done as thoroughly, effectively, and efficiently as possible. This can be endangered by multitasking. The *Los Angeles Times* article cites research that documents that "multi-tasking can prevent students from learning subjects in great depth" (Gaither, 2006). The problem with this is that it is deep learning "that stimulates reasoning, analysis and foresight" (Gaither, 2006). These are the skills that employers are saying recent college graduates have not developed. By learning how to study effectively, in addition to higher grades, you will be increasing your critical thinking, analytical, and problem-solving skills.

Don't waste your time staring without focus at your computer screen, tablet, book, or notes or being distracted by friends or family or Facebook or your smartphone or other surrounding distractions. If you find yourself not studying effectively, take a break, get some exercise, go to sleep, relocate to a different place, or just turn your phone off. Do whatever it takes so that you will study effectively when you need to.

Beware the distractive dangers of multitasking.

 ## One Final Tip to Raise Your Grades

Many of the best students achieve at the highest levels because they are spending much more time on their school work. Let's look more closely at a suggestion from Chapter 2 about doing extra practice problems. Say that a math professor assigns 30 homework problems for one class; many of the best students will do extra problems for the additional practice. There are workbooks available for many college classes, and the workbooks have additional problems and exercises. So here is one of the other best kept secret tips about the top students: Before starting their assigned homework, top students will (1) read the explanatory pages in the auxiliary workbook for additional explanation of the material; (2) do many of the problems in the extra workbook, checking the answers against the solved problems at the back (which ideally will show the steps for working each of the problems); and then (3) turn to the assigned homework reading in the course textbook and the assigned homework problems.

If these students do 20 extra problems *before* doing their homework, so that they will have done twice as many as the other students and double the number assigned for homework, how do you think this will affect these students' performance when the tests and exams roll around? Exactly! They will have had more practice. They will be quicker on the tests and exams. By being able to work through their tests and exams more quickly, these top students buy time so that they will have *more time* for the tough problems, for the complex questions, for the difficult parts of the test or exam. Remember that the tough parts of your tests and exams require that you think more critically, more creatively, and more thoroughly; to do this, you need more time on these problems and questions and essays than on the easier ones.

So remember to study in smart, deliberative and strategic ways. Take charge and make your studying work for you.

4 Strategic Credentialing

Majors, Minors, Skill Sets

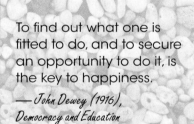

I call therefore a complete and generous Education that which fits a man to perform justly, skillfully and magnanimously all the offices both private and public of peace and war.

— *John Milton (1644), Of Education*

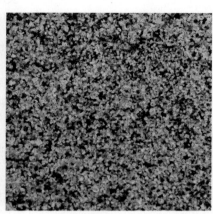

To find out what one is fitted to do, and to secure an opportunity to do it, is the key to happiness.

— *John Dewey (1916), Democracy and Education*

Students will understand the crucial importance in developing strong and relevant skills and smart and strategic credentials for the 21st-century workplace:

1. **Credentialing, Skills, and Accomplishments:** Gain smart credentials, strategic skill set development, and significant accomplishments that showcase what you have learned and achieved.

2. **College as a Strong Foundation:** Appreciate your college years seriously and holistically as a preparatory foundation for the rest of your life.

3. **Hard and Soft Skill Development:** Utilize your time in college to develop both the hard and soft skills that will best prepare you for your post-college life and career.

4. **Personal Assessments of Experiences, Abilities, Skills, and Interests:** Select courses, programs of study, and organizational involvement in order to ensure that you build on your abilities, minimize your weaknesses, and increase your skills.

5. **Flexibility and Adaptability:** Be open to learning new things, trying new ways, and adapting within an increasingly dynamic world and workplace.

6. **Smart Program and Class Selection:** Make creative and strategic choices regarding majors, minors, and courses.

7. **Academic Program Fit:** Choose fields of study that fit your abilities, your interests, and the difference you want to make in the world.

Many people believe that a student's choice of a major is the most important decision to make as an undergraduate. It is an important decision, but the world is changing very quickly in this 21st century. It is crucial that you understand these changes and how they will affect your future career and work life. As a college student, you will make choices regarding your fields of study and specific skill sets that you want to develop before you graduate. But as you will learn in this chapter, often this is less about what you choose for your major and more about your overall learning experience in college.

College is an educational transition between secondary education and career work that follows college. Regardless of your major, undergraduate education is essentially a training program for your postgraduate life. Treating college as an extension of adolescence—with extreme partying and limited studying—may have worked in the past for children of the wealthy, whose parents and family friends would open career doors for them. However the increasingly complex and skilled demands of the 21st century make the partying lifestyle a terrible choice for students seeking the needed skills for the workplace. In a study done at Rensselaer Polytechnic Institute, graduates were surveyed to see what skills were most important to them in the workplace and what they wished they had learned in college: "Graduates who were a year out of college wished they had gotten more technical skills. Those who were five years out wanted more management skills. But alumni who were 10 to 20 years into their careers wanted more cultural literacy, 'because they were traveling all over the world, working with cultures they never experienced before'" (Carlson, 2013, p. A32).

Smart Credentialing, Strategic Skill Set Development, and Significant Accomplishments

These four S's should govern your undergraduate experience: You want to make Successful, Smart, Strategic, and Significant choices so that your college years and future career will be defined in terms of Success, Smarts, Strategy, and Significance. Specifically, your highly successful trajectory in college involves smart credentialing, strategic skill set development, and significant accomplishments.

Smart credentialing includes academic majors, minors, concentrations, certificates, honor society memberships, pre-professional training programs, and other forms of academic credentialing. Remember that your smart credentialing is important not because of the titles and awards in and of themselves, but because of what they represent: your hard work and discipline, your extensive studying and learning, and your executive decision making that made these credentials possible.

Strategic skill set development moves beyond the arena of credentialing to detail specific areas of developed skills of value for the workplace and your chosen career, such as strong communication skills, critical and creative thinking, data analytics, strong computer skills, and teamwork and leadership skills.

Significant accomplishments showcase your learning (both academic and experiential): You may have presented research at a conference, worked closely with a professor on a book project, been president of a student organization, organized and run a volunteer service activity, had a solo music recital even though not a music major, won a national competition in debate and public speaking, worked with inner city boys each summer at a Boy Scout camp and during the year as a Scout leader, received training and worked as a tutor for dyslexic children, trained for and ran a marathon each year in college, or even started a small business.

Smart Credentialing
+ Strategic Skill Set Development
+ Significant Accomplishments
= A Successful College Trajectory

While many students arrive at college already knowing what they want to major in, others may make it all the way to their junior year still unsure of the academic and career directions for their future lives. Whether you are a student already set on a major field of study even before starting college or you are still considering various options well into your college years, this chapter is important for you!

If you already have a major and career path, now is the time to diversify your assets. Because you have a major that you are happy with, this chapter will help you explore additional options to increase your various skill sets, your academic credentials, and your knowledge base.

If you have a major but are still unsure about your future career, now is the time to capitalize on your interests and abilities. You are in the fortunate position of a student with a major field of study, so this chapter will help you to strengthen your developing skills, increase your academic credentials, and broaden your potential employer base.

If you are still unsure of your major, now is the time to explore your interests and maximize your strengths. Because you are still exploring various options for your major in college, this chapter will help you to hone in on your strengths and abilities, to explore diverse career paths, and to make strategic academic decisions that will work for you. First, you need to understand two facts about today:

1. The 21st century offers new and exciting career and job opportunities. There is so much that is possible today that we couldn't even imagine just a generation or two ago.

2. The 21st century presents new and challenging career path obstacles. This can be scary, but it shouldn't be. You just need to learn how to jump over the obstacles in your way or to avoid them altogether.

To respond to these opportunities and challenges of the 21st century and the contemporary marketplace, you need to focus on increasing your skill sets and building on your strengths in order to ensure your relevance for the job market today and into the future. It really does go back to the four S's of this chapter: Your highly *successful* trajectory in college revolves around *smart* credentialing, *strategic* skill set development, and *significant* accomplishments.

College as a Strong Foundation for Life beyond College

You want your college work to provide you with solid academic insurance against the challenges of the 21st-century workplace. To this end, you want to insure your future by making strategic decisions today. The nine years of primary or grade school are preparation for four years of secondary education in high school. The four years of high school are preparation for your undergraduate years in college. Your undergraduate time in college is preparation for the rest of your life!

- K-8 primary school years: nine years to prepare for the next four years of secondary school. This is a 9:4 ratio.
- College prep secondary school: four years to prepare for the next four years of undergraduate college education. This is a 4:4 ratio.
- College: four years to prepare for 40 or more years of work. This is a 4:40 ratio.

So you see, your time at college is *very* important. For most college graduates, the equivalent of four years of full-time academic study provides a foundation for the next *forty years* of your work life. You want to make the best of those critical undergraduate years to build a strong, broad, and long-lasting educational experience.

Strategic Skill Set Development of Hard and Soft Skills

Strategic skill set development involves your mastery of specific hard and soft skills. Hard skills are the tools and methodologies of the trade—the skills that are often specific to your major and career path. Soft skills are the broader skills that are important for all people. For example, strong critical thinking, analytical ability, and creative problem solving are soft skills that are relevant and valuable for any person, but these are soft skills that are of heightened value in the technology driven dynamism of today's workplace.

Education expert Tony Wagner (2013), current Innovation Education Fellow at the Technology and Entrepreneurship Center at Harvard University, has researched the state of education in the United States in relation to education in other countries. He has also focused on specific skills needed by college graduates for use in the 21st-century workplace. Among those skills are creative and critical thinking, problem-solving skills, collaboration and networking, strong communications skills, curiosity, adaptability, and an entrepreneurial spirit. He explains that all of these are needed in and relevant to most skilled jobs today.

Additionally, Dan Berrett (2013) reports in *The Chronicle for Higher Education* that "increasingly, education experts also want students to develop . . . another] skill, integrative thinking" because "the ability to see connections between disparate methodologies and ways of knowing allows students to generate new ideas and novel theories" (p. A20). Employers relate that more and more college graduates have not developed their abilities in these critical "soft skills."

Those students who excel academically and socially in college are those students who do develop many of these skills through their classwork and in their organizational involvement. There are different majors and minors to select from. There are areas of concentration within majors and certificate programs that certify participation and learning from specific workshops and other learning programs. There are study abroad programs, foreign language study, and other globalization initiatives to take advantage of. There are student organizations, volunteerism opportunities, and other extracurricular activities on and off campus.

Be involved. Have fun. But make strategic decisions regarding what you study, what you do, and what you are interested in.

Think about the skills, information, experiences that will work for you. You want to explore different learning opportunities to increase your skill sets. This will make you a more attractive job candidate. This will make you a more interesting applicant to graduate or professional school. This will make you a more effective employee in your chosen line of work.

To increase your skill sets, consider the following opportunities:

- A second major or a new minor to increase your knowledge base
- A certification or concentration to demonstrate your knowledge in a particular area

While you are an undergraduate student, you have opportunities that you will never again have, in the same ways and to the same degree, at any other time in your life.

- Foreign language study to a proficient level (possibly including study abroad)
- International experience through study abroad programs and travel
- Additional computer, tablet, and mobile skills (either through classes, informal workshops, or work at your campus help desk)
- Additional English and communications classes to improve your written and oral communication skills to highly proficient levels
- Involvement with diverse organizations, ideally with leadership opportunities

A student's undergraduate years provide so many opportunities for growth. Explore new areas for skill development. Capitalize on what you already have learned, abilities that you already have developed, and things that you have already done. You want to have a good sense of your strengths and weaknesses, your passions, your skills, and your natural abilities.

Personal Assessments of Experiences, Abilities, Skills, and Interests

Every student arrives at college with particular strengths. You may think that your strengths mainly reflect your natural talents. This is true, but the majority of a person's strengths are developed through their experiences in life. Think about what you have accomplished in your life and all of your experiences over the years. Think about what you have learned to do. Your strengths include both sides of the "nature versus nurture" debate, but here they are additive. Your natural abilities combined with what you've done, what you've read, and what you've learned produce the aggregate of your current set of strengths.

Every student in college has his or her specific strengths and abilities. Capitalize on your specific set of strengths, but first you need to have a clear view of what your strengths are. Most people never sit back and take stock of all of their strengths, but it is important to know what assets you bring to the table as a college student. Remember that your college years are preparation for the next 40 or more years of your work life, so you want to have a clear view of what you bring to the table so that you can make the most informed and strategic choices for your future. This exercise in human resource and strategic thinking invites you to discover and explore your current set of personal assets.

List of Past and Current Experiences

It may seem straightforward to list your past experiences. Many of you will immediately think of the jobs you've had. Some will also think of community service work. Even beyond paid and volunteer work, there are other important experiences that you've had that you should think about here.

- Have you spent time in other countries? This shows your developing global literacy and foreign language abilities.
- Have you lived in different parts of the United States, experiencing different regions, geographies, and cultures? This shows your developing cultural literacy.

- Have you performed in front of groups of people (e.g., music, dramatic performance, giving speeches, etc.)? This shows your discipline, artistic creativity, and interpersonal communication skills.

- Have you assisted others with computers, cell phones, e-readers, or music sound systems? This shows your technical knowledge and skill.

- What paid jobs have you had and for how long? Your work experience shows your responsibility and work ethic.

- What volunteer activities have you participated in and in what capacities? This shows your commitment to the betterment of your community and the world.

- What team or individual sports have you participated in? This shows your discipline, hard work, and teamwork and/or competitive competencies.

Think of the many different experiences you've had over the years. Please list 10 of your most distinctive and important experiences:

1. _____
   _____
2. _____
   _____
3. _____
   _____
4. _____
   _____
5. _____
   _____
6. _____
   _____
7. _____
   _____
8. _____
   _____
9. _____
   _____
10. _____
    _____

List of Past and Current Skills and Abilities

Now you will consider your many skills and abilities. Whether you are a traditional age 18–23-year-old student or an older and more experienced student, by now you will have amassed a significant number of skills in your lifetime. These are what you have learned from your various experiences.

- Have you played team or individual sports, developing your teamwork abilities or individual dedication as well as the specific athletic and sports abilities?

- Have you learned another language so that you can communicate orally and write in that language?

- Have you developed your artistic skills in particular areas?

- Have you mastered playing a musical instrument?

- What computer skills do you have (e.g., Word, Excel, Photoshop, PowerPoint, or website development)?

- Have you worked as a tutor, religious class teacher, or waitperson, developing your interpersonal skills?
- Have you been involved in Scouting, FFA, 4-H, or other organizations in which you have developed particular skills?
- Have you learned how to play chess competitively?
- Have you learned how to read philosophy comfortably or to write poetry?

Think of your many experiences throughout your life and what you have learned to do from these experiences. What skills have you developed? Note that from any one of your life experiences (say a job or volunteer activity), you may have developed multiple skills. It might help to begin your list in one of these two ways: "I am good at doing X" or "I have learned how to do Y." (Let me give you two of my own examples: "I fell in love with reading at an early age and became a great reader" or "My parents encouraged athletics, and I learned to be a very good softball player.") Please list 10 skills that you have learned in your life:

1. _____
   _____
2. _____
   _____
3. _____
   _____
4. _____
   _____
5. _____
   _____
6. _____
   _____
7. _____
   _____
8. _____
   _____
9. _____
   _____
10. _____
    _____

So far you've listed a number of your most significant experiences and skills that you have already developed in your life. This is a crucial part in your strategic decision making as a college student. It is important to get a clear view of what you bring to the table. These are many of your current experiential and ability assets.

What you've done and what you've learned are important, but what you really *like* to do is also an important part of the equation. So now, turn to your personal preferences: what you are interested in and what you enjoy doing. As you settle upon fields of study, the development of skills, and types of work that you will pursue, *who you are* and *what you like* are vitally important to the process.

Students who plan ahead and pursue career trajectories that are in line with their personal interests and dreams will find much greater job satisfaction than those who do not.

List of Past and Current Interests

Here you are to list your past and current interests. Try to list interests that are somewhat enduring and that have defined *who you are* and *what you like.*

- What activities have you spent time pursuing over the years simply because you enjoy the activity? This may be something as simple as sitting in your favorite Starbucks and reading or talking with friends. Even something like this is important, for it shows a tendency towards books or people, each of which is important to different fields (e.g., teaching, counseling, editing).

- Are there areas of the arts that you especially enjoy (whether as a performer or as an arts lover)? Which forms of the arts are you especially attracted to?

- Are you an impassioned computer geek? Do you love tinkering with the insides of computers and helping others with their hardware and/or software problems? Is your interest in gaming? What about technology impassions you?

- Which of your volunteer activities did you absolutely love? Some love doing environmental restoration and clean-up. Others prefer working with people with different needs and interacting with them. Understanding which types of volunteerism you prefer, and why, is important.

- Do you enjoy the outdoors, swimming, camping, hiking, biking, or running?

- Do you love sports? If so, which types of athletics and sports do you prefer?

- What types of conversations energize you the most? What are the topics that you are most interested in?

Please list 10 of your different interests (past and current) that have helped to define who you are and how you enjoy spending your time:

1. _____
   _____
2. _____
   _____
3. _____
   _____
4. _____
   _____
5. _____
   _____
6. _____
   _____
7. _____
   _____
8. _____
   _____
9. _____
   _____
10. _____
   _____

By listing the assets that you already bring to the table, you will begin to look closely at *who you are.* Remember that your assets include your natural gifts, your learned skills and developed abilities, and your interests and likes.

Having a better picture of your experiences, background, and skill sets is important for your strategic decision making in college. This affects not only what you major in but also what activities you decide to participate in and also what extra classes you might take, even what topics you might select for your research papers and projects and your creative and artistic work in your different classes. The more information that you bring to the table about yourself makes your college years and later life that much more strategic.

Skills for the World Today and the Future

Here are two important facts about your future:

1. **If you are a college student today, the majority of your parents' lives and your professors' lives were lived in the 20th century.** This may make their lives seem less relevant to you, but actually it makes their lives that much *more important* to you. You need a strong foundation to stand on as you go forward through your life and throughout the 21st century. That foundation is made up of everything that you have learned and experienced. Draw upon their experience and knowledge and then update it for today.

2. **If you are a college student today, the majority of your life will be lived in the 21st century.** This really is exciting! There are new opportunities for you as a member of this fast-changing global civilization. There are new challenges, but also amazing possibilities: new knowledge that was unknown in the 20th century, careers and jobs that did not exist in the 20th century, and experiences that were not possible in previous centuries.

Remember that you want to ensure that your assets will be relevant for the job market today and into the future. Jenny Blake (2011), a Career Development Program Manager at Google and the author of a popular blog about life after college advises, "Anticipate the skills you will need 6 months or 1 year from now. Be proactive about seeking learning opportunities to position yourself for a new role or promotion in the future" (p. 51). Think about your desired career path and specific skill sets that you can develop and/or heighten while you are in college.

As you explore your career and learning options, you want to gain as clear a picture not only of yourself, but also of the world today and the world as it is evolving forward into the future. There are fields of study and careers that my generation could not even imagine when I was an undergraduate. For example, needed and growing fields today include statistical analytics and data mining, network and cyber security, environmental engineering, mobile apps software developers, preventive health care and well-being, publishing technologies, and digital pedagogy. What this means for you is to hone in on specific skills and skill sets that you would like to develop that will be of direct use for you in your post-college work and life. You could take a number of classes in statistics, computer science, and quantitative analysis to develop strengths in data analytics and data mining for use in many job sectors today. Or you could develop your skills in a new language for use in your career with geographic and international mobility and reach.

You also want to develop a strong foundation of knowledge. In order to gain an informed and correct view of the world today and a good sense of the future, you need to have solid knowledge of the past. You can develop your knowledge and understanding of the past and present, along with helpful glimmers into the future, in various ways: by close and engaged reading of various texts and your smart utilization of the wealth of legitimate information accessible via digital media; by watching movies, videos, and television; by listening to lectures of others' knowledge, experiences, and stories; by taking different classes (both in your fields of study and also other classes); and simply by engaging in conversations with a variety of people.

Try to learn as much as you can about the world today and its changes through time, both changes that happened in the past and those that are anticipated in the future. What you learn and how you think will come together in important ways as you make your strategic choices regarding your fields of study in college.

It is crucial that you make the best choices possible regarding your academic majors, minors, concentrations, certificate programs, and other forms of academic credentialing. And to do this most strategically, you want to base your decisions on knowledge and a clarity of understanding about yourself and the world—the present world, the world as it has been in the past, and the future world that is unfolding.

Flexibility and Adaptability: Be Open to Learning New Things

You must always be open to learning new things, even if they seem to contradict your prior understandings regarding specific topics. Be open to finding truth, and accept that some of your previous views about a particular topic may have been false.

As you know, I am a professor and a scholar in my fields of expertise. As such, I contribute to the learning in my respective fields of study. When I conduct my research as a literary scholar and literary critic, I learn from the work of my peers and predecessors. In some cases, I see mistakes that have been made in the past, so I work to learn from those and help to move scholarship in my fields forward in new ways. Does this mean that my work is always completely correct, even though it passes the review of my peers? Of course not. There will be mistakes—although hopefully not too many. And I trust that other scholars, today and those who will use my work in the future, will build on it, affirming what is correct and still useful while making the needed corrections where my findings or methodology may have been partial or even wrong.

I have recently been working on a project that looks at the poetry of select Anishinaabe poets, contemporary and historical. After finishing my early work on this project, I sent my research to a specialist in the Anishinaabe language for her expert and professional review. This leading scholar of the language and culture responded with extensive comments, noting areas where correction and reconsideration were needed. So my task was to return to the project and tackle those challenges to make the work that much stronger, accurate, and, thereby, of greater value to others.

We should always be open to acknowledging where we may have been wrong about something, where we may have made mistakes, where we can learn new things, where new ideas and understandings can be incorporated into our work, and where we can continue to learn and grow throughout our lives. Ideally, you want your college years to help you develop the foundation for a life rich and open to learning both in college and beyond.

In college, you will have the opportunity to learn lessons from many of the greatest minds throughout time. You want to take advantage of those educational opportunities as fully as possible in order to develop as strong a foundation of learning during your college years as you can. This means looking outside yourself and your world view. Learn about other cultures to help you better understand those cultures and also your own culture. Learn about the past to help you understand today and tomorrow.

There is one remarkably easy way to learn about the past, but unfortunately it has become a forgotten relic for many people: simply talking with people about their past experiences. Of course, you can also accomplish this by reading, checking out various websites, watching videos, and attending lectures and presentations.

As you do all this, you want to practice your skills in listening, reading, and watching closely, thoughtfully, and empathically. Try to think of questions that you could raise about what you are learning, and use your questions and thoughts to put those histories into the context of their times and into relevance for today.

Try to understand those histories in relation to your own life, family, and immediate community. You can even ask someone who tells you a story from the past, "Why is this important to me? Why is this relevant today?" And see what they say. You also want to find out as much as you can about other people's work experiences: currently and in the past. You want to learn as much as possible from others' experiences. Remember, people like to talk about what they do, people like others to be interested in them, and people like to be asked about their life experiences.

Let's look at how this learning relates specifically to your decisions regarding your future work life. Let's also look at how this learning relates specifically to your decisions regarding your major and minor fields of study and even specific classes that you will take. Here are some strategic conversations that you can initiate to heighten your knowledge base and give you a better view of the workplace for today and throughout your life:

- Talk with your parents and grandparents about their work experiences, about their current and past jobs, about what has changed since they were your age. You want to have a solid picture of today, but to do so, you also need to understand how the world is and has been changing.

- Meet the specialists at your college's or university's career centers. Sit down with them one on one. Make a list of questions before your meeting. Find out how they can help you. Also take advantage of the career center's open house and other events.

- Make sure that you attend a number of the job fairs at your college or university. You can even do this as a freshman. Spiff up and put on your interview outfit to visit the job fair and enter into conversations with various employers. Even as a freshman, you may impress a potential employer so much that you are invited to apply for an internship for the summer between your freshman and sophomore years!

- Think of family, friends, various relatives, and other people you have met at home, at school, in your community, and at jobs. Find out whether any of those people are in fields that you are interested in, and make an appointment with them to talk about their work. You may be able to job shadow them or learn about possible internships or available positions.

- Talk with your friends and fellow students about their majors, their classes, what they are learning, the organizations they are involved with, their internships and other valuable college experiences, and what jobs and careers they hope to have in the future.

- Meet with your professors outside of class. Talk with them about what they do and about what professionals in your major do outside in the real world. Ask your professors for their suggestions about how to be better prepared in your chosen field. And take their suggestions seriously.

What are all of these bullet points really about? Networking! It is never too early to begin strategic networking. This topic will be explored in greater detail in Chapter 8: "Networking and Mentoring: Teamwork, Leadership, Strategic Relationships," because networking is important to your work life.

Smart Major, Minor, Course Selection

Now that you have looked at your own personal set of experiences, skills and abilities, and interests and have explored various guidance and directions for fact gathering about the workplace (past, present, and future), you are positioned to make some strategic decisions regarding your major and other courses of study in college.

While you are in college, select fields of study that will propel you to the job and career that you seek. To do this, you need to select the *right* major. If you want to work designing car engines, a mechanical engineering degree makes a lot of sense. If you only major in creative writing, that will not get you an engineering job nor will it give you the primary skills you need to work in mechanical engineering. If you want to work in professional writing, an English degree makes a lot of sense. If you only major in mechanical engineering, that will not get you a professional writing job nor will it give you the primary skills you need to work in professional writing.

If you have a major that you are totally committed to, there might be other majors and minors that you could explore as possible areas to consider adding. One student of mine was an engineering major, but had a passion for music. After working on these exercises, that student decided to add a music minor. The creativity involved in the music minor will be a great asset to an engineer. In fact, my grandfather during the 20th century was a highly skilled electrical engineer at Bell Labs; he was also a highly skilled cellist who played in quartets throughout his life. Music heightened his creativity which, in turn, heightened his ability as an engineer.

> "I came to college, but I don't really know what type of career I want. I know that I need to get a job and pay my bills and that I don't want to continue working at Starbucks for my entire life, even though it is a great company. I am interested in a lot of different things, and I want to make a difference in the world, but I have NO idea what to major in! I don't even know what kind of job I want! And I have absolutely no idea how to map out a career plan!"

If you do not yet have a clear career path and chosen major, do not worry. Explore different options. You can simply select two or three areas with the intent to develop specific hard and soft skills for your future, even though you may not be ready to settle on a specific career.

Choosing a major, mapping out a career plan—these are difficult and serious decisions to make. College is a stressful time, especially in young adults' lives as their transition from adolescence to adulthood solidifies. Some people discover a passion for a career early on. Some musicians know in middle school that they want to pursue a lifetime of music. Some young athletes know that they want a particular sport to be their life work. Some young people arrive at college already knowing that they want to be biomedical engineers or pharmacists or history teachers or artists. This is terrific, but it is important to understand that it is also very okay to be in the situation where you do not know what you want to do!

This is perfectly fine because this means you are in the position of being able to explore different options, and the process of exploration and discovery is fun, energizing, and even exciting.

So far in this chapter, you have looked at who you are (your experiences, skills/abilities, and interests). Now, you want to bring those together *strategically* as you explore various options. Remember that even if you are not completely sure about your career plans, you can move in strategic directions by developing specific skill sets in specific areas that will move you forward toward a wonderful career.

Please take a moment to review your self-assessment worksheets from earlier in this chapter. Based on your interests and abilities, you can now consider possible majors and fields of study in college that just might work well for you.

First, let's eliminate some right off the bat. When you look at all of the major fields of study in college, it can be overwhelming to pick one out of, say, 50 or more departments. But if you can narrow down the field, it will start to become much easier to select viable options for you.

At this point, I'd like you to think of 15 majors that you know with 100 percent certainty do not fit you. To review the range of options, go to your prospective or current college's or university's website for the list of departments and majors. If you are still having trouble eliminating 15, you can go to a larger university's website for additional majors and departments that may not exist at your college. Please list 15 majors that you can eliminate from your consideration:

1. _____
2. _____
3. _____
4. _____
5. _____
6. _____
7. _____
8. _____
9. _____
10. _____
11. _____
12. _____
13. _____
14. _____
15. _____

Now that you've ruled these out, we can now turn to some of the majors that are still viable possibilities for you. Do not worry right now about what career you want to settle on. This is still exploratory brainstorming at this point in order to imagine a range of possibilities. For now, you simply want to think about a number of possible fields of study that you know you would enjoy and that you could excel in (even if it would take hard work).

Please list 10 majors or fields of study that you would be good at, that you would be interested in, and/or that would offer valuable learning opportunities for you:

1. _____
2. _____
3. _____
4. _____
5. _____
6. _____
7. _____
8. _____
9. _____
10. _____

Of course, you cannot choose all 10 of these to major in, but there are creative ways to navigate your college years with an interesting mix of chosen areas of study. It is possible to have multiple majors and minors, but you have to narrow the field down to a manageable number, especially if you expect to graduate with the equivalent of four or five years of full-time study. If you are not on the 20-year plan, you will need to narrow your list down from 10 possibilities. Look over your list of 10 major options, and review it with an eye towards your top choices. Narrow down your list to your top five possible majors.

Please list five majors that you are very interested in. Try to put these in rank order with 1 being your top choice.

1. _____
2. _____
3. _____
4. _____
5. _____

You now have a clear view of your leading areas of focus as a college student. And do not worry about needing to choose just one. The 21st century is less about narrowing your study to one specific field and more about the convergence of different areas of learning and a mix of different skills sets. The dynamism of the workplace today requires a diversity of skills and breadth of knowledge. And most colleges and universities provide ways for you to develop a diversity of skill sets, such as having a major, a minor, and a couple of concentrations.

Looking over your short list, you will want to go meet with the heads of the departments that oversee each of these majors and talk with them about their departments' fields of study for undergraduates. You want to find out about the departments' different options for you: majors (some departments offer more than one), minors, concentrations, and certificate programs. Ask about career trajectories for majors and minors. Ask about the types of jobs that recent graduates have gotten. Ask about possible internships, co-op opportunities, work-study jobs, and faculty mentoring options such as undergraduate research. Ask questions. Find out as much as you can. Approach these meetings like a skilled and *strategic* interviewer. What you find out will be very helpful over the course of your decision-making process.

After you meet with the department representatives, you may still be considering multiple majors. If so, this is an opportunity for strategic diversification. You want a diversified portfolio of knowledge, experience, and skill sets when you graduate. So consider signing up for a mix of majors, minors, and other learning options.

If you have not yet finished your freshman year, it is important for you to understand that you do not need to worry about selecting your major or minor fields of study right off the bat as a first-year student. Many of the early classes you take will count toward general education and core curriculum requirements and will be helpful in considering various majors and minors. And many programs do not even let you declare their major until your sophomore year. However, if you do know early on that there are several fields that you are especially interested in, you need to start taking classes in those areas right away. This will help in (1) moving you forward in those fields and (2) helping you see whether one or more can be removed from consideration. After one semester, you may realize that one specific choice really is not a fit for you or that you want to change one option down to a minor rather than a major.

No matter what, keep your options open as you explore various possibilities during your years in college. This will help you maximize the return on your college investment.

Each semester, take some time to sit and think about your classes and fields of study. Talk with your professors about what you are learning and possible career opportunities. Go to the career center at your school during your first year as a student and ask them what they can do *for you* even during your freshman and sophomore years.

Inquire about applied learning opportunities to gain an experiential advantage. Employers want graduates with hands-on experience in their fields rather than those who only have the academic learning. Remember that every college graduate has a college degree, but not every college graduate has relevant and valuable experiential learning opportunities (work study in your department, co-op and internships, independent study and mentoring with a professor, undergraduate research experience).

You may be asking, "If I already know what I want to major in, why do I need to think any more about my major or other fields of study? Aren't I done with this? Isn't one major enough?" Well, you may have arrived in college knowing just what you want to study, or you may have gone through the above exercises and have begun to hone in on your preferred major. Either way, whatever you select as your major, it is important for you to think about ways in which you can diversify your portfolio of learning.

You want to graduate with a strategically selected set of skills and assets. Your most important assets as a college graduate will be: (1) your academic credentials, including chosen majors, minors, concentrations, and certificates; and (2) your experiential strengths—namely your work, internship, research, organizational, and volunteer experiences.

Remember the three S's in Succe**SS**:

> *Smart Credentialing*
> *+ Strategic Skill Set Development*
> *+ Significant Accomplishments*
> *= A Successful College Trajectory*

Even if you know for sure what you want to major in, it is important for you to spend strategic time considering other options to add to your total college learning portfolio: additional academic credentialing, additional skill and knowledge development, additional learning and experiential accomplishments. This will give you the strong college foundation to approach the job market and/or graduate and professional schools as a distinctively viable and successful candidate, unlike the unemployed young man wearing his business suit and holding the "LOOKING FOR A JOB" sign.

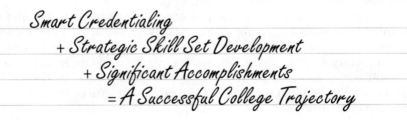

Review the material and worksheets in this chapter as you deliberate regarding majors, minors, concentrations, or other academic credentialing (e.g., being in your college's leadership, global scholars, study abroad, or other notable programs). Increase your skill sets while you are in college. A student's undergraduate years provide unique opportunities for both a breadth and depth of learning. Remember that you will never have the same opportunities to increase and diversify your skill sets with the same degree of opportunities as exist in college, so be strategic, and make college work for you. Take smart advantage of these opportunities while you can, and have a great and successful time learning and growing in college!

Settling on the Right Fields of Study

Build on your abilities, your interests, and the contributions that you want to make in the world in order to achieve a truly fulfilling career and life.

Your chosen fields of study need to be WHAT YOU CAN DO:

Make sure that your fields of study in college will work well with your strengths and abilities. Engineering may be the right fit if you are very good at mathematics. English may be the right fit if you are a very good reader and writer. Theater may be a great fit for you if you are skilled in any of the various arenas of the performance arts.

Your chosen fields of study need to be WHAT YOU WANT TO DO:

Make sure that your fields of study in college will work well with your interests and desires. If you love to travel to different countries and learn about different cultures and languages, then foreign language study fits your interests. If you love cooking and nutrition and aspects of personal health, then nutrition, dietetics, or another health science would fit your interests. If you are fascinated by the aesthetic and physical design of buildings, then architecture might be the right fit for your interests.

Your chosen fields of study, ideally, need to fit with THE DIFFERENCE THAT YOU WANT TO MAKE IN THE WORLD:

When you are in the workforce, what you do is less for you and more for others. You work as a contributing member of society. Your work helps to propel the world forward in valuable ways. Regardless of what field you choose and regardless of the type of job you have, if you perceive your work as a service to others, it will be that much more rewarding. Take some time while you are in college and then throughout your postgraduate years to review your choices and see how you can always make the world a better place as you study and as you do your job.

In the article "How to Assess the Real Payoff of a College Degree," Joseph R. Urgo, president of St. Mary's College of Maryland, emphasizes the importance of college experiences in developing students as significant contributing players in their communities and the world. President Urgo explains that "college is for students to decide what and how they want to contribute to society, to the economy, to their communities, and to the well-being of their families" (Carlson, 2013, p. A31).

When I was a teaching assistant at the University of New Mexico, one of my students who was Native American stopped by during office hours to talk with me. We spent a bit of time going over her recent work, which was very strong. Then after some time had passed, she turned to me and said, "I'm having trouble picking a major." She then said, "I need to find a major that will help my people." By this, she meant that she wanted to get an appropriate major that would be of service to her tribal community. We then spent some time exploring the options. Over the next few years, she eventually decided that going to law school and becoming a lawyer would be a good fit for her and provide a tangible way for her to be of service to her community.

That particular office hours meeting affected me greatly. It was the first time that a student had communicated that the most important factor in picking a major was not primarily about their interests and desires but rather about how they would be of greatest service to others. I was deeply touched by that student's perspective. It did not mean that she would pick an area in which she had no interest and no strengths, but rather that, in taking those issues into account, the most important consideration for her was to help, to be part of the solution consciously and deliberatively.

I have noticed that many Millennial-generation students have very much a similar orientation—that of wanting to make a difference in the world. This can be done through many different choices in your fields of study, whether you decide on education or engineering, health sciences or the humanities, business or law. It is simply an orientation toward the world, your communities, and your families—an orientation in which you view your education, your work, and your career as a means toward the betterment of us all. Such an approach is a gift to you because, in this way, your choices and your life work will matter that much more—to you, to your family, to your community, and to the world. And accordingly, with an attitude of service, your education and your work then become a gift of yours that you offer outward each day.

5 Communication Skills

Oral, Written, Digital

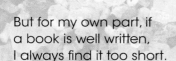

But for my own part, if
a book is well written,
I always find it too short.

— *Jane Austen, Catherine, pub. post. 1993*

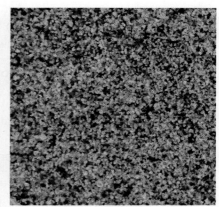

Everything that can be thought at all can be thought clearly.
Everything that can be said can be said clearly.
Whereof one cannot speak, thereof one must be silent.

The limits of my language mean the limits of my world.

— *Ludwig Wittgenstein (1922), Tractatus (4.116, 7, and 5.6)*

The single biggest problem
in communication is the
illusion that it has taken
place.

— *George Bernard Shaw (1856–1950)*

1. **Strong Professional Communication Skills:** Take advantage of the opportunities in college to improve your communication skills, especially in your communication and English classes, and strive to excel in those classes.

2. **The Omnipresence of Communication Events:** Utilize your college years to develop and improve your oral, written, and digital communication.

3. **Modes of Communication: Oral, Written, Digital, and Interpretative Listening and Reading:** Approach college strategically and work hard to improve your communication skills in each of these four modes.

4. **Five Key Oral Communication Rules:** (1) Build relationships and learn to communicate and behave professionally; (2) avoid under communicating; (3) be clear and complete; (4) pay focused attention when reading, viewing, and listening; (5) listen more than you speak.

5. **Group/Team Work:** Take advantage of group/team experiences for smart and strategic teamwork and leadership skill development.

6. **Writing Fundamentals:** Propel your written communication to greater levels of effectiveness and success with practice, effort, and attention to nine key elements of effective writing.

7. **Writing as a Process:** Practice the process of writing from initial brainstorming through multiple drafts and to your final revisions, proofreading, and production.

8. **Specific Writing Tips:** Minimize writing errors and maximize your communication presentations and "readability."

9. **Digital Communication and Information Literacy:** Ensure successful access, evaluation, and comprehension of information, including its accuracy and reliability, and ensure the absence of plagiarism in your own communication.

The most important skill set for you to develop for your career and future life involves the skills of effective and professional communications. College provides you with distinctive opportunities to learn, develop, and practice the professional skills needed in the job market. In virtually every class you take, you will be given a range of assignments and requirements that, if taken seriously, will help you improve the range of your communication skills. And most colleges and universities see this as "mission critical" with required course work in these areas for every student.

Reading assignments help you learn how to be a more effective reader and interpreter of what you read. Writing assignments help you learn how to be a better writer and written communicator. Digital communication assignments and everyday use of email and the Internet (Google docs, online classes, course sites, etc.) help you improve your digital communications, your interpretive and evaluative assessments of online material, and your own professional digital presence. In-class work, student organizations, volunteerism, internships, undergraduate research and creative production, and various projects will help you improve as a better interpersonal communicator and team member.

Throughout your life, the extent to which you develop and perfect your communication skills will determine, in many ways, the success that you will achieve in your career, your community life, and on the social and home fronts.

During your undergraduate college years, you will have many opportunities to develop and improve your communication skills. You want to take smart and strategic advantage of these as much as possible. Whether it is in composition and speech communication courses, in your conversations with your professors, or in your student organization meetings, you want to finely hone your oral, written, and digital communications to achieve the results you desire.

Strong Professional Communication Skills

Strong professional communication skills are essential to any career plan you have; are vital to any successful, fulfilling, and happy life; can be significantly improved through smart and strategic choices while you are in college; and should be developed and improved throughout your life.

In a recent article in *The Chronicle of Higher Education,* Robert J. Sternberg explains that "overwhelmingly, the thinking, problem-solving, and communication skills a job candidate has acquired in college are more important than the specific field in which the applicant earned a degree" (Sternberg, 2013). And Professor Tony Wagner, codirector of Harvard University's Change Leadership Group, goes further, delineating what he terms "survival skills students need for their future" (Wagner, 2013):

- Critical thinking and problem solving
- Collaboration across networks and leading by influence
- Agility and adaptability
- Initiative and entrepreneurialism
- Effective oral and written communication
- Accessing and analyzing information
- Curiosity and imagination

Of these seven core skill areas that students need to develop in college for their future work lives, which do you think are distinctively practiced and developed in English composition/writing and speech communications classes? Take a moment to review the list. Pick out those skills that you think can be significantly heightened in writing and communications classes. How many did you pick?

Were you able to decide that at least five of the seven are especially developed in writing and speech classes? If you bring intelligence and commitment to your communication and writing classes, you will (1) improve your oral and written communication skills, (2) learn how to access and analyze information and information sources, (3) finely hone your critical-thinking and problem-solving skills, (4) practice your skills in collaboration and leadership through group and team work, and (5) expand your imagination and curiosity in relation to a variety of topics.

Today, employers are increasingly seeking college graduates with these "so-called soft skills—those who can work well in teams, write and speak with clarity, adapt quickly to changes in technology and business conditions and interact with colleagues from different countries and cultures" (Wiseman, 2013, n.p.). Note that all four of these highly desired skills are communications based, whether oral, written, or digital.

These are the skills that are vital to the successful functioning of a nation that is based on democratic principles and reliant upon an educated citizenry. These are the skills that employers are seeking in those they hire and that are crucial to organizational success. These are the skills that are among the most important in the workplace, in your communities, and in your families. And in your college classes, you can develop these vital skills *and* even receive your college classes credit for doing so. What a deal!

Say that you attend a college or university where you are required to take core curriculum, general education or first-year writing or speech classes. Be excited about your communication and composition classes. Bring a positive attitude and a strong work ethic to these classes, appreciating that your college or university is providing you with hands-on opportunities to improve in these areas. Take these classes seriously, and put out the effort necessary to excel in all of your speech communications, composition, and other writing classes.

Even if your performance in high school English classes was not exceptional, and even if you have always struggled with English, *if* you work hard and take advantage of the additional resources at your school (faculty office hours, tutoring services, writing centers, etc.), you can begin to achieve mastery in these areas. Even the great violinist Yasha Heifitz had to start out as a beginning violinist. Over the years, I have seen very weak writers come into a freshman composition class, work exhaustively to improve their writing, and then develop into assured, fluent, and polished writers by the end of one or two semesters.

You never want to use your poor English skills as an excuse to settle for merely average or mediocre work in class. You may need to work harder in certain classes than do other students, but so what? Everyone has different strengths and weaknesses. If you have to work harder in specific classes, that is what it takes. So just roll up your sleeves, visit the tutoring service on campus, and make a commitment that you will do the hard work necessary to produce top-quality work. As a bonus, you will have a great talking point to tell your future employers about your exceptional work ethic and your commitment to succeed despite adversity.

The Omnipresence of Communication Events

Human life is largely defined in terms of interpersonal communications. Think about how omnipresent communication is throughout your life. You communicate with family members at home and with your roommates at school. You communicate with friends and acquaintances on a daily basis in your classes, in dining halls, on campus, and in your everyday socializing. You communicate with your professors, bosses, advisors, and mentors regarding classwork, internships, research, and jobs. Communication occurs when you listen, read, surf the Internet, and receive messages and updates from social media.

Every day you have in-person conversations. Most days, you communicate with others digitally via social networking sites, text messaging on your cell phones, and traditional email. Almost every day, you read many things whether online or in print. And most days, you do some writing even if it is just Facebook, Skype, Twitter, and text messaging.

There may be no facet that is more important to your success in college and beyond than the vital necessity of strong communication skills. Your skills in interpersonal, digital, and print communications affect virtually all aspects of your life. So take smart and strategic advantage of the many communication experiences that are available to you in college. Utilize these communications opportunities in smart ways, whether they occur in class, on campus, during projects, in your research and creative work, in campus clubs and other organizations, or in your jobs, internships, and volunteer work. In this way, you will practice and perfect your oral, written, and digital communication skills.

Remember that when CEOs of major corporations are asked about the needed skills of employees, one of the essential areas that chief executives raise is the need for excellent communications skills. The encouraging news here, especially for those of you who do not view yourselves as strong writers, readers, or speakers, is that, like any skill, communication skills, including interpersonal relationships and multicultural literacy skills, can readily become stronger simply through effort. (Do note, however, that these skills will also weaken through inactivity and lack of intentional practice.) To strengthen them is really very easy: practice, practice, practice.

All colleges and universities understand the importance of strong communication skills for their students and graduates, hence the reasoning that most schools require specific courses that will help their students to develop their skills in these areas. So remember to take advantage of these opportunities. Work hard to develop your communication skills as much as possible while you are in college, because these skills will be directly relevant and valuable to you throughout your life.

Modes of Communication

There are four predominant modes of communication: oral, written, digital, and interpretative listening and reading.

Before you graduate from college, you should ensure that you have strong skills in each of these four areas. While you are in college, pay attention to all of the occasions available to you for improving your developing communication abilities in each mode. During your undergraduate years, you will have many such opportunities both in your academics and in your extracurriculars, because communication is at the center of both your studies and your interpersonal human relations. Look for intensive opportunities for professional communication skills development—whether in your academic classes, in your student organizations, in your internships and jobs, or in your everyday interactions (whether in person or online). Regardless of your major in college and regardless of your required course work it is your responsibility to do whatever necessary as a college student to improve your skills in each of these four areas prior to graduation.

Oral Communication

▶ Demonstrate respect, interest, commitment, focus, empathy, and a clarity of purpose, intent, and meaning.

You can develop these skills in speech communications and other communications courses as well as classes in theater, education, and law/pre-law, among others. Many student organizations also provide opportunities where you can develop your oral communication skills: debate and speech team, tutoring on campus and at off-campus schools, theater productions, and so on. Since oral communication is inherently inter-personal with peers, subordinates, and bosses/instructors, your practice in class, in extracurriculars, in your volunteer activities will all help you develop your interper-sonal relations for successful communication practice.

Writing

▶ Demonstrate coherent and focused meaning, effective and logically structured organization, clarity in the expression of content, attention to audience, commitment to the process of writing, and correct grammar, punctuation, and spelling.

Because there are many opportunities to improve your writing throughout your college years, you can develop and improve key skills for your career and life. In many of your classes, you will have writing projects (print and digital). These will take different forms (essay exams, term papers, memos and emails, project reports, lab reports, undergradu-ate research articles, etc.). Take advantage of the various writing classes (composition, expository writing, argumentative writing, business writing, technical writing, creative writing) offered at your school. Do not forget the tutoring services, writing labs, and other resources available for writing assistance. In this way, your writing will work for you (and others) by being useful and, thereby, successful.

Digital Communication

▶ Demonstrate strong competencies in the areas of computer, tablet, mobile, and social networking communications, especially with distance, cultural, and global experience.

There are few areas of skilled jobs in the 21st century in which digital technology is not a key component. Although most college students are very tech savvy these days, you should explore digital tools to heighten and broaden your skill sets, especially technolo-gies that are most relevant for your desired career (Excel, LinkedIn, Drop Box, Google Drive, Twitter, Skype, Webex, PowerPoint, online class platforms, MOOCs, analytics and data mining). You will have opportunities to learn and develop highly effective skills in these areas—both in your classes and student organizations. Technology opens up the world to you in ways otherwise not possible; take advantage of the ways by which you can develop your global and multicultural competencies as a student.

Interpretative Listening and Reading

▶ Demonstrate focused and appreciative attention; correct understanding; strong analytical, emotional, creative, and critical-thinking skills; and readiness to ask questions to ensure correct understanding.

Develop your listening and reading skills. Classes in English, communications, foreign languages, psychology, and philosophy, among others, are helpful in these areas. Inter-active media and other digital communications courses provide training in the intersec-tions of visual and textual modalities. Classes in literary criticism and theory, semiotics, social psychology, cultural communications, ethnic studies, and women's studies are some that broaden and deepen your skills of interpretation and understanding.

Five Key Oral Communication Rules

Communication is a tricky business and, as a college student, you need to review and evaluate how you communicate. Successful communication, regardless of the form it takes, requires practice and hard work. To become good at any skill requires effort, practice, and hard work. In the book *Engaging Ideas: The Professor's Guide to Integrating Writing, Critical Thinking, and Active Learning in the Classroom*, John C. Bean (2011) explains that successful writers are those who step up to the plate and do the hard work necessary to write, rewrite, revise, reconceptualize, redo, re-envision, and recraft their writing and their ideas: "Great writers do extensive rewriting, the final products often being substantially different from the first drafts" (p. 33). Whatever you do improves with practice, repetition, focus, time, and effort.

By following five key rules of communication, you can improve your overall communication skills in strategic and effective ways, both for use while you are in college and for use on the job and in graduate or professional school. By taking them to heart in your everyday communications events—when you read, when you have a conversation, when you are in a meeting, when you are in class (listening or speaking), when you are writing (essays, email, reports, webpages, blogs, tweets), when you are giving a presentation, when you are online (reading, listening, viewing)—you will develop your communication skills with intentionality and in smart and strategic ways.

Relationship Building

▶ Build relationships and learn to communicate and behave professionally.

The most important fact for you to understand about strong communication skills is that your successful communications are based upon your relationship-building skills, and both (communications and relationships) require a regularity of focused and attentive practice. Understanding this rule is vitally important because when you communicate to others, you need to be aware of the relational factors of interpersonal, intergroup, interorganizational, and intercultural communications to ensure that your communications are successful.

As Wittgenstein and other philosophers of language have made poignantly clear, there is no such thing as a private language. Language is a tool for communicating, and communication involves more than one person. Just as "it takes two to tango," it takes at least two to communicate. Dancing requires expertise in the physical skills of dance, but when one dances the tango with another, the dance is significantly informed by the interactions between the two people. It is the relational element that becomes foundational and central to the totality of the tango. All successful communications, like the tango, involve a functional and effective relationship.

This is true of the diverse verbal forms of interpersonal communications, whether written, oral, or digital. A speaker speaks to a listener. A writer writes to a reader. A blogger blogs to readers. YouTube videos are sent outward to viewers. Think of the phrase "social media." This refers to digital technologies that mediate and facilitate *social* relations.

In your speech communications classes, you will be reminded to think of your listeners. In your writing classes, you will be reminded to think of your reading audience. In your digital communications and social media classes, you will be asked to pay special attention to those for whom your webpages, other textual posts, and online videos are intended.

Think about the different people with whom you communicate. You speak differently to your relatives than you do to your friends or to your bosses or to your professors.

This is as it should be, for each conversation "takes two to tango" and is developed within the specific context of the conversation and is co-directed by the participants. Each person contributes to the conversation and guides it in various directions. The success of the conversation, however, is primarily determined by the extent to which each person's contribution is consciously directed to the others.

When someone speaks to you in a connected way, your engagement is stronger and your understanding is clearer. In a back-and-forth conversation, if the other person stops paying attention, you will usually pick up on that because the conversation will no longer be collaborative.

This is evident in the example of the classroom setting. When a professor is lecturing, the success of that lecture occurs when students pay close attention and are interactive participants. For example, when your professor is lecturing, you and several other students may have a quizzical look on your faces at one particular point. When the professor sees those facial responses, she may actually stop and ask for questions or simply take some time for additional clarifying details or explanations. In this way, simply by paying close attention and facially demonstrating your responses to a lecture, needed clarification is provided and student understanding is, thereby, increased. During discussion, when a class session is more explicitly interactive, the relational component is more obvious, but it is integral to heightened student learning regardless of the class session's format.

When you are receiving and interpreting someone else's words, whether in class or in more informal settings, your responsibility is to take seriously your side of the communication relationship. Be gracious, respectful, and pay close attention to the words that you are hearing or reading. And when you are the speaker or writer, whether it is written, oral, or digital communication, maintain clear and focused attention on whomever is receiving your words. Make sure that your words and text are crafted in ways that ensure their successful delivery, reception, comprehension, and appreciation. You do not want your words to be sent out into a void. You want others to want to connect with your words. You want others to value and learn from your contributions. And, in turn, you want to give the same respect to others' contributions and words.

Take advantage of college to practice and develop professionalism in your communications. Practice relating with your professors with the professional decorum that is expected in the workplace. You want your communications to be effective and to present you in the best light: This means being respectful, appreciative, and responsible. Let's look at a concrete example. When you email one of your instructors, which of the following emails do you think is more professional?

> Hey! This is Sue in your class. I missed class because I had to study for an exam. Did I miss anything? I'll be in class next week and will give you yesterday's assignment then. Bye!

> Professor Brill de Ramírez,

> This is Susan Smith from your ENG 101 class. Unfortunately, I missed yesterday's class. I have already contacted Darrion Jones to get notes from that class. I will stop by during your office hours later today for clarification to make sure that I do not miss anything.

> The absence was unexpected and unavoidable. I assure you it will not happen again. I will look forward to speaking with you this afternoon.

> Respectfully,

> Susan Smith

The first email is informal, disrespectful of the professor (whose name is not even included anywhere in an email), and not personalized at all. The student does not give her full name nor does she identify the class, so the professor may not even know who the student is. The email also communicates that the student devalues the class, intimating that the class session may not have had anything that she *might* have missed. And in stating that she ditched class in order to study for another class, she further communicates how much she devalues the class and the professor's time, and indicates that her other class is the higher priority for her. Finally, she assumes that her late assignment will automatically be accepted.

Whether it is in class, in your digital communications, in your instructor's office, or elsewhere on or off campus, you want your communications with your instructors to be respectful, interested, appreciative, deferential without being obsequious, and friendly and pleasant. In other words, you want your communications to be academic and professional. And when you collaborate with your fellow students on projects, you also want your work to be collegially professional. You want to utilize the range of your communication experiences to step up and improve your professional decorum. It is important, and it counts for a lot in the workplace.

Avoid Undercommunication

▶ As a rule, it is better to risk over communicating. Never under communicate, for this almost certainly ensures that the intended communication will fail. Over communication, while not ideal, is far better than inadequate communication.

Within the framework of an in-person conversation, you are very aware of your listener's responses. Once the distance between the participants in a communications event is increased due to distances in geography or time or mediated technology, then it is harder for you to know whether your communications have been (1) received, (2) understood, (3) valued, and (4) acted upon. Depending on the degree of distancing between your initial iteration and the reception of your message, you will need to determine how to make sure that the specific communication has, in fact, been received, understood, valued, and acted upon.

Because communication is relational, the most important factor in communication is being very aware of your listeners' responses. Because of the distancing inherent in your written and digital communications, you will need to anticipate, as best you can, your readers' responses as you craft your writing, your email, your blog, and your text message.

There will be many times when you will need to repeat yourself to ensure that relevant and important information is getting through to everyone, especially in the workplace. Let's say that you issue an oral directive at a meeting to your staff at work. It is entirely reasonable to follow that up with an email with that same directive, along with a request that they provide updates regarding their responses to your directive. It is also wise to provide clear deadlines regarding when you want such reports. Such deadlines create a valuable and strategic timeline that creates a regularity of reminders so that important work is neither forgotten nor delayed.

If you are in a group or on a team working on a class project with a set deadline and a week goes by with no contact from certain group members, remember that it is better to risk overcommunicating than undercommunicating. If you are the team leader, you can contact your fellow group members and ask where they are on their parts of the project. If you are a team member and you are worried that certain team members may not be pulling their weight, either contact the team leader to look into the situation or, when there is no team leader, you can simply contact everyone giving them an update on what you've been working on and asking everyone to provide their own updates. You can also offer your assistance to particular team members whom you believe may need some additional prodding or other help to contribute more fully to the project.

Be Clear and Complete

▶ You have the responsibility to make sure that your listeners and readers can reasonably and correctly understand what you have said and written. Be clear, focused, and provide sufficient background and context for your listeners' and readers' understanding.

When sending communications, you know what you are thinking, what you are saying, what you are writing, what you are texting. But this does not mean that your listeners and readers will understand what you are trying to communicate in the way that you intend. Remember that you are not speaking/writing to yourself. You are speaking and writing to others, so you need to prepare your words so that they are most likely to be interpreted and understood as closely as possible to your intended meaning. This means that you need to remember to *clarify* and *repeat* when needed.

You do this by crafting your words carefully, clearly, and coherently to ensure, as best you can, that they say what you have intended. And then you have the additional responsibility to double check others' understandings of what you have said, written, and texted.

Focus When Receiving Communications

▶ You have the responsibility to pay focused attention to what is said to you and to what you read and view. With sufficient cultural literacy and contextual background, if you pay close attention, then you can reasonably expect to understand what you hear, read, and view.

When receiving communications at your end of the communications continuum, *you* have the responsibility to make sure that what you have heard and read is correct. Remember to listen and read with focus, with attention, and with interest. This means paying attention:

- Do not check Facebook during class time.
- Do not text a friend when you are with another person.
- Focus on a conversation you are having with a friend at lunch. (Do not take a non-emergency phone call when there is someone else right there with you.)
- Listen intently in class to your instructor, to your group mates, and to other students' comments and questions.
- Do not turn pages in a textbook if you are not really focusing intently on the material and understanding what you are reading.
- Reread a paragraph in a textbook several times to make sure that you understand it. Write down any questions that you have about the reading to bring to your study group, to class, or to your instructor's office hours.
- Do whatever it takes for you to be focused on the communication task at hand.
- Do not be distracted and do multitasking unnecessarily when what is required at the moment is doing one thing very well.

On the reception end of the communications process, remember to clarify, clarify, clarify. Understanding is key. This means rereading a paragraph multiple times when necessary. This means taking a break if you are losing your focus during a study session, and doing whatever necessary to regain your focus so that you are able to get back to your work with focus and understanding.

Multitasking has become an increasingly serious problem for students' focused communications. For example, the intrusions of multiple distractions are challenging student abilities to focus when they read. Naomi S. Baron (2013), a linguistics professor and executive director of American University's Center for Teaching, Research, and Learning, reports from her research that students prefer "doing substantial reading . . . on platforms that lacked Internet connectivity . . . [The students] judged it easier to concentrate" without the ease of Internet distractions (p. 197). When you have reading to do for class or on the job, you are responsible for doing the reading well. Choose when and where and how to do the reading so that you get the most out of it and can contribute strongly in class and at work.

The distractive dangers of digital multitasking are also true regarding oral communications. You have the responsibility to make sure that you are paying attention to others and in class. Do not ask questions if those questions arise because you were not paying attention in class or had not completed the assigned readings. Certainly ask questions when needed, but do so *after* you have first read *and* reread the assignment closely and intently to see whether the answer to your question is already clearly addressed there.

Over the last few years, I have noticed more students asking questions in class about classwork and homework even though the answers to their questions have been explained orally in class and are right in front of them on the assignment sheet, on the board, on the syllabus, and on the course website. In their questions, these students demonstrate to their instructors and to the other students in class that they are not paying attention. You want to do well in class. You want the respect and esteem of your professors and your classmates. One easy way to do this is simply to pay attention in class, to pay attention to your course work and to pay attention to *all* of the course materials that are provided . . . and to do so thoroughly and with understanding.

Listen Intently and Courteously

▶ Listen more than you speak. Listen intently and with focus to everyone. Value each person's contribution, even when you disagree with them . . . especially when you disagree with them. And remember to listen courteously, critically, and empathically.

You've probably heard the saying that "You should listen twice as much as you speak because you have two ears and just one mouth." The exact proportion should vary depending on the circumstances, but what is important is to pay attention to each of your communication events, to assess each situation, and to determine your most effective listening approach and tactic for each specific communication event.

Each person is different and has his or her own communication style. This is one of the most wonderful aspects of communicating. Like snowflakes, no two communication events are identical to each other. They are determined by the participants, the time and place, and context. Each conversation that you have, each meeting that you are involved in, and each chat that you have are distinct communication events with their own unique parameters and requirements. You will have to be smart and intuitive and sensitive to know how much to speak and listen in each conversation and dialogue that you have with others.

As a speaker: speak clearly, repeat, reframe, reiterate, clarify, explain. As a listener: listen intently, pay attention, ask for clarification, ask for reiteration.

- **Listen intently.** In other words, pay very close attention to make sure that you are hearing everything and that everything that you hear, you are hearing correctly. Work to avoid distractions so that you can focus better. In class, that may mean changing where you sit.

- **Listen critically.** Listen carefully to understand *what* is being explicitly said: the data and facts, the logic and reasoning, the support and evidence. Listen intently in order to pick up on the speaker's paralinguistic cues as they contribute to your interpretations of what is being said. Process what you are hearing in terms of what you have previously learned and understood. Note down questions, points of logical inconsistency, and additional facts that may support, contradict, or develop the speaker's points.

- **Listen empathetically.** Listen carefully to understand the implicit meanings that a speaker is conveying. Being familiar with a speaker's demographic and psychographic background is extremely helpful. Paralinguistic behaviors are especially important here (e.g., body language, eye contact, head and hand movements, posture, etc.). Give others the benefit of the doubt as best you can; even when someone speaks angrily or judgmentally or is otherwise demonstrating ill will to you or others, remember that we are all imperfect souls struggling though this world. Be caring in your listening and fair in your judgment.

■ **Listen perceptively.** Distinguish between what is important to remember and what is less significant. Make smart determinations regarding what is important to record in your notes for future reference and what does not need recording (facts that you know are in the course text readings, points that are on the posted PowerPoint slides and outline, and other details that are extraneous). Definitely note ideas of your own that are sparked by what you hear.

■ **And be prepared.** If the listening event is a class, make sure that you have completed any relevant readings or assignments ahead of time, so that you can make smart note-taking choices. If the listening event is a meeting, make sure that you review relevant materials prior to the meeting. Do not take up important meeting time with questions that would have been resolved ahead of time simply by having been more prepared. Make sure that you are up-to-date with knowledge and information. In some cases, you will want to prepare your questions ahead of time. If you are a presenter, try to anticipate possible questions, and prepare your answers ahead of time. Regardless of whether it is a class session, a group or team meeting, or a formal presentation, make sure that you are sufficiently informed and that you build in information flexibility where needed.

Remember that you want to make sure that your communications are successful in both directions: you → saying/writing/texting and you ← listening/reading.

 ## Group/Team Work

If you're like most people, you probably just groaned at the mere mention of group work. OK, now that you're done groaning, it's time to think about how to approach group work in a mature, appreciative, and strategic way. Remember that during your college years, you have many opportunities to develop, practice, and improve your communication abilities. One key skill set that you want to take seriously and advance as much as possible while you are still in college includes your teamwork and leadership skills.

Highly developed teamwork skills are among the most important skills sought by employers today. In "Firms Seek Grads Who Can Think Fast, Work in Teams," Paul Wiseman (2013) quotes Mona Mourshed, leader of the education practice at the global consultancy McKinsey & Co., who "remembers one employer saying: 'I have never fired an engineer for bad engineering, but I have fired an engineer for lack of teamwork' . . . People have to work together. They have to collaborate."

In group work in your classes and on project teams, you have opportunities to practice your teamwork and leadership skills. Take advantage of each teamwork experience to practice, develop, and improve your own teamwork performance skills—both in your internal interpersonal communications with your group members (oral, written, and digital) and in your team's collaboratively written, oral, and digital work that you present in class or online and that you turn in for grading.

Teamwork Guideposts

- Work hard to improve and develop your teamwork and leadership and communication skills as much as possible while you are in college.
- Assess your teamwork and leadership strengths and weaknesses so that you can build on your strengths and work out as many bugs in your performance as a team player and leader.
- Value and appreciate group work and project team assignments as significant experiential learning opportunities during college.
- Hit the ground running when you work in teams in your internships so that you demonstrate to potential employers the teamwork skills that you have already developed.
- Before you apply for internships and other jobs, reflect on your group experiences so that, in interviews, you can talk comfortably and effectively about being a team player, about how much you have learned to value team activities and teamwork skills, and about specific examples in which you were able to improve your teamwork skills and contribute in big ways to your team's productivity.

Teamwork Skills to Practice

- Value each team member.
- Listen appreciatively to others' contributions.
- Be highly prepared for meetings.
- Contribute thoughtfully, intentionally, and selflessly.
- Focus on the team, the team project, and the end product (not on yourself).
- Work for team cohesiveness and harmony combined with strategic utilization of member skills, abilities, and knowledge.

If you are part of a short-term group work exercise or even just a brief group discussion that is held in class, perform at the highest of levels, thereby demonstrating your commitment to excellence even in such small assignments. View these short-term group exercises as excellent practice opportunities for you to develop your interpersonal communication and teamwork skills. Remember to arrive in class having done *all* of the assigned homework and having done it very well. Hit the ground running by being thoroughly prepared. Be one of the students in class whom others value in their groups.

"Aren't you glad we had this meeting to resolve our conflict?"

If you have a job while you are a student, demonstrate to your boss that you are a key team player in the workplace: that when your work is done, you step up to help others; that when you work in teams, your leadership abilities help everyone to perform better; and that others respect you and want to work with you. With any luck, your boss will write a letter of recommendation for you in which he or she expresses that your teamwork skills are exemplary—exactly what any employer would desire.

If you are part of a semester-long project team, step up and be the kind of team member with whom you would want to work. Be highly prepared at each stage of the project. Encourage and informally lead your teammates to perform at ever higher levels. Demonstrate to your teammates your strong time-management skills, your hard work ethic, your collaborative spirit, your interest in the project, and your appreciation of whatever each team member brings to the project. You want your teammates to communicate in end-of-project evaluations that you were, without a doubt, one of the strongest and most highly valued team members.

If you are involved in a particular initiative as part of a student organization, a volunteer group, or an internship assignment, demonstrate that you are a team player and that you will shoulder your responsibilities efficiently, successfully, *and* with interest. You want to be viewed as a team member who values teammates' participation, encourages teammates' interest and motivation, and contributes to teammates' heightened productivity. You want to be viewed as a leader and also as a key team player willing to do even the smallest of jobs when needed.

Communication Worksheets

The following worksheets shed light on your everyday communications experiences. It is important to have a clearer view of your own communication style, needs, strengths, and weaknesses. This will provide insight into your distinctive manner of communicating and how to develop your communication style in smart and strategic ways. As you fill out the following worksheets, specific details will emerge that will help you to see your communications experiences more fully (those with whom you communicate most regularly, the modes by which you communicate with different persons, etc.).

Begin by listing ten different people with whom you speak in an average week (e.g., friends, family, roommates, instructors, advisors, coaches, teammates, classmates, bosses, co-workers, customers). Include interactions that are in person, on the phone, or digital (texts, FB, chat, Skype, etc.). For each person, include the amount of time each week that you spend communicating. For example, you may write "Professor Doe, time after class and during office hours: 30 minutes/week."

1. _____
2. _____
3. _____
4. _____
5. _____
6. _____
7. _____
8. _____
9. _____
10. _____

It is important to have a clear view of the ways by which you communicate. The following list will help you begin to discern your primary modes of communications and the diverse modes used with different persons. List the 15 people with whom you communicate most regularly. For each person, delineate the modes of communications most commonly used with them. For example, if the majority of your time in class with one professor is spent mainly listening and taking notes, then you would note, "writing and listening." If your class is discussion based and you are an active participant, then your interactions with your instructor would reflect interactive oral communications. If you spend your time with one friend texting via your cell phone, then you would note, "digital communications."

1. _____
2. _____
3. _____
4. _____
5. _____
6. _____
7. _____
8. _____
9. _____

10. _____
_____

11. _____
_____

12. _____
_____

13. _____
_____

14. _____
_____

15. _____
_____

For the same 15 individuals, please identify your communications with them as primarily effective & comfortable (E/C), ineffective & uncomfortable (I/U), or a mix (M).

For those in the first (E/C) category—those with whom you have really effective, friendly, positive, collegial, and productive communications—describe your relationships with these individuals in a few words (mutual respect, caring, focused listening, etc.).

For those in the second (I/U) category—those with whom you have more problematic communications—describe your relationships with these individuals in a few words (distanced and distancing, edgy, conflictive, etc.).

For those in the third (M) category—those with whom your communications are more mixed (at times, comfortable and effective; at other times, conflictive, distanced, uncomfortable)—please describe your relationships with these specific individuals in a few words, as in the following example.

Y. Chavez	(E/C)	Mutual respect, honesty, sincerity
N. Smith	(I/U)	Jealousy, dishonesty, backstabbing
J. Doe	(M)	Caring, respectful, at times judgmental, impatient

1. _____
_____

2. _____
_____

3. _____
_____

4. _____
_____

5. _____
_____

6. _____
_____

7. _____
_____

8. _____
_____

9. _____
_____

10. _____
_____

11. _____
_____
12. _____
_____
13. _____
_____
14. _____
_____
15. _____
_____

Do not worry if there are some people with whom you have negative communications patterns. Everyone has some individuals with whom communications are challenging or even seriously problematic. Fortunately, you have many opportunities every day to practice your communication skills. For those with whom having positive and effective communications is especially difficult, you can improve your communications with those persons or minimize negative contact with them. Let's look at one example.

Select one of the people with whom you have difficult communications. Describe one situation in which you had a positive communications experience (conversation, meeting, interview, etc.) with him or her. Note where you were, the time of day, and the length of the communication event; describe the communications event in your own words, including the topic and who initiated it. In other words, tell the story of what happened during the successful communications event. Then explain what you think contributed to the positive nature of this one communications event with this person.

_____
_____
_____
_____
_____
_____

Now describe one situation in which you had a negative communications experience with that person. What is different about the positive experience versus the negative experience in your interactions with that person? Note any contributing factors.

_____
_____
_____
_____
_____
_____

Looking over the descriptions of the two different communications events with the same person, in what ways were you different in the positive example? It is important to understand how you are behaving so that you can see how best to behave and communicate in order to maximize the effectiveness of your communications with that person and with others with whom you have challenging relationships. You cannot change the other person, but you can change yourself.

In the cases of those individuals with whom you have more consistently problematic relationships, you may need to minimize or avoid altogether your communication with those individuals or, if possible, seek to improve your communications with them by working on your side of the communications equation.

Now let's turn to those individuals with whom you have consistently positive interactions. List five people you know who always seem to bring a positive attitude whenever they interact with others and who are consistently upbeat and positive influences on you. Briefly describe the qualities that you see that make these individuals especially positive communicators (e.g., "she listens closely to what I say," "she looks directly eye-to-eye and sits in an open and comfortable way," "she always says something positive about me or something I've done").

1. _____
   _____
2. _____
   _____
3. _____
   _____
4. _____
   _____
5. _____
   _____

These individuals are your role models for positive and effective communications. Pay close attention to how they communicate, and think about what in their communications styles might work for you in your own communications experiences with others. In thinking about these people, select one or two things you want to change in your communications with others, and then practice, practice, practice.

1. _____
   _____
2. _____
   _____

Please note that there are many resources available to help you improve your own communications styles. The classic Dale Carnegie book *How to Win Friends and Influence People* is still as current as ever, with key tips for effective communications. I recommend that you read this book, and over the years return to it again and again.

 # Writing Fundamentals

While you are in college, definitely take advantage of the various writing classes available to you for more extensive guidance and practice. You need to understand that there are few classes in college that will be of greater benefit to you in the workplace, in your community life, and in your family life than your speech and composition classes. The primary focus in your composition classes is writing (whether the classes are in expository, argumentative, business, technical, creative, digital, or multimedia composition), and the benefits of an improved writing *process* are far greater than the actual written *product*. Indeed, "the writing process itself provides one of the best ways to help students learn the active, dialogic thinking skills valued in academic life" (Bean, 2011, p. 24).

In the next few pages, you will learn strategic pointers to (1) help you to improve your writing and (2) help you understand why you want to make the most of your composition classes. Appreciate any opportunity to improve your writing. I am a senior professor who has published many articles, book chapters, and books. I am also an English professor. Yes, I am an accomplished writer. This means that I have successfully learned the process of writing—thinking, drafting, revising, rethinking, and revising yet again. And the vast majority of my published work has been rewritten and revised multiple times with each iteration improving on the prior version. Proficient writing, like any skill, requires practice and effort.

Your highest priorities in writing are centered in the process of writing and its content (facts and examples, development, organization, voice, etc.). But do not underestimate the importance of the mechanics of writing. In a recent issue of *Lingua Franca: Language and Writing in Academe,* Anne Curzan explains that students have the responsibility "to pay close attention to language at the level of the sentence, learn from their own work, consult available resources about grammar and style, and engage in a conversation with [their professor] (and themselves) about the details of their writing and of standard edited academic prose" (2013, n.p.).

If you plan on becoming an English professor, creative writer, or professional writer—and will spend your adulthood writing and rewriting—then you will have many years to develop and fine tune your writing craft. If, on the other hand, your plans lie in other directions, wouldn't it make sense to take significant advantage of the writing classes, writing centers, and writing tutors that are available to you while you are a college student? Wouldn't it be wise for virtually any college student to put 100 percent into each composition class?

As a student who desires many different things in life, you want to work as hard as possible to develop and improve your writing skills to the highest levels in your writing classes and in any projects in which you have the opportunities to practice your writing skills (term papers, essay exams, webpages, email, reports, résumés, etc.). And beyond the explicitly required composition/writing classes at your college, wouldn't it make sense to consider taking an extra composition class or two for added writing practice, guidance, and expertise? Remember that you want to make smart and strategic choices that will help prepare you in big ways for your future life.

Now let's turn to some specific guidance regarding your writing. Remember that the relational or interpersonal/intergroup nature of writing is paramount, so the following nine key elements of writing begin with your express attention to your audience—the individual or people to whom your writing is addressed.

Your Audience

▶ From the outset, focus relationally on your audience (and team members, if any).

Know your audience's and team members' demographics and psychographics to help you anticipate how they will understand, interpret, and respond to your writing. Familiarity with your intended audience is crucial to your determinations of content, form, style, voice, and word choice. Remember that you want your writing to speak *to* and speak *with* your readers as if in a dialogue or conversation. By crafting your writing with an empathetic voice, your writing will be more accessible to your readers. This will make your writing that much more informative and persuasive. If your written assignment is a team project, by working collaboratively with your team members, you will help the writing to be that much more unified and coherent.

Your Attitude

▶ Demonstrate a sincere generosity of spirit and a respectful tone in your writing.

Begin with a positive attitude towards your writing project. You want your writing to be honest, sincere, straightforward, trustworthy, enthusiastic, and informed. This is also necessary for your reader to approach what you have written with an open mind, an amenable attitude, and a considerate response. You want the style of your writing and the tone of what is written to reflect the importance of your words and your interest in sharing your words with your readers. If you struggle in this area, then you either need to change your approach to your topic or change your topic altogether. Your responsibility is to bring enthusiasm to the task at hand and throw yourself wholly into the research and writing so that what you produce is interesting, inspired, and informed.

Your Brainstorming Process

▶ Brainstorm your initial ideas, topics, directions, orientation, length, and structure.

As with any project or journey, to produce something or arrive somewhere, you need to begin with a plan. To do this, you need to begin with as many ideas, facts, and conjectures as possible. Brainstorming is like mapping out the many different places you want to see on a journey. Once you have a clear view of those places, then you can map out a planned itinerary. Once you have a clear view of the different ideas, facts, and arguments that you want to include in your writing, then you can begin to map out and plan your writing project in a variety of forms, such as an outline. This will help ensure that your writing draws upon the strongest and most relevant of your ideas and information. This will lead to focused, robust, and engaged writing.

Your Understanding

▶ Run with your ideas; develop them as fully as possible: write about what you know.

You want to thoroughly develop or research your ideas so that you have a deep understanding of your topic. When you *know* your topic very well, you will be able communicate what you know that much more clearly and completely to your reader. Your understanding of your subject matter needs to be well developed in order for your writing to be developed. If your knowledge of your topic is slim, then your writing will not be as strong. You want to be able to determine what are the strongest, most valid, most relevant, most interesting, and most important facts, information, arguments, and quotations to incorporate in your written documents—and to do this, your background knowledge is key.

Your Word Choices

▶ Use clear and simple language.

You want your writing to be accessible to your reader. Based on your knowledge of your intended/expected audience, you want to use an appropriate writing style and suitable language choice. Try to avoid unnecessary jargon. In some cases, there will be specific technical terminology that you will want to use. When you use more complex professional language, determine whether your audience will need to have a specific term or phrase explained (parenthetically or in a note). You want to make sure that you use more specialized and challenging terminology where it is necessary, effective, efficient, and coherent.

Your Equanimity or Fairness of Judgment

▶ Craft a balanced and fair presentation of your topic.

It is really important that you approach your topic with an open mind, being open to change the direction of your presentation if the facts, data, hypotheses, interpretations, and theories indicate that your prior understanding was incomplete or even wrong. Be careful to avoid the trap of inflexible, preconceived ideas, opinions, and prejudices of your own that will skew or altogether prevent your understanding and your writing from being as factual, balanced, accurate, and fair as you want your work to be. If your mindset is open minded, with an attitude of discovery, then your writing will be effective and truly fair and balanced.

Your Accurate and Substantial Information

▶ Provide sufficient evidence that is reliable, valid, and accurate.

Your facts provide the foundation of your work. You want that foundation to be rock solid. This means that the facts, data, and information on which your statements and claims are based must be factual, reasonable, logical, and correct. When you find information that you want to incorporate into your writing, double check to be sure that it is reliable. Much of the information available online is questionable. Examine and evaluate the source of the information in order to determine its accuracy and legitimacy. Whether you are writing about an anecdotal experience shared with you by a friend or arguing the effectiveness of a particular procedure in your field of study, make sure that what you include in your writing is reliable, valid, and accurate.

Recent research documents an alarming finding that more and more students do not know how to analyze their sources in order to determine which are authoritative, reliable, and most efficacious to use in a paper or project (Berrett, 2012). Writing faculty Sandra Jamieson and Rebecca Moore Howard point out that students across the United States are demonstrating serious problems with reading such that texts are misunderstood, with serious consequences for both the analysis and evaluation of information (Berrett, 2012, p. A29). This adversely affects students' abilities to utilize the information within those texts that have been poorly read.

The situation is even more dire with employers and professors lamenting the extent to which college students are not taking the importance of high-quality writing and research seriously. Jamieson, professor and chair of the English department at Drew University and the co-principal investigator of the Citation Project, reports that, across a diversity of institutions and with different instructors, first-year composition students are not significantly improving their writing abilities (Berrett, 2012, p. A29). Marta Deyrup and Beth Bloom (2013) make this very claim in their edited collection *Successful Strategies for Teaching Undergraduate Research* in which virtually every contributor documents the difficulties that undergraduate students demonstrate in their abilities to find, understand, evaluate, and utilize information sources for their research papers. For example, in her essay "Research Questions and the Research Question: What Are We Teaching When We Teach Research?" Heidi L.M. Jacobs notes the value that research and writing provide students, while pointing to the extent to which many undergraduate research projects end up being approached by students as little more than tedious writing assignments: "The research assignment carries with it tremendous possibilities for student engagement. In its ideal form, it builds on natural curiosity, encourages exploration, and positions students as critical thinkers and active creators of knowledge" (2013, p. 5). You can significantly improve your writing, but only if you step up and make a serious commitment to that process. Required and elective composition classes provide the best environments in which to develop your writing. Many students make strategic choices to take additional composition classes in order to raise their writing to higher levels. Employers value student résumés that exhibit top communication skills.

Your Format

▶ Present your material in an appropriate form and length.

This moves us further into the realm of digital communications. Based on the specifications of your writing assignment (e.g., email, formal letter, résumé and vitas, proposal, or report), you will need to determine whether the writing is to be crafted for a digital or print presentation. As you do your preparatory writing, drafting, and revising, you need to take into account the requisite form and length of the final product. Even short emails benefit from multiple drafts and revisions. Depending on the content, importance, and sensitivity of your subject matter, you want to evaluate the extent to which your writing merits multiple drafts, revisions, and collaborative input from others.

Your Presentation

▶ Produce a polished, effective, and professional visual presentation of the written product.

You want your final written product to be visually appealing and, thereby, effective. Use spacing (line and paragraph breaks, margins, indentation), headings, font choice, and visual aids (graphs, charts, tables, photos, and video) to productive and effective ends. Be careful to neither overuse nor underuse visuals. Remember that presentation is important, *but* it will not compensate for inadequate content and poor argumentation. Start with a solid written product; then present your work well.

Writing as a Process

Writing is a process that involves multiple stages and culminates in a final product. It begins with initial brainstorming of ideas and continues through multiple drafts and all the way to final revisions, edits, and proofreading.

Writers who are successful and experienced are those who have learned the crucial lessons of the writing process and of revising ideas, information, organization, and the written product. "Expert writers do extensive rewriting, the final products often being substantially different from the first drafts" (Bean, 2011, p. 33). If you take the various stages seriously, provide sufficient time and effort for each stage, and make the needed adjustments and corrections along the way, you will be able to produce much more successful written products. The critical element here is to take the time necessary for each stage so that you will be sufficiently prepared by the time you move to the next stage.

Brainstorm→
        think→
               research→
                        draft→
                              rethink→
                                    research→
                                          review→
                                              redraft→
                                                  revise→
                                                          edit→
                                                          polish→
                                                                proofread.

The very process of writing is crucial to the successful development of your ideas, and the very process of writing is crucial to the successful presentation of those ideas. The influential writing specialist Peter Elbow in his book *Writing with Power: Techniques for Mastering the Writing Process* (Oxford University Press, 1981) explains this in terms of the intertwined process of creation and critique:

> Writing calls on two skills that are so different that they usually conflict with each other: creating and criticizing. In other words, writing calls on the ability to create

words and ideas out of yourself, but it also calls on the ability to criticize them in order to decide which ones to use. . . . Most of the time it helps to separate the creating and criticizing processes so they don't interfere with each other: first write freely and uncritically so that you can generate as many words and ideas as possible without worrying whether they are good; then turn around and adopt a critical frame of mind and thoroughly revise what you have written. (p. 7)

This process is enormously effective. Like breathing, writing is an inflow and outflow process. As you think and then write and then think again and write some more as the writing stimulates further ideas that then are added to the writing. Inflow and outflow, inspiration and expiration, thinking and writing.

One of the most commonly used resources for writing assistance is the award-winning Purdue Online Writing Lab (OWL) at http://owl.english.purdue.edu. Most of your writing questions will find answers there. Visit the Purdue OWL site or other online writing labs and familiarize yourself with their range of resources. You will also find very clear explanations for many of your specific writing questions at Pearson's free and open access site Pearson Writing.com: Writing Resources for Students: http://media.pearsoncmg.com/long/pearsonwriting/. This robust site offers a wealth of resources for students in first-year writing courses (Pearson Education, 2011).

Remember to visit the writing center at your own college or university and learn about the resources that they offer, such as tutoring and workshops. You want to improve your writing as much as possible while you are an undergraduate so that your writing skills will be well polished by the time you apply for internships and post-college jobs. You want your writing to demonstrate your intelligence, your hard work, and your successful communication skills.

Pioneering writing specialist Mina Shaughnessy (1977) tells us that most students only make a few errors in their writing. Even though a student's essay may have many errors, those errors usually are repetitions of just a few different errors. It is especially valuable for you to look over your writing to discover the specific errors that you make. You do not need to memorize everything in a grammar textbook, but you do need to put forth the effort to understand what your typical errors are and how to correct them. The next section reviews a few common writing errors that many students make. If you can learn and correct these few errors, then you can turn the greater part of your focus towards the *content*, *process*, and *style* of your writing—the areas where you want to pay most attention.

Specific Writing Tips

By learning the following rules, you will minimize your writing errors to improve the readability of your writing. Writing errors can take an otherwise thoughtful and well-developed piece of writing and make it difficult for your reader to read. Your ideas and researched information deserve a polished and error-free presentation.

Punctuation and Mechanics

Punctuation rules have varied somewhat over time. But what is most important for you to understand is that all punctuation indicates various pausal spacing in the writing. The pauses indicated by punctuation identify areas in the writing where a reader would naturally pause in the reading (or where most speakers would naturally pause in their speaking). In many cases, these pauses are crucial to understanding the meaning of a sentence.

Commas After most *introductory phrases or clauses,* use a comma before the main independent clause. If you have an introductory dependent clause (like this), use a comma to separate it from the main independent clause. Note that the two previous sentences both demonstrate the placement of a comma after an introductory phrase (in the case of the first sentence) or introductory clause (in the case of the second sentence). Also note that when you read the first two sentences (and this one) aloud, you will hear a slight pause where the commas occur. The placement of the commas indicates a slight oral pause to help guide your reader and to announce and give emphasis to the beginning of the main part of the sentence—which comes immediately after the comma. I recommend that you reread this paragraph and see how this works in order to understand this comma rule more fully.

You want to use a comma to separate different items in *lists, series, or other strings of words or phrases.* Note how this is done in the previous sentence to demonstrate this punctuation rule. The final comma is optional because the conjunction "or" or "and" is sufficient. Most students follow this rule consistently, so we need say no more here.

A smart stylistic and contextual choice is to include *two independent clauses* that are closely related in meaning within one sentence, but use *a comma with a coordinating conjunction* (e.g., *and, or, nor, for, but, yet, so*) to conjoin them. Note how this is done in the previous sentence and in this one, and also note that what comes before and after the "comma-conjunction" link are two separate independent clauses that are kept in one sentence to show that they are closely and meaningfully related. In other words, each of the independent clauses is a complete idea and could stand alone as a separate sentence, but (as in each sentence in this paragraph) the independent clauses are meaningfully related and therefore combined within the one sentence.

Semicolons As in the previous rule, often you will have *two independent clauses* that you want to keep closely together in one sentence; the two clauses are closely related in meaning and can also be stylistically connected with the punctuation of a semicolon and *without a coordinating conjunction.* It is okay to have two independent clauses in one sentence; just make sure that you separate them with a semicolon (not a comma). Note how this is done with the semicolon in all three of the sentences in this paragraph; what comes before and after the semicolon are two separate independent clauses that are conjoined by the semicolon to keep them more closely related within the boundaries of one sentence.

Parentheses (or Commas) Use parentheses and commas to set off *a nonrestrictive (and, thereby, nonessential) word or phrase* in a sentence. Nonrestrictive parts of a sentence are nonessential elements (such as explanations, added descriptions, examples) that can be taken out of the sentence without affecting the main meaning of the sentence. Note how this is done with the parentheses in the previous sentences and with the two commas in the first sentence to set off the word *thereby.* The main idea of each of these sentences is communicated without the added information in the nonrestrictive phrases or words.

Colons and Dashes Both the colon and the dash are used to *point in a directive manner* to some related idea—as is done here. What comes in front of the colon or dash must be an independent clause: both of these sentences show how that is done. The difference between the colon and the dash is subtle. The colon has been described as a more masculine form of punctuation in that it is a harder stop than the dash. The dash is more connective, more of a bridge, and has been described as a more feminine form of punctuation. Both have their roles to play in your writing. On this note, I have a question for you: which one of these two forms of punctuation was made famous in Emily Dickinson's poetry—the colon or the dash?

Apostrophes Remember the difference between *its* (possessive) and *it's* (contraction of "it is"). The difference in spelling is minor but important because their meanings are very different. These two words are two of the most commonly confused.

Possessive Pronouns	Pronoun Contractions of the Verb "To Be"
my	I'm
your	you're
his	he's
her/hers	she's
its	**it's**
our	we're
your	you're
their/theirs	they're

The easiest way to remember the difference between *its* and *it's* is to remember this friendly mnemonic listing of pronouns:

If you can remember that *its* goes with *his,* and if you can remember that *it's* goes with *he's,* then you will be able to remember when to use *its* (with its correct format) and when to use *it's* (because it's really time to start remembering this).

Identifying Titles

Many students have difficulty understanding how to correctly identify titles of books, articles, websites, videos, and so on. If you cite a book chapter, but you erroneously underline or italicize the chapter title, your reader will think that what you are citing is not a chapter but rather the title of the complete book. This becomes very confusing. Let's say that you are submitting a professional report and include citations and references for some of your sources, which will be useful for your coworkers who want to know more. If you misidentify a chapter as a book, your coworkers will have trouble finding the chapter to use. Then time will be wasted as they continue to try to track the information down or as they contact you and have you spend time tracking down the source.

Think about Michael Jackson's famous album *Thriller* with the equally famous video and title song "Thriller." If you are writing about the pioneering gothic music tune "Thriller," but you erroneously identify it as *Thriller*, your reader will think that you are writing about the album. Remember that you want your writing to be clear, coherent, and correct. By using the correct identification system for the title, your writing is clearer to your reader.

Let's say that you are doing research for a class paper or for a project in the workplace and you find an especially helpful article that includes references to other valuable publications on the topic. You want to look up one of the referenced publications to use in your paper, but the author incorrectly identified it as an article when it is really a book. That one error makes it hard for you to track down the source, so you end up not being able to use what otherwise might have been very useful for your work. Understanding the rules for identifying titles, and remembering how to identify them correctly, is really not that difficult. All you need to know is the difference between parts and wholes.

- Underline or *italicize* the names of books, movies, plays, television shows, CDs, magazines, journals, newspapers, websites, and blogs. You can decide whether to underline a title or italicize it—just be consistent throughout your document. Both conventions are acceptable, but italicizing titles is used most commonly now. The one time where you absolutely need to underline titles is in a handwritten document because italicizing handwritten text would not be as clear as underlining.

- Use quotation marks to mark the beginning and ending of titles of shorter pieces (e.g., short stories, articles, chapters, poems, speeches, episodes, news stories, webpages, blog entries).

<u>Underline</u>/*Italicize* **Wholes**	**Use "Quotation Marks" for Parts**
The Poems of Edgar Allan Poe (book)	"The Raven" (poem)
Thriller (CD title)	"Thriller" (song or video)
Make College Work for You (book)	"Communication Skills" (chapter)
Friends (television show)	"The One Where Rachel Finds Out" (episode)

Documentation

There are several commonly accepted styles for documenting the references in your writing. The three most common are the APA (American Psychological Association), MLA (Modern Language Association), and Chicago (*The Chicago Manual of Style*). Check to see which professional style your professors mandate for your work in their respective classes. Grammar handbooks will provide the information you need to organize and format your references, works cited, and bibliography pages. The American Psychological Association provides an online guide for APA style at www. apastyle.org. The Modern Language Association provides its own handbook for the MLA style: www.mlahandbook.org. And the University of Chicago has an online version of *The Chicago Manual of Style* at www.chicagomanualofstyle.org. You can also find additional help at the Purdue OWL site and many other online resources.

Plagiarism

Review your writing to make sure that all quoted text is properly cited, documented, and in quotation marks. You want to make sure that your writing consists of your own original writing with *all* supporting information, quotations, and paraphrases properly cited. This is a very large issue, well beyond the purview of this chapter's communications overview. Most colleges and universities have writing centers where you can go for additional assistance in ensuring that your writing is absolutely plagiarism free. If there is no writing center, go to the English or communications department for guidance.

Today with the advantages of digital technology,
> **it is much easier to plagiarize—whether intentionally or inadvertently.**

Today with the advantages of digital technology,
> **it is much easier to catch plagiarized text in student work.**

So it is more important than ever that you follow these rules:

1. Understand what plagiarism is and how to avoid it.
2. Make sure that your writing is your own.
3. Make sure that your quotations and paraphrases are properly cited.
4. Make sure that your outside information is properly cited.

Digital Platforms

The world has been transformed very quickly in technologically driven directions. This has radically transformed human communications, both simplifying and complicating how, when, what, and to whom we communicate. In "Reading, in a Digital Archive of One's Own," Jim Collins (2013) explains that "the force of media convergence . . . makes anyone holding a portable device a reader-viewer-listener" (p. 212).

The speed of transformation is such that we are still figuring out how to live and work in healthy, productive, effective, balanced, and ethical ways in this information-and-technology-powered world. The world of a college student has become redefined in terms of new technology. Facebook and other social networking sites are omnipresent, along with texting and various video communications platforms (e.g., Skype, Yahoo Messenger, and WebEx). More and more textbooks are read digitally, as you might be doing with this text.

Accessing and Evaluating Information Digitally

Reading is done via the Internet, e-readers, tablets, smartphones, and course sites (Blackboard, Sakai, Moodle, and publisher sites such as Pearson's MyLabs). The ease of access to increasing amounts of information is mind-boggling. This is all unbelievably wonderful. More and more of the world's knowledge and information is increasingly available to increasing numbers of people. A young woman in a less developed country who has limited access to public education could nevertheless gain knowledge and education through the Internet—as many around the world are doing via the massive open online courses (MOOCs) of Coursera, Udacity, and edX.

Much of what is available online is valuable, accurate, informative, and much is worthless, inaccurate, and misinforming. Your responsibility when you access information online is actually simple. Unless you are an expert in a specific field already, you do not need to worry about confirming the correctness of the information. Your responsibility is to evaluate the legitimacy, authenticity, and authority of the source of the information.

If the information source is a peer-reviewed scholarly journal or publisher, accept the article or book as authoritative. If the information source is an authoritative organization, accept the information as reliable. In both of these cases, only use information if a bibliography of peer-reviewed sources is provided that documents the legitimacy of the information in the text. For sources that are not scholarly (e.g., Wikipedia, magazines, newspapers, most websites), you must dig to determine the source of any information that you want to use. If you cannot find a rock solid source, then it is best to err on the side of caution and not use that information.

Once you determine that a source is legitimate and authoritative, then you can accept the information as accurate, unless you find other legitimate authorities who indicate otherwise. This is true whether the information is accessed digitally or via a print medium, but the proliferation of misinformation and disinformation available digitally makes your evaluative job that much more necessary.

Use the following guidelines when evaluating sources.

1. **If you are an authority, then critique.** In fields in which you are an authority, you can intelligently, knowledgably, and valuably evaluate and critique what is presented by another authority in your field. Legitimate authorities have the responsibility to be current in their fields and to move the fields of science, the arts, and knowledge production forward—making new discoveries; developing new ideas, methodologies, and products; creating new art, music, and literature; and correcting the mistakes of others (past and current).

2. **If you are not an authority, then evaluate authenticity.** In fields in which you are not an authority, your job is to evaluate the extent to which authorities are, in fact, legitimate and authentic authorities. When an individual or organization lists scholarly publications and sources, are the journals and publishers highly regarded peer-reviewed sources or not? Is the authority a highly respected authority? What evidence is there for this? What is the person's training? What is the individual's current position? Is the scholar or organization respected and highly regarded within their respective field of expertise? You need to ask these hard questions in order to determine the degree of the authority's legitimacy, authenticity, and expertise. This process will help you learn to determine who is a legitimate authority in their respective fields and what information is more and less trustworthy.

3. **If you are not an authority, then trust authorities' knowledge.** In fields where you are not an authority, respect legitimate authority: their expertise and knowledge.

Legitimate experts and authorities provide the invaluable information and data that move the world forward. Indeed, as a college student, your primary responsibility is to learn from experts and get a great education. You benefit each day from the expertise of your faculty. If your instructor gives you advice, accept it, learn from it, and improve your work.

4. **If you are not an authority, then do not argue against legitimate experts.** In those fields in which we are not authorities, our role is not to argue with legitimate authorities, but rather to accept their findings. Any needed correction of their research is the job of the other legitimate authorities. Our job is to be informed about what legitimate authorities say.

Crafting and Transmitting Information Digitally

Each year, the degree to which communications are sent digitally is increasing. Although the accuracy of content is important, the predominant changes with the shift to digital realms are in accessibility and visuality. Information does need to be accurate, but the presentation, the "look" of the material is far more important than in many traditional print forms. And the extent to which online communication is widely accessible (even when it is intended to be private) necessitates far greater care in terms of discretion and tact.

The specific platforms of textual and digital writing vary, and, with that, the presentation too must fit the technological format. It would be valuable to seek out classes at your college or other places (whether "brick and mortar" or online) to improve your familiarity and proficiency in digital communications. Staying current is particularly important in areas such as graphics and webpage design. Whether your digital communications are in the form of email, text messaging, blogs, online video, or posts to social networking sites, you want your communications to be effective.

The Importance of Strong Communication Skills

This chapter ends with an invitation: I would like you to set yourself a goal toward significantly improving your communication skills while you are in college. Regardless of your current strengths and weaknesses in the various areas of communications and composition, take advantage of the opportunities at your college for growth, improvement, and development. Look for additional course work workshops, certificate programs that will help you improve your individual and group communication skills.

There may be no other fact of our times that is more important for you to remember regarding your successful and effective communications than this:

Understand the public and long life of digital communications
Whatever is put in digital form and sent out online has a permanency and accessibility that endures in a myriad of ways and with many diverse and unintended consequences. You must take this very seriously.

1. **Tact, discretion, restraint, circumspection, caution.** What you want to say does not always need to be said online. What can be said online does not always need to be said at all. It is important that your digital communications are socially and professionally appropriate. Discretion is indeed the better part of valor. This cannot be repeated enough: Whatever you put in digital form is not private.

   Be smart and strategic, judicious and diplomatic, restrained and respectful in your online communications. Only put in digital form what you are comfortable having future employers read. Keep everything else oral.

2. **Presentation, appearance, structure, form, the visual look.** A major difference between digital communication forms and print text is that online text is much more visually acute. The "look" of online communications is essential in its effectiveness. Its appearance determines its attractiveness, its accessibility, its meaning, and its overall communications success.

   Even writing rules have to adapt for the medium. For example, a complete and coherent print paragraph might need to be broken up into three separate units for effective presentation on a webpage. In a scholarly article in a text journal, a paragraph might have over 300 words and a sentence might extend for many lines. In contrast, paragraphing and sentencing are best abbreviated in their digitized, visual forms. Open space, choice of font, images, and links are much more important in digital publications.

3. **Permanency, imperishability, timelessness, eternity, infinity and beyond.** This also cannot be said enough regarding any digital texts and images: What is sent out digitally has a permanence far beyond the initially intended transmission. Tattoos last a long time, but they can be removed far more easily than you can erase any text or image that has been sent out into the electronic ether of the online cosmos.

   Regarding online communications, it really is vitally important to be smart and strategic and take a long-term view of the digital temporal horizon. Be careful. Protect yourself and your future. It is important.

Remember that what you do in college is important for what you will accomplish in life. It is about the many ways that you will contribute to the forward progress of the world. It is about the many ways that you will help to make the world a better place.

The renowned Native American writer Leslie Marmon Silko (1981) has beautifully articulated the effective power of language in human communications, namely "the boundless capacity of language which, through storytelling, brings us together, despite great distances between cultures, despite great distances in time" (p. 72). It is through language that we knit together the fabric of the world. Be smart and strategic, and utilize the opportunities in college to improve your oral, written, digital, and interpretative communications capabilities.

6 Campus Activity

Clubs, the Arts, Athletics

It isn't what we say or think that defines us, but what we do.

— Jane Austen (1811), Sense and Sensibility

Education, therefore, is a process of living and not a preparation for future living.

— John Dewey (1897), "My Pedagogic Creed"

1. **The Breadth and Depth of Experience:** Live your college experience fully to gain a complete undergraduate education.

2. **The Larger Significance of Experience:** Live your college experience and act in ways that contribute to the betterment of your communities and the world—both now and for what you will do in the future.

3. **Extracurriculars and Skill Set Development:** Gain invaluable skills from campus involvement in the areas of communications, socialization, cultural competencies, leadership and teamwork.

4. **Student Organizations and Clubs:** Be active in several organizations on campus, including one that is selective or one in which you hold a leadership position.

5. **Volunteerism and Student Leadership:** Take advantage of the many opportunities on campus to volunteer, be of service to others, and practice servant leadership.

6. **Extracurricular Lectures and Arts Events:** Attend as many extracurricular lectures and arts events as possible to expand your knowledge, increase your cultural literacy, and enrich your college (and post-college) life.

7. **Undergraduate Research and Creative Production:** Experience the intensive learning, problem-solving, and creative thinking opportunities through undergraduate research and creative production.

8. **Physical Fitness, Athletics, and Team Sports:** Participate in physical fitness, athletics, and team sports opportunities that are widely available on most campuses for student overall wellness and fitness.

Studying may be your #1 job in college, but extracurricular activities can be as important to your future life and career. While you are a college student, you want to take advantage of the special opportunities that are available to you through your college's or university's resources to develop and practice your own professional/personal management and civic mindedness, both of which are vital to your professional networking and mentoring endeavors and, even more importantly, to the successful functioning of any community and nation.

Your on-campus activities that occur outside of the physical classroom or digital class platform will take one of two forms: (1) activities either largely or wholly extracurricular and unconnected to your classes (e.g., student organizations and clubs, intramural athletic competitions, concerts, and other arts events), or (2) activities directly related to your academic learning in the form of experiential and service learning or other heightened undergraduate research and creative production opportunities (e.g., your performance in a musical, lab work as part of a faculty led research project, and presentation of your work at an on-campus student expo).

■ The Breadth and Depth of a Complete Undergraduate Education

A complete undergraduate education reflects a breadth and depth of learning and experience in both your academics and extracurriculars. It is critical that you understand that the success of your time in college and beyond is largely determined by your activities outside of class.

Throughout time, education has been understood to combine ideas with practice, book learning with applied learning, and theory with praxis. Most classes will combine both in some ways: a lesson with practice problems, literary theory with interpretive essays that use literary critical methods, statistical analytics interwoven with psychology methods, or learning about stage design and applying that knowledge for an actual dramatic performance. Many people think that college is just about getting a degree and performing successfully in class. These are indeed important. But college is much more than just your academic studies.

College is about the skilled,
        informed,
                thoughtful person that you are becoming.
College is about the educated,
        well-rounded,
                cultured person that you are becoming.
College is about the mature,
        disciplined,
                responsible person that you are becoming.

Your college years offer you many diverse ways to successfully traverse this period by increasing your knowledge base in your fields of study and more broadly about the world; expanding your appreciation of the fine arts (music, painting, sculpture, dance, drama, etc.); developing your disciplined study and work habits (in your academics, extracurriculars, and jobs); solidifying your commitment to volunteerism, service activities, and civic mindedness; and supporting your physical fitness and health (individual exercise, intramural teams, fitness classes).

The extensive period of undergraduate education (the equivalent of four to five years of traditional full-time study or 120 or more credit hours of study) permits this unique combination of breadth and depth. It is in graduate and professional schools where the focus is primarily or solely on depth of learning in a specific area in order to train students for specific careers.

In high school, there are many extracurricular activities that help teenagers to become well-rounded people: athletics to support physical fitness and team work skills, and many other clubs that support and build on school work (e.g., Scholastic Bowl, Spanish club, yearbook, newspaper, chess club, robotics club, Future Farmers of America, etc.). This is also true in college, but whereas most high school clubs are usually connected in some way to the learning in class, at the college level, extracurricular activities offer a much broader range of experiential opportunities.

Remember that, in college, what you do outside of class is as important as what you do in class. You want a well-rounded educational experience that will well prepare you for your future:

- Be involved in various campus organizations.
- Have experiential opportunities that demonstrate your responsibility, drive, and leadership.
- Take advantage of as many extra on-campus experiential learning and artistic events as possible (e.g., lectures, concerts, performance, poetry readings, and museum and art gallery shows). After college, you will have to pay a great deal of money for many of these kinds of events. At college, many of these are free or, at the least, inexpensive.
- Remember the crucial role of being a civically minded citizen who practices giving back by being involved in various volunteer activities and classes that incorporate service learning.

All this is important because, after college, what you do outside of the workplace is often as important as what you do at work. So it is important for you to develop and practice this balance during your undergraduate years in order to establish a strong foundation for your life after college. A crucial part of your college experience is your own personal development and growth, and much of this takes place outside of class.

- Live fully
- Think deeply
- Love college life
- Expand your horizons
- Learn more about the world
- Get to know a diversity of students
- Learn more about different places and cultures
- Be involved in a variety of social and service organizations
- Experience new things and learn as much as you can during college
- Take advantage of the many extracurricular activities at your university
- Attend lectures to become a more informed citizen about past and current events
- Learn about music, literature, painting, opera, theater, and the other fine arts

Even before you begin college, you should begin to think about the many different things that you would like to experience in college, about what you would like to try out, and about diverse cultural events that you think you probably should experience or learn about at this stage in your life.

Once you get to college, you need to begin thinking seriously about how to get the most out of your college years. As a college student, you are no longer a child. So you need to start thinking strategically about your course work *and* your life outside of the classroom.

How You Live and What You Do Matter

Who you are matters. You matter—in fact, a great deal! What you do in college and throughout your life can make your community and the world a better place. So you want to act as if you matter. You deserve to be successful, but you will need to put forth effort to accomplish it. How you live and act as a college student is only partially about you and your desired lifestyle; the other part is about the needs in the world and the difference that you will make in the world, both during college and beyond. You are needed for the betterment of the world.

The world needs each and every person to work hard and be successful and involved in his or her communities. By developing a strong foundation of learning and maturation during your college years, you will be of greater value and benefit to your job, to your community, to your nation, and to the world.

Extracurricular activities at your school contribute to the mature and educated human being that you are becoming. Here are a few examples to consider:

■ If you have never developed an appreciation for classical music, college would be the perfect time to learn this skill. You could take a class in the music department that would give you many opportunities to learn about and listen to wonderful music. You could go to various classical music concerts and recitals on campus. Or you could befriend a music major and attend classical concerts together off campus. If you take a required general education class in music appreciation, do not blow off the class; you may develop an appreciation of different types of music, even opera! ☺

■ If you spent years learning a foreign language in high school, college is the perfect time to develop that burgeoning skill through a foreign language major or minor. Even if you are not a foreign language major or minor, you could join other students at a weekly French/Spanish/Arabic/Chinese lunch table where the students and faculty practice speaking the language. You could go to the foreign language films available on campus. You could even sign up to live on a dorm floor especially designed for students to practice a specific foreign language.

■ If you are planning to work in a business-related field, you could take on financial or leadership responsibilities in one of the organizations with which you are involved. You could run for election as an organization's treasurer or president. In many organizations, such roles do not require an election and the membership appreciates all interested volunteers. Without taking on an executive role, you could step forward in a leadership capacity to oversee a particular event or one aspect of an event, such as the design, printing, and posting of print flyers or digital announcements for an event. The hands-on leadership activity just in this one example demonstrates valuable skills in effective communications, marketing, and advertising.

The Benefits of Campus Involvement

The benefits of campus involvement are manifold, including heightened socialization and communication skills, deepened experiential learning opportunities, and leadership and teamwork experience. Students who participate in extracurriculars are often many of the most successful students academically.

In their research into undergraduate student success in the journal *Studies in Higher Education*, Hounsell, Christie, Cree, McCune, and Tett (2008) explain that student involvement on campus often leads to higher grades because club involvement and a community of like-minded friends help students to be more engaged in school. Their research affirms "that engagement with learning is a subjective experience, bound up with other life events and experiences"—further pointing to its "social situatedness" (p. 579). University of Michigan psychology professor Alexander W. Astin (1993) found the same results a decade earlier when he affirmed that positive peer interactions and extracurricular activities such as intramural sports, Greek life, and other student organizations contribute positively to a student's successful academics and a higher G.P.A. (Astin, 1993; Wang & Shively, 2009). Much of the success of active student involvement on campus is a direct result of these students' commitment to more disciplined and balanced daily and weekly schedules.

Extracurricular involvement is paramount for ensuring that your undergraduate years are fulfilling and broadly successful. Dr. John C. Hitt, president of the University of Central Florida, explains that his undergraduate experience as a college athlete led to his later successes in life, teaching him how to balance out his many duties, achieving beyond stress, and learning from failure: "As an offensive lineman, I learned the power of persistence, the rewards of hard work, and the hard lesson that one doesn't always win" (Carlson, 2013, p. A28). The research of Caldwell, Darling, and Smith (2005) bears this out, noting that extracurricular activities provide students with opportunities otherwise unavailable to them, including strong "social networks" (p. 52).

The many and diverse benefits that come from your smart and strategic extracurricular activities as a college student are invaluable to you and your communities both while you are in college and beyond:

■ **Socialization and communication skills.** By being involved, you will interact with students whom you would not get to know otherwise. Throughout your life, you will be interacting with and working with many different people. You want to take strategic advantage of your college years to develop your global and multicultural literacy and overall people skills so that you will be that much more comfortable and experienced when you enter your post-baccalaureate work life.

■ **Experiential learning opportunities for skill set development and practice.** As a student, you can gain experience in communications, finance, accounting, art, marketing, management, education, and areas related to your fields of study.

■ **Leadership opportunities.** In positions such as organization chair, vice chair, secretary, treasurer, board member, project team leader, and strategist, you will get experience in team building, leadership, and conflict resolution.

■ **Teamwork experience.** Campus organizations and clubs give you group work experience during regular meetings, smaller meetings focused on specific tasks, the implementation phase of specific projects, and new member recruitment.

These four areas of personal development are crucial needs that employers are increasingly looking for and that employers say are skills that are underdeveloped in far too many job applicants. So look out for opportunities for strategic skill set development that will make college work for you in big and complete ways.

Extracurricular activity is vitally important in achieving productive, balanced, rewarding, and joyful college lives. In many cases, the most involved students are not only the most successful academically but also those who are the happiest with their overall college experience. Choose to have a rich and fulfilling college life.

Student Organizations and Clubs

At most colleges and universities, there will be a plethora of student organizations from which to choose. They include academically oriented groups that are often aligned with specific academic departments and programs, socially active organizations with various agendas, religious groups aligned with specific religious affiliations, various intellectually stimulating groups (e.g., honor societies, political and governmental groups, creative arts organizations, and cultural groups), athletic and other competitive groups, leisure activity groups, Greek organizations (fraternities, sororities, and co-ed affiliations), and organizations that are explicitly oriented towards volunteerism and service (tutoring, Circle K, Big Brothers/Big Sisters, Habitat for Humanity, etc.).

You want to be involved, but the proviso here is that you do not want to be overinvolved in extracurricular organizations and activities. Remember to maintain a healthy balance (as explained in Chapter 1) and to ensure that you have structured your daily and weekly schedule to accommodate at least two hours of study for each credit hour; do not let your extracurricular involvement adversely affect your studying and academic productivity. As you explore various groups, here are a number of considerations to help your selection process.

Different organizations: Get information about a number of different organizations on campus. Explore many possibilities so that you can make strategic decisions about which organizations to be involved with. Many colleges and universities have activity fairs early in the year where you can find out about the different groups. Get information about groups that focus on your areas of interest. If you are a skilled chess player, check out the chess club. If you enjoy scuba diving, see whether there is a scuba diving or outdoors club. If you are active in a faith-based organization, look into your campus's Jewish, Hindu, Buddhist, Christian, Muslim, Bahá'í, or nonsectarian religious student groups.

New areas of interest: Pick up information about groups that offer new areas of interest that you think would be valuable and of interest for you to explore. You want to expand your horizons while you are in college. If you never learned to play golf or tennis, but see that as valuable for networking later on, look into the golf or tennis club. If you would like to learn more about the fine arts, a foreign or art film club might be a viable prospect for you.

Career relevant organizations: Look into student organizations that are relevant to your prospective future career. If you are interested in working in editing or media, the student newspaper, yearbook, radio station, or creative writing journal would be valuable to you. If you are an engineering major, the robotics club, tech crew for theater productions, amateur radio club, or Habitat for Humanity would give related extracurricular experience.

Diverse organizations: As 21st-century world citizens, consider involvement with ethnically, culturally, and globally diverse organizations to develop your cultural literacy. If you know a foreign language, check out your college's French, Spanish, or Chinese club. Other groups that you could look into include ALAS (Association of Latin American Students), BSA (Black Student Alliance), Muslim Student Association, Bahá'í Student Association, anime club, or foreign film club.

Inclusive and open organizations: All student organizations are happy to provide you with more information about who they are, what they do, and how one becomes a member. Most student organizations are inclusive and open to anyone who is interested in being a member. If membership is open, you want to attend a meeting or two to meet current members and learn more about the group, what the group does, who the group's members are, what the group's needs are. In this way, you can see if a specific student group is a good fit for you.

Selective organizations: Some student organizations are selective and have certain requirements for membership. For selective organizations, you can learn whether you need to be elected to become a member (e.g., student senate, most fraternities and sororities) or if membership requires a specific G.P.A. as in the case of national honor societies (e.g., Phi Beta Kappa and Phi Kappa Phi) and discipline-specific honor societies (e.g., English's Sigma Tau Delta, theater's Alpha Psi Omega, civil engineering's Chi Epsilon, psychology's Psi Chi, nursing's Sigma Theta Tau, or biology's Beta Beta Beta). Consult with current student members to learn more about the organization in order to see whether you want to make the effort to become a member. Find out what you need to do or accomplish in order to be considered.

Volunteer service organizations: Investigate various organizations' service orientations and specific volunteer opportunities in order to be involved in ways that are of broader benefit to your community and to the world. See how you can benefit the student organization or club that you are interested in joining. You also want to see how the student organization will be of benefit to you (what you will learn, whom you will get to know, what experiences you will have, etc.).

Multiple organizational involvement: You want to learn about many different groups so that you can make smart and strategic choices about the right groups for you to join and with which to become involved. Be involved in several student organizations. Do not put all of your eggs in one basket. You want to diversify your extracurricular associations and activities. You want to become a member of several student organizations that will play to your strengths and future prospects. Think about what you want to learn, what you want to experience, and what strengths you want to demonstrate to future employers. Think about organizational membership and future networking possibilities.

Balanced involvement: Evaluate your chosen groups and make strategic decisions regarding the responsibilities you will take on. Do not do too much! Balance your work load intelligently (schoolwork, part-time job, volunteerism, and other extracurricular activities). Decide when to be a rank-and-file foot soldier in a group and when to take on a leadership role. Practice your strategic time-management skills in knowing when to say, "No, I'd love to, but I cannot take on that responsibility right now."

Strategic involvement: Select your key student organizations strategically. It is not a bad idea to select one for valuable experiences and networking, one to expand your horizons and knowledge base, and one just for fun. It is a good strategy to be a member of at least one selective student organization in addition to at least one or two other organizations on campus.

Leadership opportunities: The role you play in a student organization can take different forms, depending on your level of involvement and the amount of responsibility that you are willing to take on. Be a very active member in at least a couple of organizations in which you can move into some leadership role. Taking on additional responsibilities demonstrates your organizational abilities, your time-management skills, your accomplishments, and your level of commitment to an organization. Ideally, you want to achieve some leadership roles in these organizations. By moving up in responsibility, you also demonstrate your involvement over the course of several years. This shows a steadiness and commitment that is also valued by employers.

If you are already attending college or if you are still in the looking stage, for the next exercise, look over the student organizations at your college or the colleges that you are interested in attending.

Please list 10 student organizations that you would be interested in finding out more about and possibly getting involved with. Make strategic choices here, but also select some groups just for fun.

1. _____
2. _____
3. _____
4. _____
5. _____
6. _____
7. _____
8. _____
9. _____
10. _____

Please review this list and find out some additional information about each of these student organizations. Find out how often the groups meet, what their activities are throughout the school year, and how involved members are expected to be.

Now based on this additional information, narrow your list down to your top five student organizations for which you will attend at least one meeting to explore possible membership and involvement. List your top five to contact and visit. Include the name of the student organization and the dates and times of the next two meetings.

1. _____
2. _____
3. _____

4. _____

   _____

5. _____

   _____

Best kept secret about student organizations: If you learn about a student organization that you would really like to be a member of BUT your college does not have it at your college, you can explore the possibilities in creating such a group on your campus. Being a founding member of a student organization is a great opportunity to bring an additional resource to your college, and it also shows your initiative, drive, leadership, and organizational abilities. Employers value creativity and entrepreneurship; starting up a student organization demonstrates your abilities in these areas as well.

Volunteerism and Servant Leadership

Throughout your life, you will have many opportunities to give back to society for all that you have received in the form of education, experiences, free public events, access to parks and forest lands, and access to many museums and other cultural venues. As a student, you receive invaluable learning opportunities in your classes and other experiences on campus. In return for all that you receive as a student, you give back financially through your tuition and later in your support as alumni, but this is really a pittance in relation to all that you can gain during your college years. Your involvement on campus and your volunteerism and service are central to your side of the equation—your giving back. It is very much like breathing: inhalation and exhalation. Both are part of the same life giving act. In much the same way, living is a process of receiving and giving, and an enriched life includes giving back through volunteerism and service.

When you were growing up, you benefited from activities such as Boy Scouts, Girl Scouts, 4-H, Little League and school athletics, Scholastic Bowl, debate team, school band and orchestra, chess club, Spanish club, student newspaper, and other activities made possible and supported by adult mentors. Looking back through the first two decades of your life, you will see that you have benefitted from the support of many adults throughout your life. Children require assistance from many adults to support their development and growth, but young children are not the only ones who need help.

The world is not a perfect place. Life is filled with many challenges. Each person has to struggle at times in life, but beyond your own life, there are many problems and challenges in need of remedies throughout the world. Look at your community. There are many areas that need help: children needing positive role models and tutors, the natural environment needing restorative help, food banks and food kitchens needing volunteers, and community service agencies and projects needing additional support personnel.

You can volunteer on campus. When you get out of a class, you can simply walk across campus to an organization meeting to plan a service activity. Or after breakfast in the dining hall, you can simply walk to the student center or main classroom building to staff an informational and fundraising table. For much of your volunteering on campus, you do not even need to drive anywhere: the activity is right on campus.

While you are a college student, volunteering is easier than it will be at any other time in your life.

If you become a member of a service-oriented organization on campus, your volunteer activities will be set up to accommodate your semester time frame so that you will not leave things hanging when you go home for term breaks or summer vacation. The main events and service projects will usually be scheduled during the regular semester or quarter of study—and rarely around final exam times.

You can also schedule your volunteer activities around your studying needs. For example, you could decide to log some hours at a fundraising Halloween spook house for neighborhood children while keeping your final weeks of the fall semester free for finishing up term papers, projects, and exams. Or you could spend a few Saturday mornings assisting local naturalists in restoring native habitat while keeping your weekdays and Sundays free for intensive studying. Or you could tutor at a nearby elementary school for two hours each week, fitting that schedule around your class schedule. Remember that you want to be smart and strategic with your scheduling; do not agree to a significant amount of volunteer hours around the time when you have a major exam period or semester project due date.

Rationale: The "Why"

- **Heightened integrity.** In life, much of a person's integrity is defined in terms of what he or she does for others without the expectation of remuneration or other gain.

- **Foundation for a well-lived life.** Your volunteerism in college gives you the opportunity to practice and solidify what will become a life well lived in service to others.

- **Ennobling character.** Service to others is ennobling and helps to mature a person in important ways. When the volunteerism is offered in a collaborative manner, it is ennobling for both the giver and the receiver.

- **Communities and people in need.** Civic-minded people perform vitally needed service to their communities and world. You are needed. What you can do counts. What you do is important.

- **Empathy and caring.** People matter. Those you help matter. Thank you for the volunteerism and service that you have already offered to the world and your communities. Thank you for the volunteerism and service in which you are currently involved. Thank you for your future service to your families, to your communities, to the world.

- **Deepened understanding.** Your lived engagement with your community through volunteerism and service deepens and solidifies your connection to your community and gives you a deeper understanding of the realities of the world.

- **Renewal of perspective.** Helping others puts life and the everyday into a renewed, broadened, and often reoriented focus. This helps to define how you view the world; it also defines how you view yourself. Note that for many, volunteerism and service to others actually lower their own stress levels.

- **Valuable experience.** Your volunteerism gives you valuable experiences that your future employers will take seriously. This shows your time-management skills, empathy, experiential activity, teamwork, energy, and commitment.

- **Ethical orientation.** Volunteerism and service demonstrate your commitment to ethics while also increasing your ethical practice and orientation.

Logistics: The "How"

- **Service-oriented organizations and clubs.** Some student organizations are expressly designed with service at the center of what they do. These organizations will provide many ways for you to volunteer and help out.

- **Student organizations and clubs.** The majority of student organizations and clubs on campus provide at least some service opportunities in which you can be involved—whether in a leadership or support role.

- **Strategic selection of service activities.** Pick volunteer activities that draw on your strengths and that will give you valuable experience. You want to be of the greatest service to an organization. If you are a skilled athlete, then consider assisting in an after-school athletic program. If you are a skilled writer, consider assisting in a service agency's creation of a fundraising brochure, grant writing application, or assisting children with their reading and writing. If you are good with math and finance, volunteer to serve as the treasurer of a service organization.

- **Service learning.** Most colleges and universities incorporate service into the academic side of college life. Some of your professors will incorporate service-learning activities into the course work for a class. Some institutions have a broad service-learning component structured into their general education or core curriculum program. Look for classes that include service learning.

  What distinguishes service learning from regular volunteerism is that it includes service plus reflection on the volunteer work done. This is important, because it provides you the added understanding about what you have done, why it is important, and what you have learned from it. In this way, you will be better able to communicate the value of the service to future employers or in application essays to graduate school or professional school. Deeply appreciate any service-learning opportunities in your course curriculum.

- **Other students' past experiences.** Talk with other students about their current and past involvement in service on campus. Other students are a major resource for additional information about service opportunities for students at your institution.

- **Student activities office.** Check out your college's or university's student activities office for suggestions for your volunteerism. Check out the office's webpages or simply stop by the office. The personnel in the office are always happy to meet new students and help them connect with campus organizations and off-campus groups involved in volunteerism.

- **Strategic scheduling.** Remember to schedule your volunteer hours strategically so that they do not impede your academic success. Plan ahead so that the preponderance of your volunteer time occurs on days, weeks, weekends that work well with your studying and other scheduled activities. Make your volunteerism work for you as well as for others. While you do want to give of yourself to others, you want to do so in a way that does not negatively impact your own life.

Volunteerism Worksheets

In order to get a good idea of some strategic areas in which you might want to get involved with volunteerism in college, please list 10 volunteer activities that you have already been involved in. These can be projects organized by a student club, an outside organization such as Scouts, or a religious affiliation. Your service activities can also be those times when you helped others study, listened to their problems, cooked or cleaned for them, and so on.

1. _____
   _____

2. _____
   _____

3. _____
   _____

4. _____
   _____

5. _____
   _____

6. _____
   _____

7. _____
   _____

8. _____
   _____

9. _____
   _____

10. _____
    _____

Now look over your college website or the website of your prospective colleges to review the different student organizations that offer service activities to their members. Note that almost all student organizations provide such opportunities for students. At many schools, there are special programs for students interested in a heightened level of service. If you would like more information about certain groups and opportunities, contact the student activities office.

Once you have the needed information to consider a few organizations for your volunteer work, please list five different student organizations and their volunteerism initiatives and service projects that you are interested in.

1. _____
   _____

2. _____
   _____

3. _____
   _____

4. _____
   _____

5. _____
   _____

With your completed Volunteerism Worksheets, you now have some specific ideas, direction, and plans for your involvement with organizations and groups that will provide the structure for some volunteerism and service as part of your college career.

Extracurricular Lectures and Arts Events

Outside of your class work and organizational involvement, there will be many opportunities for additional learning and the broadening of your horizons while you are a college student. There will be lectures on different topics, often scheduled over the lunch hour or in the late afternoons and evenings. There will also be many opportunities for various arts events: art gallery openings, theater performances, films, poetry readings, dance performances, and music concerts. Take advantage of as many of these as possible. Many of these events on campus are free!

Regardless of your fields of study or your planned career path, learning more about the world and the arts and humanities will benefit your life in many ways.

■ **Right brain/left brain balance.** Competencies in the arts provide intuitive, imaginative, and creative thinking skills, which are a crucial balance to the more ratiocinative (logical, rational, linear, critical thinking) work of college study. Even if you are not an accomplished musician or artist, you can expand your competencies in this area simply by increased exposure to diverse arts events. So go to that museum opening or that jazz or classical music performance. Work out a schedule so that you will be able to incorporate the arts into your life on a regular basis. You could even combine this with exercise through that Zumba or yoga class or an international folk dancing or ballroom dancing club.

■ **Heightened creativity.** Increased exposure to the arts contributes to your own creativity (including the development of your crucial creative and critical-thinking abilities). Employers are increasingly seeking job candidates who have demonstrated developed abilities in creative thinking for use in the dynamic and diverse 21st-century workplace. So, consider taking that arts appreciation or beginning pottery class. Or, even better, plan to add a minor or a strategic grouping of several classes to develop a skill set in a creative area.

■ **Stronger academic performance.** Recent research suggests that the fine arts contribute to stronger academic performance in your classes (Dana Foundation, 2008). Indeed, involvement in the arts has been documented to improve long-term memory, increased attention spans, and greater openmindedness to a diversity of ideas and opportunities. So expand your horizons in whatever arts directions you prefer, but arrange your schedule to make this possible.

■ **Cultural diversity competency.** As a cultured person, you will be more prepared to interact with a diversity of persons from various cultures and ethnic and religious backgrounds. Your experiences on campus that broaden your comfort zone and educate you about the diversity of the world will also communicate to employers that you have competencies in global diversity and in working with people of diverse background and cultures. So go to ethnic and cultural events on campus, enjoy different foods, meet new people, and learn about cultures that previously you may have known little about. Sign up for classes in various areas of cultural studies to develop your global and diversity competencies further.

■ **Broadly educated and cultured person.** As you learn more about various intellectual topics through different lectures and symposia on campus and as you have various aesthetic experiences in the form of concerts, art gallery shows, foreign and art films, and performances, you will become a more broadly educated and cultured person who is interested in and committed to a life of learning, and who is able to think, understand, and converse with greater depth and breadth. So check out that foreign film or documentary, attend that contemporary affairs lecture on campus by a leading scholar, and get to know many of the other students who are also attending these events by choice. In this way, you will get to know other students who, like yourself, are consciously working to get the most out of the college experience.

When I was a student, I attended a lecture by a leading scholar in a field connected to my major. After the presentation, I asked a thoughtful question based on a recent research paper I had written. The lecturer praised the direction of the question. After the Q&A was over, I went up and thanked him for his presentation and work, noting how much I had learned from an essay of his that I had used in my paper. I then said that I would love to have the opportunity to talk with him further about the topic. He said that he had to go to the airport, but that he thought he would have time for lunch, and he invited me to have lunch with him! So you never know what might come out of strategic attendance at various events on campus.

Pay attention to what is going on around you, what events are coming up, and what you can reasonably fit into your regular schedule. Contact your relevant academic department and college websites to find out about lectures and arts events that you might be interested in. Check their websites for weekly updates and the college's or university's website for daily events on campus. You have the responsibility to step up and make the effort to develop your cultural and global appreciation and literacy.

As an undergraduate, it is very easy to develop new tastes in music or some other art form. For example, as a seventeen year old, I knew that I did not like opera at all! However, I knew that there were many educated and cultured people who greatly valued and *enjoyed* opera. I figured that either (a) all of those people were wrong and opera was, as I thought, a painful way to spend an evening, or (b) all those opera fans were right and there might actually be some aesthetic pleasure found in attending an opera. Well, I wasn't so foolish as to decide that I actually knew more than all those far more educated people who enjoyed opera. So I figured that I had better take a class in opera appreciation. I doubted that I'd become an opera devotee, but I figured that I would learn more about that art form and learn how to find *some* value in it.

It actually worked. Over the course of the semester, I learned more than I thought I would. I took the course as a non-credit student. [It was cheaper to do that. And my aim was to expand my knowledge and appreciation of the art form, not simply to get credits for graduation.] The class was at night, and a number of the other students in the class were musicians and even singers. I met some very interesting people, and by the end of the semester, I had become a beginning opera *aficionada* [admirer or fan]. This one course made a significant difference in my cultural literacy and competency. Make smart choices of your own, and see how to expand your cultural horizons while you are in college.

If your friends on campus have zero interest in going with you to an opera or some other arts or informative event, find someone else to go with (maybe an acquaintance from a class or from one of the campus organizations that you are involved with), or simply go alone! People who attend events alone are more likely to meet the people sitting next to them and to make new acquaintances that way. This will provide you with the opportunity to practice your networking and communications skills, both of which are enriching behaviors. Remember that relationships are foundational to well-being. And you might even meet a person who will become important to you later on in life. You never know whom you might meet.

Now let's explore some possible areas for your attendance at extracurricular events. The following lists invite you to explore the intellectual and cultural possibilities that you will want to take advantage of in college. Find out what events are occurring, organize your schedule in order to participate, and then actually attend the specific events with interest and focus. These two lists will give you some beginning ideas and direction in strategically focusing your extracurricular lectures and arts events attendance.

List five current or past historical events (local, regional, national, or global) that you would like to learn more about.

1. _____
   _____
2. _____
   _____
3. _____
   _____
4. _____
   _____
5. _____
   _____

List five different types of creative and fine arts that you would like to learn more about (classical music, poetry, hip hop, sculpture, jazz, theatre, folk music, opera, film, painting, ballet, modern dance, ballroom dance, etc.). These may include arts that you know little of or arts with which you are already familiar and would like to explore further.

1. _____
   _____

2. _____
   _____

3. _____
   _____

4. _____
   _____

5. _____
   _____

You now have two beginning lists of events on campus that will expand your cultural horizons and increase your cultural literacy and intellectual capital. The opportunities to do this during your undergraduate years are phenomenal, so take advantage of many of these lectures, debates, concerts, and other arts events.

Remember that the extent to which you can develop your intellectual and cultural capital (e.g., your knowledge of contemporary national and world affairs; your familiarity with national and world history; and your literary, performance, and fine arts exposure and appreciation) will further your personal development as a *humane*, ethical, and cultured person while preparing you for a full and enriched life conversant with many of the diverse accomplishments of humankind across different cultures and throughout time.

Undergraduate Research and Creative Production

One of the most exciting opportunities for undergraduates is the intensive learning experience of undergraduate research and creative production. This is where undergraduate students are able to explore the fields in which they are most informed and interested with greater depth, increased time and attention, more specific results, and heightened learning outcomes.

In the majority of cases, undergraduate research and creative production are directly relevant to a student's major or minor fields of study. A strong foundation of knowledge and skills is requisite for the work involved in substantive research and creative production. But there are also opportunities in select lower-level and general education/core curriculum classes for such heightened learning experiences.

Often undergraduate research and creative production are initiated as part of a course (e.g., a significant term project, performance, or portfolio production). In its more intensive and extensive forms, undergraduate student research and creative production are undertaken under the *aegis* (supervision) of a faculty supervisor and take place outside of your classes, perhaps as an independent study project, a summer research internship, or a required capstone activity for your major (e.g., a major dramatic performance, lab work as a research assistant to a professor or as a lead researcher for your own project, a senior recital, or a term paper revised for a conference presentation or for publication in an undergraduate research journal).

You may be thinking, "This sounds like more work than I can handle right now. I'm swamped with studying, being in student organizations, attending occasional arts events and lectures, and working part-time! I don't see how I can also get involved with research or serious creative production."

This is an excellent point. Time is the crucial element for successful, full, and fulfilling lives in college and beyond. After all, there really are only 24 hours in the day and seven days in the week, and you only can do so much. Make sure that you fit your activities into a schedule that works for you. This being said, I think that you will look more seriously into the possibility of getting involved in such intensive undergraduate learning opportunities once you understand the significant benefits that come from such activity.

Benefits: The "Why"

- **Discovery.** You will discover the palpable excitement of personal discovery! Remember when you learned something as a little child, and would be so excited that you wanted to tell everyone? Let me share one story about a little girl whose substantial efforts proved the success of such hard work. I watched this toddler reach for a brightly colored plastic cup on a couch. The cup was out of her reach. The mother looked down, saw the girl's effort, and reached toward the cup. But what do you think the mother did? No, she did not simply give the little girl the cup. This mother understood the value of effort, hard work, and discovery. So the mother made sure that the little girl was watching her, then she pushed the cup a bit closer so that it was not as far away on the couch.

Watching this, the little girl reached for the cup again, just barely touching it with her fingertips. She squealed and jumped up and down! She was so excited that she was able to touch the cup. Her mother gave her a nod of encouragement, and the little girl reached a third time for the cup with all of her might . . . and grabbed that cup! The little girl was so excited about her success that you would have thought she had just awakened to a full Christmas stocking full of candy and toys! This is the sort of excitement that comes from great effort and success. Learning and discovery are important, but when learning and discovery come from great effort, the joy of success is that much greater.

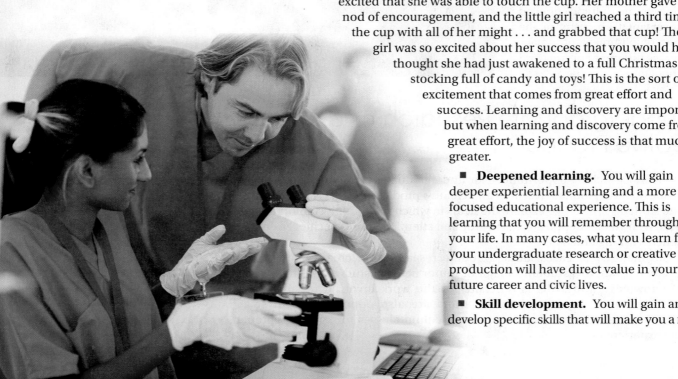

- **Deepened learning.** You will gain deeper experiential learning and a more focused educational experience. This is learning that you will remember throughout your life. In many cases, what you learn from your undergraduate research or creative production will have direct value in your future career and civic lives.

- **Skill development.** You will gain and develop specific skills that will make you a much more attractive candidate for jobs or subsequent educational programs. Your work in this area demonstrates your competencies in specific research methods and/or the craft of creative production. And the intensive work in undergraduate research and creative production activities heightens and demonstrates your critical- and creative-thinking abilities and your problem-solving skills.

■ **Faculty mentors.** You will get to know one or more faculty members more closely through the interactions related to the research project. This faculty member may become an important mentor for you by (1) giving you career guidance regarding internships, jobs, and graduate/professional schools; (2) providing you with especially strong letters of reference that can speak directly to your intelligence, work ethic, and experience; and (3) helping you gain expertise in your chosen field of study.

■ **Professional networking.** You will get to know other students who are involved in intensive research and creative production, perhaps in collaborative research ventures or as you present your projects and findings at the same departmental colloquium or college/university expo. These students will be strategic persons to consider adding to your growing professional network.

■ **Enjoyment.** Students who have done undergraduate research report that it was one of the most fulfilling and rewarding parts of their undergraduate years.

Logistics: The "How"

■ **Term paper or course project.** Term papers and projects for classes are generally not considered actual undergraduate research. These assignments are designed to give you beginning practice in the methodologies of your major. This being said, you could ratchet up the work you are already doing on one term paper or course project. You could meet with your professor and see how you can intensify your efforts to produce an even more developed product, perhaps developed enough to present and be competitive in your university's student research expo or in an undergraduate research or creative writing journal.

■ **Independent study.** Seriously consider opportunities for independent study courses with one of your professors. The intensive research or creative work counts as one of your three-credit-hour courses. Instead of taking an additional upper-level class in your major, you get the opportunity to work closely with one of your professors doing work at a higher level.

The quality of independent study varies from student to student. Inform your professor that you want your independent study with her or him to be at a very high level and that you would like to produce work to present at your school's student research expo or even at a professional conference. If you are interested in taking your work to the highest of levels, then consult with your faculty member about what would be necessary in order to produce work that would contribute to the field and that you would be able to publish in a national peer-reviewed undergraduate journal.

■ **Summer projects.** Talk with faculty in your major department to explore the possibilities for intensive learning opportunities during the summer. Such summer research usually leaves enough time for you to have a part-time job throughout the summer or to take one class. In many cases, colleges and universities provide funding for undergraduate research and creative production projects during the summer. Inquire about whether your school has such paid internships and research positions. The summer periods move quickly, so be careful not to overschedule your summers; remember that you want to do well at whatever you are doing, so be careful to pace yourself.

■ **Presentation of your work.** Investigate the various opportunities to present your research or creative production at your college or university. Many schools have a student expo where students give poster presentations. Usually these expos reflect a wide variety of majors across campus. Some departments have smaller colloquia where their majors and minors can present their work. If this does not exist at your school or department, talk with your fellow majors and faculty to start such an initiative! It will be a great line item for your résumé. In the arena of creative production, explore poetry readings and art gallery presentations, on campus and off.

You may also want to explore larger and more prestigious venues for presentation of your work. There are various regional and national conferences in your discipline. There are also conferences that focus on undergraduate research, including the prestigious Posters on the Hill, in which leading undergraduates from around the United States have the opportunity to present their research and creative production in Washington, D.C.

■ **Publication.** Depending on the success of your research and creative production, you might explore the possibilities for publication. Your department or university may have internal journals and websites to showcase undergraduate research and creative work. If your work is very successful, you may want to seek out even more competitive venues for publication. There are a number of very highly regarded journals that showcase undergraduate work.

There are, of course, the nationally and internationally peer-reviewed journals and other publications that present groundbreaking new work. Consult with your professor regarding the appropriate places for you to consider submitting your work for possible publication.

Undergraduate Research and Creative Production Worksheets

Over the course of your college years, try to take advantage of any possible undergraduate research opportunities, whether they are part of your classes or a separate initiative. I'd like you to spend some time thinking about possible opportunities for undergraduate research or creative production.

List five different areas of research and creative production that you would be interested in participating in (either that you have not yet done or that you would like to do at a higher or deeper level). These can be projects that are part of your professor's research, an outgrowth of a term paper or project of your own that you would like to develop further, or a musical or other arts accomplishment of yours that you would like to take to the next level. Please list the specific area of research (an exploration into Jane Austen's critique of British imperialism and colonization or a research project exploring specific chemicals and their genetic effects) or creative production (special on-campus recitals for local or regional arts groups or youth groups).

1. _____

   _____

2. _____

   _____

3. _____

_____

4. _____

_____

5. _____

_____

Now that you have thought a bit about possible areas for additional research and creative production, I'd like you to think about professors and other professionals at your college and university. It would be helpful to go online and review available short biographies, vitas (academic résumés), and websites that will tell you more about specific faculty members. You can also do an online search to learn about your faculty members' publications, presentations, and other professional work.

Please list five faculty members with whom you would be interested in working on a research project or creative production. List their main areas of expertise and any particular projects that you know of that you would be interested in working on with those professors' assistance, oversight, or mentorship.

1. _____

_____

2. _____

_____

3. _____

_____

4. _____

_____

5. _____

_____

Athletics and Fitness Activities

The most successful students are those who are the most involved on campus. This includes taking charge of their physical fitness and wellness through various activities. While you are a college student, you have a plethora of fitness options available to you on campus, and most of these do not require any additional cost because they are funded through your student activity fees. (There will usually be fees for "added-value" fitness options, such as personal trainers, club sport costs, or certain fitness classes.) There should be a fitness and sports option that fits for virtually any student, and they are available at different times to accommodate student schedules. Find the option that works for you and your overall fitness and wellness plan.

- **Intercollegiate athletics.** This is the gold star of physical fitness activities on campus. Student athletes who participate in intercollegiate varsity sports usually join their teams before they arrive on campus. Some teams provide "walk-on" options for promising athletes who have not been previously recruited nor given scholarships. If you are not on an intercollegiate varsity team, there are many ways that you can support one or more teams as a cheerleader, band member, or as part of a fan group.

- **Intramural sports.** Organized campus intramural sports provide opportunities for students to participate in competitive sporting events on campus. Some schools have established leagues and tournaments in specific sports. Unlike intercollegiate varsity athletic teams, intramural sports are open to all students, with play at varying levels.

■ **Club sports.** Many colleges and universities register official student organizations that are focused on athletics and sports endeavors. Some are team oriented and may include competitions against clubs and teams at other schools. Other fitness clubs are noncompetitive. All of these clubs maintain their commitment to student physical fitness combined with the equally important social benefits that come from group engagement. These club sports range from basketball, soccer, and hockey to fencing, martial arts, running, fishing, and ultimate Frisbee.

■ **Group fitness classes.** You will find a range of fitness classes to choose from at most schools. The types of fitness classes that are popular today include Zumba, kickboxing, spinning, and yoga. Whether you are seeking a program to improve or maintain your current fitness level, you should be able to find fitness classes that will work for your desired goals. If, however, there is a certain type of fitness class that you seek on campus that is not already provided, you can take the initiative to start such a class or look for off-campus options.

■ **Personal trainers.** Many schools have personal trainers at their athletic facilities. Whether you are interested in working closely with a trainer to jump-start your fitness program or to raise your fitness up to the next level, working with an individual trainer is an excellent option while you are in college—especially with trainers who expect to schedule training sessions around student schedules. Note that trainers work with their clients to put together overall fitness and wellness plans, so you would get additional information and guidance regarding diet and nutrition, heart health, and strategies to relieve stress.

Create an individualized fitness program that is suited to you. List five athletic and sports activities that you would be interested in participating in at your college or university. Please note whether this is a group activity; if so, note whether there is a group on campus or whether you would need to start a club or seek a group off campus.

1. _____
   _____
2. _____
   _____
3. _____
   _____
4. _____
   _____
5. _____
   _____

 ## Keeping a Balance

An important *caveat* (warning or qualification) to your involvement in campus activities outside of class is that, although extracurricular activities are important, you should not let them get in the way of your class work! Make sure that you stay current and on top of your schoolwork, and fit your extracurricular and co-curricular activities around your class work.

Remember that you want to achieve a strategic balance between your course work and your other activities. College gives you the time to practice achieving this balance. To accomplish this successfully often requires little more than a clear and focused weekly schedule that you adhere to. Your success in this area will prepare you for achieving success after college. And as you discipline yourself to excel in your classes and also be involved in valuable extracurricular activities, you will find that you are better prepared to achieve balance in your life after college. Learning to juggle school and extracurricular activities (and a job if you are working while you are taking classes) is your training for balancing your future work life with your personal life and volunteer activities.

Time management.

This will take practice.

There will be difficult periods.

You will have times when it all seems too much,

or too hard,

or too overwhelming.

This is okay. It's part of the process. You just need to review what you are doing, what is working, what is not working, what you need to do differently, where you need to work harder, and which activity you need to eliminate so that what is important is done and is done well. A full and balanced life involves a great deal of trial and error, but in the process, you will achieve great satisfaction as you see your life evolve and grow in deeply meaningful ways.

7 Off-Campus Endeavors

Internships, Jobs, Volunteerism

The unexamined life is not worth living.

I am not an Athenian or a Greek, but a citizen of the world.

— *Socrates (470–399 B.C.E.)*

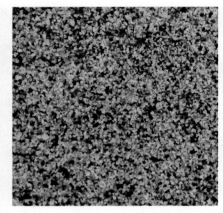

If there is an end for all we do, it will be the good achievable by action.

— *Aristotle (384–322 B.C.E.)*

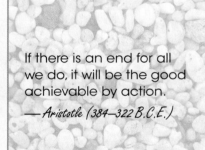

Failure is instructive. The person who really thinks learns quite as much from his failures as from his successes.

— *John Dewey (1859–1952)*

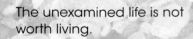

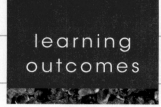

learning outcomes

1. **Off-Campus Experiential Learning:** Participate and benefit from the range of off-campus experiential learning opportunities.

2. **Co-op and Internship Placements:** Take advantage of direct career-related co-op and internship placements—the gold standard for "on-the-job" training for college students.

3. **Part-Time and Full-Time Jobs:** Maximize the benefits of your paid job experience while you are still in college—demonstrating strong skills in time management, communications, cultural competencies, teamwork, and leadership.

4. **Volunteerism and Community Service:** Demonstrate and practice civic mindedness through off-campus volunteerism, community service, and servant leadership.

5. **Curricularly Connected Experiential and Service-Learning Activities:** Profit from various off-campus experiential and service-learning activities that are connected to your classes.

College students gain valuable experiential learning through on-campus activities, and potential employers value this experience and the level of commitment they expect on the job. But employers also want to see experiential performance in actual work performance in internships, volunteerism, and jobs. Although your grades and campus involvement may make you an appealing candidate for internships, it is your performance in workplace internships that demonstrates your value as a prospective employee.

Your off-campus endeavors provide employers with hands-on evidence of the quality of your performance that they will be able to reasonably expect from you in the workplace. Additionally, in your student organizations on campus, most of those you interact with are also students, often your own age, and with similar interests. But when you are employed in the real world, you will be working with people of different backgrounds, ages, genders, beliefs, ethnicities, educational backgrounds, and nationalities. Off-campus activities can offer the rich diversity that will prepare you well for your 21st-century jobs and career.

▨ Participate and Benefit from a Range of Off-Campus Experiential Activities

Your off-campus activities provide a range of benefits for your growth and maturation. You learn from different situations and challenges, become familiar with a diversity of people, and gain real-world work experience. You are also able to put into practice much of what you have been learning in your classes.

Additionally, you will develop important skills valued by employers and valuable on résumés, such as business communications, problem solving, time management, and critical-thinking skills. In balancing school and off-campus responsibilities, you strengthen and fine tune your time-management skills, which are increasingly crucial in the dynamic time pressures of many workplaces.

Over a century ago, Lydia Moss Bradley founded the university where I work, Bradley University, to guide each student toward "an independent, industrious and useful life by the aid of a practical knowledge of the useful arts and sciences." This really is what college education is about: the period of transitional training between high school and professional work lives. Ideally students will be able to use their college educations in strategic ways to position themselves for meaningful and productive post-college lives. In the world today, there are serious needs, globally and in our own communities and families. College education provides the tools for each student to develop talents, skills, and abilities in order to be of service in the world, whether that is in the workforce, within the family, or in one's civic-minded community life.

Back in simpler times, young people would apprentice under a skilled person, thereby learning a lifelong trade. Today, the needs in the workplace are much more complex, demanding more of each person. What was the teaching of a master craftsperson now takes place in college through your learning from your professors, lecturers, and teaching assistants. The on-the-job practice occurs through the various forms of experiential learning opportunities, whether connected to academics or extracurricular. This is why you want to utilize your college years strategically to develop multiple skills and have diverse, enriching, and instructive experiences.

As a student, you want as many substantive hands-on experiences as possible to prepare you for your post-college lives and work. Seek out such productive experiences during which you can practice the skills that you will need in the workplace.

You may ask, "How does my part-time job in the library or at a local restaurant or at the mall relate to my future career as an engineer, photographer, or accountant?" This is an excellent question. Nowadays, most students have part-time or even full-time jobs while they are in college. Often employees in jobs that are unrelated to their future career plans do not take those jobs as seriously as they should and may view those jobs as little more than a means towards a paycheck. Yes, it is necessary to be able to pay the bills and be financially able to attend college, but there are ways that you can transform your temporary and lower-skilled jobs into valuable experiential training.

Regardless of the type or level of off-campus work (whether paid or unpaid), you are gaining invaluable skills in many areas: team-building and teamwork skills; critical-thinking and assessment skills; communication and listening skills; interpretation and evaluation skills; reliability and time-management skills; and patience, respect, and discipline. Think about all of this for a minute.

Say that when you are applying for jobs or internships, you have a letter of recommendation from the boss from your off-campus job saying that *you* are one of the most impressive employees that he or she has ever worked with, that *you* have amazing interpersonal skills, that *you* can defuse difficult situations and turn them into solid positives, that *you* have the drive and discipline that always gets the job done and done well, that *you* are flexible and always open to new ideas, willing and able to change course when necessary, and that *you* quickly gained the respect and esteem of every person with whom you have worked because of your abilities to do your job well and your willingness to assist others. Doesn't this sound like a person you would love to hire? Doesn't this sound like the employee you would love to be?

Don't worry if you make some mistakes during your off-campus experiences. Don't be concerned if you rub some people the wrong way or if you do not excel right off the bat. These are the experiences where you want to learn from your mistakes. You want to grow and improve in your performance. You want to mature, so that, over time, your supervisor will write an *absolutely glowing recommendation* for you that speaks positively about your remarkable progress.

Concerns about the professionalism of today's college students run rampant. A recent survey of faculty conducted from the Center for Professional Excellence at York College reports that "more than one-third (38.3 percent) said they felt that fewer than half of their upper-level students exhibited qualities associated with being professional in the workplace. . . . The qualities the respondents most strongly associated with being professional included having good interpersonal skills, being focused and attentive, being dependable in completing tasks on schedule, and displaying a work ethic" (Schnoebelen, 2013, p. A21). These are the very skills that you want to develop and practice in your off-campus, on-campus, and in-class performance.

Take advantage of as many opportunities as possible while you are in college to develop your mature and professional attitude and behavior. These applied learning opportunities help you develop, improve, solidify, and practice, practice, practice your work attitude and ethic. Take this seriously. Do not ever look at your work as just a job. Do not look at volunteer activities as just something required for a class or by your fraternity or sorority. Put your heart into all of these activities. Do your best and produce a top-level product in your performance.

Analogous to your on-campus involvement, your extracurricular activities off campus will be much easier for you during your college years than they will be later on in your life when you will have additional family, work, and community responsibilities. Use your time in college strategically and take advantage of your flexible college schedule to gain added value through important work experiences, regardless of whether those are paid, volunteer, or for credit.

Co-op and Internship Placements

Co-op and internship placements are the gold star among off-campus work because these are almost always related to your major field of study. They provide you with a direct opportunity to work in your chosen field of work, give you invaluable career trajectory networking connections, and can lead to a job offer from those with whom you have interned.

Companies and government agencies love co-op students and interns. While you get to practice your learning and become familiar with a workplace and its particular culture, the benefits you bring to the company or agency are substantial. You bring very current and state-of-the-art knowledge from your studies and experiential learning as a college student. You provide the energy, enthusiasm, and drive of someone at the beginning of their career. You are affordable, either working just for college credit and experience or receiving a lower salary than you would get as a new, full-time employee in that job. You give your superiors the opportunity to observe you on the job, which helps them decide whether you are someone they might want to employ full time upon your graduation.

Salman Khan, founder of the Khan Academy and a leading pioneer in current trends in global education, points out how important internships are to employers today: "Because of the demand for talent and the recognition that college degrees and high GPAs are not the best predictor of creativity, intellect, or passion, top employers have begun to treat summer internships as something of a farm league. They observe students actually working and make offers to those who perform the best. Employers know that working with a student is an infinitely better assessment than any degree or transcript" (Khan, 2012, pp. 234–235).

Do not underestimate the importance of these on-the-job experiential learning opportunities. A recent *Wall Street Journal* article states that "Nearly 40% of this year's entry-level positions

will be filled by former interns, according to a survey by the National Association of Colleges and Employers" (Light, 2011). In his book *The One World Schoolhouse: Education Reimagined*, Khan discusses one of the world's top engineering schools: the University of Waterloo in Canada. He points out that Waterloo's understanding of the importance of internships and co-ops is such that "by graduation, a typical Waterloo grad will have spent six internships lasting a combined twenty-four months at major companies"—many of which are companies in the United States! Khan then contrasts this level of experience with American students, who typically have just three to six months of internships (Khan, 2012, pp. 236–237). If you are not a Waterloo student, do not despair. There is much that you can do to heighten and broaden your experiential learning. And you can do this in a variety of ways. First, let's continue reviewing co-op and internship placements; then we'll look at other off-campus experiential learning opportunities that you will want to explore and take advantage of.

Co-op and internship placements vary in a few ways, although the differences are not as sharp as they used to be. The traditional difference between co-op positions and internships is in how they relate to your studies. Co-operative education is usually more explicitly intertwined with your studies, and internships are almost exclusively work oriented.

Co-op or Co-operative Education Placements

Co-operative education involves placement in real-world jobs as part of your studies. Often these apprenticeships are unpaid. But they provide you with actual experience, on-the-job training, networking and mentoring opportunities in your field, and, in most cases, academic credit for the work. These positions are designed to put into practice the knowledge and skills that you have been learning in your classes. The name "co-op" indicates the collaborative nature between your studies and their application in the real world.

Co-op arrangements can take place during the school year, either as a part-time position that you schedule with your classes or as a full-time position during a semester or year. Some co-operative education arrangements may take place during the summer. Most of these are procured with the assistance of the relevant administrators and faculty at your college or university. Co-op arrangements are much less common than internships.

Internships

Internships are entry-level positions in your field. They are often paid positions. Many colleges and universities work actively to assist their students in applying for internships. In many cases, you will be able to arrange internship interviews during career and job fairs at your school. Some schools help to set up your first interviews on campus. When you arrive on campus as a first-year student, begin exploring the internship possibilities right away. In order to find internships that you would qualify for, there are several crucial resources that you want to tap.

Co-op and Internship Procurement Resources

You can find out about prospective co-op positions and internships in several ways.

- **Your school's career or job placement center.** Many internships will be advertised on the website of your college's career or placement center; visit

the website and familiarize yourself with the resources made available to students and alumni. Stop by the career center during your first semester on campus. Introduce yourself, and present staff with your résumé that details your accomplishments from high school through your current work (academic and experiential). Work with them early on to explore valuable internships and other experiential learning opportunities that they will know about and that may not be posted on the website nor accessible online. Often there are internships available even on campus.

■ **Your academic advisor.** Meet with your academic advisor early on. Most colleges and universities provide advisors for all of their students. Many of these advisors are professors or other professional staff. Visit with your advisor a couple of times each semester. You may even learn about possible internships that are not listed at the career center, perhaps one that involves working with a professor in your department.

■ **Your professors and the department chairs in your major and minor fields.** The professors, lecturers, and teaching assistants who teach your classes and the department chair in the departments in which you are majoring and minoring are additional resources with whom to consult about possible internships and other experiential learning opportunities.

■ **Internet searches.** Do not forget to conduct your own research into possible internships in you field(s) of study and your desired career path. Conduct broad Internet searches for internships, including specific company and government websites. Select those companies and agencies that you would like to have as a future employer. Once you track down additional possibilities, bring that information to your advisor and your campus career center for assistance in procuring your desired internship.

■ **Relatives and friends.** Do not forget the importance of your own professional networking and mentoring contacts. Your relatives, friends, coworkers, and bosses are valuable resources as well. Inquire among them for possible placement leads. I knew one young man who procured a prestigious internship through family connections. Once in the internship, he impressed his superiors at the company by working harder and more successfully than any other intern. Who do you think was the first intern who was offered a job upon graduation? A relative helped him get the internship, but the young man earned the permanent position himself through his distinguished performance as an intern.

Some students land impressive internships as early as the summer between their freshman and sophomore years! This is pretty rare, but possible. So begin your investigations into internship possibilities as soon as possible. When you arrive on campus as a first-year or new transfer student, find out the following:

■ What types of internships and co-op positions are available and how to get one
■ What employers are looking for when they choose their interns
■ What you need to do to be one of the best candidates for career-related internships
■ What knowledge, job skills, and behaviors on the job will distinguish you as an intern

Then begin your professional networking! Get to know lots of people. Ask them questions about themselves. A student who sits next to you in class may have a father who works in the field you are interested in; you could ask to meet the father and ask him questions about the field and career prospects. He just might have some helpful tips, and perhaps even opportunities in his own company! You never know who might turn out to be a very good friend down the road. You never know which networking connection might connect you to the internship or job you want. You never know whom you might be able to help with their own networking needs. Chapter 8: "Networking and Mentoring: Teamwork, Leadership, Strategic Relationships," provides explicit guidance for your professional networking in college.

Co-op and Internship Placement Worksheets

List 10 individuals—relatives, friends, acquaintances, or coworkers—who are potential resources for you regarding co-op and/or internship possibilities and who are people with whom you will want to stay in contact.

1. _____
   _____
2. _____
   _____
3. _____
   _____
4. _____
   _____
5. _____
   _____
6. _____
   _____
7. _____
   _____
8. _____
   _____
9. _____
   _____
10. _____
    _____

List five websites that you have reviewed and that you will want to return to. These can be general sites with a range of internship opportunities, or they can be specific to a particular company or agency that you hope to work for:

1. _____
   _____
2. _____
   _____
3. _____
   _____
4. _____
   _____
5. _____
   _____

List five upcoming events that relate specifically to information about co-op or internship placements that will be helpful to you. These might be job fairs, special presentations given for students with your majors, general informational meetings for all students, or résumé development sessions. Make sure that you put these in your calendar!

1. _____
   _____
2. _____
   _____
3. _____
   _____
4. _____
   _____
5. _____
   _____

Part-Time and Full-Time Jobs

Most college students work at some point during their college years, gaining valuable skill development and work experience even when the jobs are not directly related to future careers. Many of these jobs are full-time during the summer and part-time during the school year. Many are on campus; others are off campus. Many students today work full-time and go to school part-time or even full-time. Whatever configuration of work and school that you have, you want to make your job *work for you*.

There are a number of factors that you want to have in the forefront of your mind as you think about your various jobs and on-the-job performance. It really doesn't matter all that much whether your job is a professional position, whether your job is full-time, or even whether it is directly, indirectly, or not at all related to your chosen career trajectory. Regardless of what job you have, you can approach your job to make it work for you in smart and strategic ways.

- **Fit your job and schoolwork together so that both are successful.** You want to be a top student *and* a top employee. This means figuring out how to accomplish this. When you manage your time so that you are highly successful in both work and studies, you are developing the high-level time-management and prioritization skills so necessary and valued in the workplace.

- **Remember that your studies are your #1 priority!** You want to aim for success in all of your classes. You want to work hard in each of your classes. You want to learn as much as you can in each class. You want to earn the respect and esteem of all of your professors and classmates. At times, that may mean taking one fewer class in order to be successful in the others. If you have to work full-time while you are a college student, it is much better to be highly successful as a college student and graduate in five or more years than to graduate earlier but without the skills, credentials, experiences, and knowledge that will make you a desired job applicant and professional employee.

- **Ensure that your performance on the job is at the highest of levels.** Whether you are working part-time or full-time, you want to approach your jobs strategically with an eye to what you are doing well, what you can improve, and which valuable job skills you are developing and practicing.

■ **Develop your job skills.** Regardless of what jobs you have, you can develop and practice these important skills at work:

- Time management
- Strong work ethic
- Reliability
- Consistency
- Patience
- Innovation
- Caution and thoroughness
- Courage and risk taking
- Strong communication skills
- Positive attitude
- Helpfulness

Part-Time and Full-Time Job Worksheets

The following worksheets highlight a number of the important aspects of your work experience. As you fill these out, specific details will emerge that will help you to see your work experiences more fully (e.g., potential role models and mentors in the workplace, challenges and weaknesses that you will want to begin to work on, and your especial strengths in the workplace, including key accomplishments that you will want to highlight on a résumé or in a job interview). If you are at the beginning of your college career or have only had one or two jobs, return to these worksheets while you are in college and continue to fill them out as you gain more experience in the workforce.

List up to five different jobs that you've had in the past few years:

1. _____
_____
2. _____
_____
3. _____
_____
4. _____
_____
5. _____
_____

List five difficulties or problems that you had at your jobs and how you dealt with them. Explain whether you feel you dealt with the problems effectively:

1. _____
_____
_____
2. _____
_____
_____

3. _____
_____
_____
_____

4. _____
_____
_____
_____

5. _____
_____
_____
_____

List five accomplishments that you are proud of from your current job or past jobs. Note what particularly makes you proud of each accomplishment:

1. _____
_____
_____
_____

2. _____
_____
_____
_____

3. _____
_____
_____
_____

4. _____
_____
_____
_____

5. _____
_____
_____
_____

List five people with whom you've worked who have really impressed you with their commitment to excellence on the job. Include examples of something they did that really impressed you. In what ways would you like to be like them?

1. _____
_____
_____

2. _____
_____
_____
_____

3. _____
_____
_____
_____

4. _____
_____
_____
_____

5. _____
_____
_____
_____

List five strengths that you have demonstrated on the job (e.g., your time-management skills, your people skills in defusing tense situations, your computer skills that keep things running smoothly while waiting for tech support, or your patience and positive attitude that uplift your coworkers). Include a specific example that demonstrates each strength.

1. _____
_____
_____
_____

2. _____
_____
_____
_____

3. _____
_____
_____
_____

4. _____
_____
_____
_____

5. _____
_____
_____

Finally, note five performance and attitudinal areas that you expressly want to improve. For example, you might note that you need to work on discipline and time-management skills, perhaps setting up a daily schedule to practice better time management. You might simply note that you want to smile more throughout the day. You might note that you want to practice being more patient during those times that you find especially stressful.

It is helpful to get an idea of a few areas for improvement; use your jobs during college to work on these. Please include a specific example that demonstrates areas for improvement.

1. _____

2. _____

3. _____

4. _____

5. _____

You now have a good sense of the importance of all of your part-time and full-time jobs, even when they are not directly related to your desired and intended career path. When you approach your job with a heightened sense of commitment and service, your work performance concomitantly (connectedly and similarly) moves into a higher plane of accomplishment. This is also true of your off-campus volunteer and community service activities.

 # Volunteerism and Community Service

While you are an undergraduate student, develop and demonstrate your habits of civic mindedness through volunteerism and community service.

In so many ways, the spirit of volunteerism and community service, of "giving back," defines what it means to be an American. There is no other country in the world that is so distinguished by the commitment of its citizens to community service. Civic mindedness has actually defined our land for many generations. Such communalism was foundational to the survival of early European settler communities in North America, and it has been a central principle for many of our Native American tribes.

Think back to the communities in which you have lived. Think of all the adults who helped with Boy Scouts, Girl Scouts, Cub Scouts, and Brownies. Think of all the adults who helped with the many different athletics activities available for children and teens. Think of all the adults who volunteered through their churches, synagogues, mosques, and

other faith-based communities. Think of the adults who helped out in your schools by tutoring, baking, providing transportation, fundraising, and so on.

The United States, albeit not perfect, is distinguished as an incredibly caring nation. As Americans, we care about our country and other nations. We care about our families, our communities, about any person or people in need. When the American people learn about a disaster anywhere in the world, we step up to help. When we see a need, we respond with great empathy, caring, and effort. Whether it's a soup kitchen in your city, tornado-stricken communities in the Midwest and South, flooded regions along the Mississippi, tsunami-ravaged nations along the Pacific Rim, drought-ravaged regions in Africa, or the catastrophic horrors of 9/11, Americans are there helping. Perhaps this may be one of our greatest legacies for the world: to show others the power and magic of volunteerism, community service, civic-mindedness, and servant-leadership.

Being of service in the world is in many ways part of the "warp and woof" (threads running lengthwise and crosswise) of American culture and very much a part of the fundamental fabric of American college education. Volunteerism is essential to the well-functioning of our communities, nation, and world. And your volunteer activities communicate much about you as a person and about your abilities and experiences.

■ **Develop and demonstrate initiative, motivation, caring, empathy, and a life of service.** Community service during college helps you to develop and practice a life of service. During your K–12 years, much of your community service was organized and required by the adults around you, whether required service-learning hours in high school, service projects for Scouts, or volunteer activities organized by your faith-based community or your parents. In college, you have the opportunity to practice your own initiative of service. This develops and demonstrates your motivation, caring, empathy, and life of service. Those around you will value these qualities of yours; so will future employers.

Relevant historical story about service related to me by the photographer John Pack over a lunch in Gallup, New Mexico in the 1980s:

Pack recounted his time on the Diné (Navajo) reservation over twenty-five years ago. He travelled to the reservation with a dream of the photographic work that he wanted to do there, but he quickly learned the tribal ethic in Navajo country that one does not receive from a community and its people without first giving to the community.

So he procured work with a local fire department and became part of the community over a period of years—"giving back"—and in return, he was able to produce some of the most remarkable photographs ever taken of Native American people. The broader lesson here is the importance of being a fully involved member of one's community, living a life of service wherever one is.

- **Develop and demonstrate discipline, commitment, and a strong work ethic.**
Community service during college provides you with hands-on activities that deepen your work ethic. Choosing to spend free time committed to volunteerism requires a higher level of discipline and commitment. Twenty-first-century lives are very busy, and it would be easy to choose not to be active in one's community through volunteerism. When you add active volunteerism into your schedule while still excelling in your studies and other activities, this demonstrates your discipline and commitment.

    Even if your volunteer activities are not directly related to your chosen career, how you perform in your volunteer activities communicates a great deal about how you will perform on the job. If you put your heart and soul into those initiatives, your future employers will know that, in all likelihood, you will demonstrate the same rigor of effort and commitment in your job.

- **Develop related work experience, valuable networking connections, and possible mentor contacts.** Strategic community service during your college years can relate directly to your desired career path. If you are a construction engineering major, it would make a lot of sense to volunteer for an organization like Habitat for Humanity. If you are an English or education major, it would make sense to volunteer as a reading tutor at a nearby elementary school. If you are a math or computer science major, you would be a terrific resource as a volunteer to schools in your community that could use your math and computer skills. If you are a nursing or health science major, volunteer at a local hospital or nursing home. If you are majoring in the fine arts, volunteer at a local school to help with their arts instruction and events (plays, band and orchestra, art displays) or see whether you can volunteer with a local arts organization (an opera guild, a dance troupe, a theater company). When you make such a fit with your interests, skills, and career plan, you will gain related work experience, valuable networking connections, and possible mentors.

- **Develop and nurture networking opportunities.** Community service during college provides you with valuable networking opportunities. When you volunteer off campus, you will meet many people whom you would not otherwise meet. Take the initiative to get to know your fellow volunteers and your supervisors well. Do not simply hang with your school friends who might be volunteering with you. Get to know the other volunteers, the organizers, and the people being helped by the volunteer activities. As you get to know others involved with the organization, step up and ask for additional ways that you can help. Distinguish yourself as one of the most active, engaged, and interested volunteers. And down the road, you never know who among the various individuals involved in the organization might be a valuable professional connection for you.

- **Develop and grow into a mature, serious-minded, caring, and civic-minded person.** Community service during college helps you to mature in important ways. As you give back to your communities and world, your life will be enriched through self-sacrifice, and you will grow and develop into a serious-minded, caring person and an active, civic-minded citizen. As you live a life of committed service, you will emerge as an important and valued servant-leader in your respective communities, and this will provide you with additional avenues of service and a life well lived. And through these actions, your life will matter that much more.

- **Find fulfillment, joy, and rewards in volunteerism and community service.**
Community service during college can be hard work, especially as you fit it into your busy schedule of studying, work, and extracurricular on-campus activities. But it is your volunteerism that will often prove to provide many of your most rewarding, enjoyable, and fun experiences. Roll up your sleeves and work hard in your community service efforts, but remember to also take joy in that work. When you work to help remediate some of the world's problems, the realities can be very heavy

and depressing. But remember that you are making a difference. You are helping others, your community, and the world. Do not forget the gifts of humor, laughter, enjoyment, and smiles. Work with effort and commitment *and* with humor and joy. This will make your volunteerism more enjoyable for you; even more importantly, it will also make the volunteerism of those around you more enjoyable.

■ **Look for new and additional opportunities to volunteer.** Many of your on-campus student organizations will include some sort of volunteerism or community service activity. Some of these will be on campus; others will take place off campus in your local and regional communities. Even if you are already participating in service activities through your sorority, fraternity, or other student groups, it is important to step up and take further initiatives on your own to explore additional volunteer possibilities where you can make a difference, where you can utilize the knowledge and skills that you are developing, and where you can gain valuable experience. This will demonstrate your heightened caring, commitment, work ethic, and initiative.

■ **Utilize the resources on campus to find and participate in various volunteer opportunities.** Many colleges offer an annual volunteer fair where different service agencies in the community provide information about how students can become involved. Your college's career center or student affairs office might have additional information for you. Check out their websites and stop by their offices to get directed toward volunteer and community service opportunities that will work for you, that will draw upon your talents and abilities, and that will fit into your schedule.

Volunteerism and Community Service Worksheets

These worksheets highlight important aspects of your past and current volunteer experience. As you fill these out, you will see the value of your community service more fully (e.g., key accomplishments of which you are especially proud, distinguishing strengths, and possible networking and mentoring connections). If you are near the beginning of your college career or your volunteer activities are few, return to these worksheets while you are in college and continue to fill them out as you gain more service experience.

Look at those individuals you have known in your life who really distinguish themselves by their volunteerism—those who you consider to be servant-leaders. List five people with whom you've volunteered who have really impressed you with their commitment to making the world and their communities a better place. For each person, please include one example that shows that person's efforts and that really impressed you. Also note in what ways you would like to be like each of these remarkable people.

1. _____
_____
_____
_____
_____
_____

2. _____
_____
_____
_____
_____
_____
_____

3. _____
_____

_____
_____
_____
_____
4. _____
_____
_____
_____
_____
5. _____
_____
_____
_____
_____
_____

Now list the five most significant volunteer activities that you've been involved with in the past few years:

1. _____
_____
2. _____
_____
3. _____
_____
4. _____
_____
5. _____
_____

Looking over your volunteer activities that you listed, list five different problems in your communities or the world that your volunteer work helped to ameliorate. Most volunteer activities are designed to help with an explicit problem, but, in most cases, the problems are more complex than that and each effort actually provides a broader range of benefits.

1. _____
_____
_____
_____
2. _____
_____
_____
_____
3. _____
_____

4. _____

5. _____

Think of times in your own life when you have helped others. List five situations in which you made a meaningful difference in someone's life, helped to resolve a specific situation, or contributed in an especially important way to a person, group, or organization. These can be as part of an organized activity or simply moments in your life when you helped a relative, friend, co-worker, or even someone you did not know. Note what particularly makes you proud of what you did.

1. _____

2. _____

3. _____

4. _____

5. _____

Now list your volunteer and community service strengths: people skills, expertise in your major field, or your patience and positive attitude. Include a specific example that demonstrates each quality or strength. If you are having trouble thinking of five different strengths, it might be easiest to begin by describing your specific examples and then review the example with an eye towards discerning the qualities, strengths, and abilities demonstrated in what you did.

1. _____

2. _____

_____

_____

_____

3. _____

_____

_____

_____

4. _____

_____

_____

_____

5. _____

_____

_____

_____

Regarding the networking opportunities that are connected to your volunteer activities, think about the different people you've met in your volunteer work. List 10 individuals with whom you have worked in your volunteer and community service work who could be important people to maintain in your professional network.

1. _____

2. _____

3. _____

4. _____

5. _____

6. _____

7. _____

8. _____
   _____

9. _____
   _____

10. _____
    _____

Finally, look at various organizations in your community with which you are not currently involved but might like to be. Conduct online research into various community service organizations. These may be local, regional, statewide, or even national organizations. List five off-campus volunteer organizations that you would be interested in finding out more about and possibly getting involved with while you are in college. If you are in college, you may list organizations in the town, city, or region of your current college and/or groups back at home for summer volunteer initiatives.

Also consider the broader possibilities of getting involved with an organization that has more extensive reach statewide, nationally, or globally. By becoming involved with larger organizations as a volunteer, you open the door to possible future service opportunities (internships, jobs, etc.). If you are not yet in college, look at the websites of some of the colleges you are interested in and list five volunteer organizations in the towns or cities where those schools are that interest you.

1. _____
   _____
   _____

2. _____
   _____
   _____

3. _____
   _____
   _____

4. _____
   _____
   _____

5. _____
   _____
   _____

This provides you with a beginning list of possible off-campus organizations and agencies to consider becoming involved with on your own or with a friend or two. It is recommended that you find at least one off-campus organization with which to be involved during your college years.

Experiential Learning and Service Learning

Some off-campus activities originate as part of a class's course requirements in the form of experiential learning and service-learning activities. These may involve experiential learning in which you job shadow a professional in the field, attend an off-campus event related to the course work, go on a class field trip, engage in an independent study practicum, or work on a case study project in which your team is paired with a company or agency to help solve a specific business, financial, or communications problem.

You may also have the good fortune of being in a class that incorporates service learning in which there will be some volunteer activities as part of the course work. These are especially important opportunities that you want to make the most of. A recent study of service-learning that appeared in the *Journal of the Scholarship of Teaching and Learning* focused explicitly on first-year college students, documenting significant benefits for the student: "These experiences enhance academic learning and are associated with positive cognitive and social changes, including advances in moral reasoning, prosocial reasoning, and decision-making" (Dingle, Eppler, Errickson, & Ironsmith, 2011, pp. 102–111).

Much like your co-op and internship placements and your off-campus volunteerism and community service, classes that incorporate off-campus experiential and service learning components give you the opportunities to meet, assist, learn from, and work with a diverse range of people you would not otherwise get to know. These events heighten your learning through new information, alternate learning environments, and differential teaching styles.

Regardless of the nature of the specific experiential learning occurrence, approach experiential and service-learning activities in smart and strategic ways:

- **Before you go on the off-campus activity, visit relevant websites for background information.** This will communicate to others your appreciation of the learning opportunity. With your newfound background knowledge, any questions and comments that you make during the event will be that much more informed. In this way, you will distinguish yourself among your peers.

- **Make the most of each of these opportunities.** Demonstrate your effort and interest. If you are working on an applied project, work as hard as you can. If you are participating in an off-campus lecture or tour, listen carefully to the presentations, learn as much as you can, and ask thoughtful questions. Enjoy the new experiences. You want to get as much as possible out of each of them. Do not waste opportunities that are given to you.

- **At group meetings or off-campus events, take thorough notes.** Keep a record of what is happening and what you are learning. Remember to bring a notepad, laptop, tablet, or other note-taking device. There will be aspects of select experiences that you will want to remember later on for use on exams and essays. You will appreciate having taken thorough notes later.

- **Spend some of the off-campus time with your professor, instructor, or teaching assistant.** Ask thoughtful questions about what the class is doing. Comment on what you are learning and what is especially interesting and new for you. This demonstrates your interest and engagement. You want to impress your instructor with your level of engaged learning.

- **Make an effort to get to know some of the people involved in your off-campus experiential learning activity.** If you go to a theater performance, talk to some of the performers or crew afterward. Talk with others in the audience who are not in your student group. Feel free to ask someone you meet for her or his business card. You never know whom you might meet. If, say, you are being given

a tour of a water treatment facility or visiting a museum, listen carefully to the presentations. Demonstrate that you are a focused and interested visitor; ask questions that reflect your close listening skills and interest. Take some extra time to talk with people who work there.

■ **If you are participating in a volunteer activity, get to know the other volunteers and the supervisors.** Remember that you do *not* want to just hang back with your fellow students. Take advantage of what you are doing, learn as much as you can, and get to know some new and interesting people. Again, feel free to ask someone you meet for her or his business card. If you see a promising networking or mentoring contact, email your thanks, along with a brief commentary on what you learned and a follow-up question.

■ **If you are working with other students on a project for a local business, make the time to get to know the relevant people there.** Ask them attentive questions that will help your team's project. Ask for any company literature that is available, and make sure that you read it closely. Volunteer for an extra meeting with people at the company or agency to get additional information that would help your team. If an additional meeting is not warranted, volunteer to be your team's liaison with the company, but do this graciously. After any correspondence, add your teammates' names after your own.

■ **Whatever the academic requirements are for your experiential or service-learning opportunity, take them very seriously.** Do your best and participate fully in the class activity, even if the event represents only a small part of your grade or is not graded at all. You want each of your professors to respect you as a person and as a student. Whatever the class activity may be, take it seriously, responsibly, and positively!

Experiential Learning and Service-Learning Worksheets

List up to five significant experiential learning or service-learning activities that you've participated in and excelled in while in college. If you are a new college student or have not yet begun college, feel free to list such activities that you have had in high school (field trips, hands-on demonstrations, volunteering, etc.):

1. _____
   _____
2. _____
   _____
3. _____
   _____
4. _____
   _____
5. _____
   _____

Looking back over the five events listed, note one thing that you learned from each and one way that you could have performed more strategically had you already learned the material in this chapter.

For example, say that one of your classes had an off-campus visit to a museum. While there you learned that Native American cultures were much more advanced prior to conquest and colonization than you had known. Even though you sort of learned this in your class, at the activity you spent the majority of your time talking with your friends rather than focusing on the exhibits, reading the posted information, or talking with museum officials. You ended up getting relatively little out of that experiential learning opportunity. Having studied the lessons in this chapter, how would you participate differently in that event now?

1. _____
   _____
2. _____
   _____
3. _____
   _____
4. _____
   _____
5. _____
   _____

These two lists give you added information about your past performance in various experiential learning situations and areas. This helps you see where you can make your performance smarter and more strategic. They also help you to reflect upon past valuable learning opportunities that you have had and those that you will have throughout your time as a college student and throughout your life. Take this learning to heart so that your future experiential learning and service-learning opportunities will be that much more strategic and effective for you.

8 Networking and Mentoring

Teamwork, Leadership, Strategic Relationships

My idea of good company is the company of clever, well-informed people who have a great deal of conversation; that is what I call good company.

— *Jane Austen (1818), Persuasion*

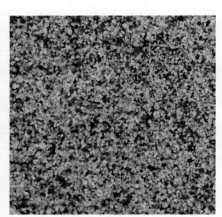

There is nothing I would not do for those who are really my friends. I have no notion of loving people by halves, it is not my nature.

— *Jane Austen (1803), Northanger Abbey*

Be true to your work and your word and your friend.

— *John Boyle O'Reilly (1891), "Rules of the Road"*

Associate yourself with people of good quality if you esteem your own Reputation, for it is better to be alone than in bad Company.

— *16th C. maxim from George Washington (1744), "Rules of Civility"*

1. **Deliberative Collaborations and Relationship Building:** Appreciate and practice intentional networking and mentoring relationships that are collaborative and two-way.

2. **Authenticity, Parity, and Diversity:** Pay attention to five guidelines for networking success: generosity, graciousness, sincerity, vitality, and diversity.

3. **Recommended Networking Practices:** Heighten success by following specific networking practices regarding courtesy, social media, in-class networking, contact information, events and meetings, and faculty office hours.

4. **Seven Key Elements for Mentoring Success:** Develop and maintain strong mentoring relationships with honesty, trustworthiness, respect, appreciation, availability, professional boundaries, and patience.

5. **Recommended Mentoring Practices:** Find and develop your mentoring relationships with specific recommendations for selection, contact, meetings, follow-up, and termination.

6. **Reciprocity with Mentors:** Manage your mentors to find opportunities to help others and also to return the favor.

When people think of networking and mentoring, they usually think of the business world. But networking and mentoring really are much larger than merely a person's professional contacts and advisors. In fact, networking and mentoring are really the warp and woof (underlying fabric) of our everyday lives. Networking and mentoring are friendship, acquaintanceship, community, support, guidance, assistance, teamwork, and leadership.

As the planet shrinks—seemingly day by day—in our increasingly technologically driven era, our lives are, too, increasingly interwoven on a global scale. As the oft-cited adage says, many sticks tied together are much stronger than one lone stick. Interpersonal connections are important for strength in numbers, but they are also crucial for happiness, diversity, information, enrichment, support, assistance, caring, and love.

Relationships are key to your future life, including your future career. Friends and associates let you know about important opportunities. You help out a colleague struggling with a project and deadline. A mentor of yours provides an especially strong recommendation. You contact a former professor about internships at your company, thereby opening doors for students at your alma mater. You serve as an informative colleague for fellow volunteers at a specific organization or agency. Professional peers whom you get to know through conferences become friends; throughout the years, you assist each other in a myriad of ways.

What all this means is that networking and mentoring are about relationships, partnerships over time. The most effective, enduring, and successful networking and mentoring relationships are built upon much more than mere self-interest or self-benefit—whether personal or professional.

Networking and Mentoring at Their Best

Many think of networking and mentoring solely in terms of climbing career ladders in the business world and as a superficial activity largely aimed at self-interest. Although this may be true in specific cases, networking and mentoring, at their best, help to knit together the fabric of humanity. They are vital for every person's life. When you network and mentor, you make and maintain connections. Even when intended to be professionally beneficial, you are still creating connections between yourself and others—and in many cases, connecting your associates with each other.

Think about this for a minute. Networking and mentoring are much bigger than just you. Look for a moment at how torn the planet is and how many peoples are divided from each other: nations at war with other nations, political and religious enmity and division, and nations and communities and families divided within themselves. We are currently observing the 150th anniversary of the American Civil War, a time when our nation was terribly divided, resulting in horrific loss of life.

You may be wondering, "What does the Civil War have to do with my professional network or mentors?" Well, as you develop and strengthen your professional network and mentoring relationships, you are bringing together people who otherwise might not have strong bonds between them. Whenever people come together in a mutual and sincere relationship, the strengthened ties that are produced yield benefits to individuals, to companies, and to communities; these benefits extend outward into the wider world, even beyond the bounds of your personal network and mentoring relationships.

Networking and mentoring relationships are important in the professional world largely due to their interpersonal and intergroup reciprocity. Never think that they are just about you. The most successful networks and mentoring relationships are never one way. They are effectively reciprocal.

Most networking and mentoring experts focus on the ways by which strong networks and mentoring relationships are beneficial to a person's life and career. This is why networking is a smart and strategic tool to begin utilizing while you are in college. In "How to Network Your Way Up the Corporate Ladder," Tara Weiss (2008) emphasizes the importance of networking early, consistently, and sincerely. Citing many experts in the field, Weiss points out that "getting ahead in your career is directly tied to whom you know." She then references Jan Vermeiren, author of *Let's Connect! A Practical Guide for Highly Effective Professional Networking* and founder of the Networking Coach website. Vermeiren asserts that "your network is the most powerful resource you can have, and it's free" (Weiss, 2008, n.p.). Regardless of your major or career plans, begin your network now.

Professional networking is about knowing whom to call when there are needs in your community, about being a vital resource for younger people starting out, and about connecting those in your network who are unknown to each other and yet whose needs and resources fit together. The stronger, wider, more diverse, and more vital your network is, the better you will be able to utilize your network for your own career progression, and even more importantly for the many ways you will be able to be of service to others throughout your life. Remember that you want to *make networking work for you*—and, in this way, you can help the others in your networks as well.

Five Guidelines for Networking: Authenticity, Parity, Diversity

You can raise your networking effectiveness through the following five guidelines for relational authenticity, parity, and diversity.

Being a Giving Person

▶ Always see how you can be of service to others.

This might be something as simple as introducing two people who will bolster and be of benefit to each other's network. It may be just a short email communicating to someone how much you valued meeting them the day before. It might be a casual discussion in which you mention an article of interest to another, which you later follow up with an email and link to the article. Or a friend may be struggling in a particular class, so you offer to study together and share/model your successful study techniques. Or another student with stellar credentials may mention not having procured an internship for the summer; so you provide a strategic contact with the internship coordinator at the company where you are interning. Over the years, your successful networking will mature so that you focus more on giving rather than receiving.

The magic of networking lies in the connectedness that comes from this kind of mutual giving: helping each other along our respective ways in life. Although it may be the case that much more intentional and strategic networking takes place in the corporate world than in other venues, intentional and deliberate networking is the very fiber that knits together families, friends, communities, and even our sorely tried world. Remember that whenever you reach out and help someone else, in whatever way possible, you have deepened a relationship and helped to knit together a bit of the fabric of humankind.

Let me share a simple story that communicates a great deal about relationality and generosity in everyday life:

A Canadian doctor was in Israel visiting the holy places to the Bahá'í Faith. He was in Haifa in the gold domed Shrine of the Báb on Mt. Carmel for prayers. There was an elderly Persian man there in prayer. As the old man began to stand up, the doctor held out his arm. Later in a motivational talk, the Canadian doctor told his audience that this is really what life is about: being of service to others, helping each other along in life, simply putting an arm out to help another up.

Mutually Beneficial Relationships

▶ Be gracious both in giving and receiving.

Effective networking is a two-way street; it is invariably reciprocal and collaborative. This means that your successful networking is never just about you. Networking is fundamentally about connections, sharing, giving, and receiving. Remember that all relationships by definition and practice involve more than one person. You want your networked relationships to be mutually beneficial.

Much like an electrical grid, the energy of interpersonal networks flows back and forth along lines of connection. The energy required to power an electrical network needs to be strong enough to maintain the flow of energy to keep the electric currents moving. Analogously, interpersonal networks require sustained and sustainable energy flows. Electricity does not flow evenly all the time; neither does the connective energy in relationships. But it cannot be neglected for extended periods without degrees of disconnection.

As a student, always be willing to help others; just pace yourself to ensure that you do not overcommit and thereby compromise your own studies and job requirements. Likewise, always be willing to accept help. Help others and accept assistance, both in moderation. Do not do so much that you end up robbing others of volition and effort. And to maintain your own strong work ethic, do not take more help than you really need.

The philosopher Ludwig Wittgenstein (1980) wrote that a writer should never do more for a reader than necessary: "Anything *your reader can do* for himself *leave* to him" (1980, p. 77, italics in orig.). In other words, there is valuable learning that comes from a reader's effort in figuring out what has been read. Through the reader's own efforts, he or she will become more engaged in the process, and what has been read will be comprehended more deeply. A writer must provide enough information and detail so that the reader can figure things out, but the best writing will leave some room for the reader's own effort.

Remember that in the prior example the younger Canadian doctor did not pick up the older man, thereby doing all the work for him. The younger man simply held out his arm to help. The old man stood up himself, but he graciously accepted the assistance and the offer of the younger man's arm. In this way, each person's selfhood and dignity are respected within the framework of assistance. There is both a graciousness in giving and a graciousness in receiving. And there is the wisdom and knowledge involved in knowing how much help to offer and give and how much help to ask for and accept.

Integrity

▶ Your networking relationships need to be based on sincerity, honesty, and trust.

Think about your relatives and friends—those whom you trust most in life. Throughout your life, establish networking relationships that are similarly trusted and secure. To do this, there are two basic rules: One involves your own integrity, the other that of those in your network. There are innumerable people whom you will meet in your lifetime. Be choosy about whom you include in your network. Select and maintain contacts whom you respect and know will "have your back."

The most effective networking relationships are grounded in sincere and honest relationships. This does not mean they are perfect, nor that your contacts need to be your best and dearest of friends. What this does mean, however, is that you want to rise to your best in how you communicate and interact with your contacts. Don't use some people who are immediately powerful while pushing others away just because they seem to be "less important." Those whom you push away right now might be especially helpful to you later on. And those who are most important today may actually prove to be less valuable or even problematic in ways you did not foresee.

Treat all you meet with respect. For long-term networking effectiveness, try not to burn bridges along the way. Be the trustworthy person who will gain the respect of all with whom you interact. See the good in each person. No one is perfect. Each person has better and lesser traits. Value each person for their better qualities.

Be the contact you would want your contacts to be for you: trustworthy, honorable, sincere, and honest. And if a contact proves untrustworthy or even toxic for you and your network, accept that there are times when it is necessary to drop individuals from your network or minimize your contact with them.

A Vibrant Network

▶ Maintain the vitality and effectiveness of your networks and contacts.

Having a vibrant and dynamic network requires a regularity of communications with your contacts and your strategic selection of those to keep in your network.

You need to decide how much contact you want to maintain with different contacts. For some, the occasional update on social media is sufficient. For others, more personally directed contact will be desired. Your contact with different persons will ebb and flow based upon the different needs and circumstances over time: strong and frequent at some times, and occasional and slight at other times.

For example, one colleague may post the need for an intern at his company, so you ask whether you can put him in direct contact with a recruiter at your alma mater so that his company can participate in your school's upcoming career fair. A need arose, and you stepped forward to provide a solution that assists your colleague and his company and that, in turn, also benefits students at your alma mater.

The Internet is a powerful tool for maintaining contact with increasing numbers of network contacts. Use your social media for easy means of maintaining connections. This is important to ensure that your contacts continue to perceive you as a current connection. And when you make a new valuable connection, do not simply drop out of sight for an extended period. You want to work with digital technology and in-person contact as you work out the best ways for you to maintain contact with your growing network connections.

If you lose contact with someone over time and later want to reconnect, definitely do so, but do so graciously and sincerely. Friends and associates like being remembered. Once you reconnect, try to maintain the contact.

There will be individuals whom you decide need to be minimized or altogether eliminated from your active network. In an electrical network, a fuse or switch may go bad and need to be replaced, or the wiring and connections in an electrical grid may need to be redirected or connected differently. Similarly, your professional network will need regular maintenance to remain a healthy and active network. Not everyone with whom you interact should be added to your professional network. Make smart and strategic choices. You may want an extensive and growing Twitter following, but it may be more advantageous to you to maintain smaller Facebook or LinkedIn networks.

In *Good to Great: Why Some Companies Make the Leap . . . and Others Don't,* Jim Collins explains that "the good-to-great leaders began the transformation by first getting the right people on the bus (and the wrong people off the bus) and then figured out where to drive it" (Collins, 2001, p. 63). Although Collins is speaking specifically about smart and strategic hiring (and firing), this guidance holds true for your own developing professional network. This does not mean that those you reject from your network are inadequate. On the contrary, it just means that they do not fit as integral parts of *your* network at *this* time.

Lateral and Hierarchized Diversity

▶ The strongest and most effective networks are diverse, both in terms of breadth and depth.

A mantra for an especially strong network is "unity with diversity." The 19th-century poet Samuel Coleridge used the phrase "unity with variety" to define beauty, like a beautifully coherent garden with a variety of flowers and plants of different types, colors, sizes, scents, and times of bloom. You want solid and enduring relationships with each of the members of your network, and you want a diverse network.

The greater the diversity reflected in your networked contacts, the greater will be the capacity and strength in your network. To this end, you want both lateral (horizontal) and hierarchized (vertical) diversity.

Hierarchized diversity is easy to understand. Your network should include those who are your lateral peers. As a college student, these would be other college students, but you also want to include in your network those who are your superiors and in positions of greater power (e.g., professors, other professionals in the workforce, college students who are ahead of you and about to enter the workforce, graduate students, older family members and older friends, and bosses) and also those who are below your current level (e.g., high school students, friends who have not gone to college but who have jobs that do not require college, and employees who report to you at your job).

A network that is constructed of persons at different points along the vertical axis of employment positionality offer diverse perspectives, experiences, and ways by which they can be of mutual benefit to you and others in your network. For example, you might give helpful advice about your college to a high school student preparing to go to college, or you might assist a friend who has already graduated from college and who is looking for an intern for his company. Remember that network relationships are mutually beneficial: Benefits go up and down the vertical axis. It is not only those higher up who help those who are lower. Everyone is able to help others in different ways, regardless of their hierarchized positions of formal power.

Lateral diversity signifies parallel network members who are dissimilar to you in significant ways. You want a diversity of perspectives, skill sets, knowledge, and experiences that are reflected by an ethnically, racially, geographically, religiously, socioeconomically, generationally, and gender diverse group of people who have different majors and minors, a diversity of types of jobs, and a range of life experiences.

Throughout your life, a myriad of needs will come to your attention. By having a diverse network, you will have a cross-section of your community. In this way, your network will be more robust in terms of diversity of experiences, skills, knowledge, and resources. In college, some of the strongest networking groups are within the Greek fraternities and sororities whose membership provides an excellent networking base. But if your formal networks do not provide a robust diversity of contacts, then you will need to seek out greater diversity in your own developing professional network. For example, if your networking community is made up primarily of other computer science majors and there are few educators in your network, then you will miss important opportunities that are related to the education domain. If a contact of yours is an elementary school principal who asks you for networking help with the development of an electronic "smart" classroom, having education specialists in your own network would be helpful.

If your formal network is gendered along male/female lines, such as in fraternities and sororities, you will need to make connections that cross the gender divide. While it is important to respect global cultural diversity—including diverse gender customs around the world—it is nevertheless important that each person develop a professional network that includes men *and* women.

The more laterally diverse your network is, the more robust it will be. If your developing network is thin in terms of diversity, you will need to think of ways that you can get to know different people. College provides one of the best environments to do this.

You can meet people in the cafeterias and dining halls. You can get to know other students in your classes. You can join different organizations that you are interested in and where you will meet different people. You can volunteer for different charities and service agencies. Just by being involved, your network will expand and become deeper, more diverse, and more robust. Consider these hypothetical networking scenarios:

■ During your sophomore year, you have a conversation with one of the best students in one of your classes. This student has always impressed you with her drive and discipline. You two talk about your future plans for law school and your immediate summer plans: your lifeguarding at the local pool and her first internship with an attorney. You ask her some questions about the internship and how she got it, and she gives you the contact information. You send her an email *the next day* thanking her for the information. Contacting the firm, you learn that they are interested in a part-time summer intern. You check, and you find out that you can adjust your lifeguarding schedule so that you can lifeguard *and* accept the part-time internship!

■ In a different class, you find yourself on a project team with three other students. Your efforts on the team distinguish you, and your group members appreciate your hard work, your positive and encouraging attitude, your intelligence, and your willingness to take on even the grunt work. Over the course of the project time frame, you get to know the other students much better, and they get to know you. When you mention your career plans, one of the members of your team mentions that her uncle works for XYZ Company in the same field as your engineering major. You ask whether her uncle would be open to hearing from a student who is studying mechanical engineering, and your teammate (who is impressed by your attitude and work) puts you in contact with her uncle. The company is local, and at your request, you get to job shadow him for the day, including a tour of the company. The next year, they develop a part-time job for you during the school year.

■ You want to be a teacher at a school not too far from home. As an education major, you reconnect with your former teachers, some of whom live in your town, but also several who live in the surrounding towns. They know many of the teachers throughout the area. As a college student, you decide to use your Facebook account strategically, only posting messages that you would be comfortable with virtually anyone reading. While you are student teaching, you send out posts about how much you love what you are doing, including posts about the magic and struggles of students, and about a few creative ideas you have successfully implemented. A few of your former teachers have been reading your posts with interest. When you then post about your beginning search for a job in the area, three of your former teachers send you information about possible leads for upcoming openings that they know about.

In Scott Carlson's article "How to Assess the Real Payoff of a College Degree," Lauren Jones, a former Miss Teen Maryland and current college student was asked about the importance of college for students. She explained that college is much more than the studying and academics: "It's for better career opportunities and networking. . . . The people you meet here are going to be people who are influential after you graduate" (Carlson, 2013, p. A28). Belgian networking specialist Vermeiren, underscores that more often than not, it will be "people from your network [who] can connect you with the people you need to reach your goals" (cited in Weiss, 2008, para. 4). Do not undervalue the importance of networking while you are in college.

 # Recommended Networking Practices

To create and sustain successful networking and professional relationships, you should employ these key practices:

Courtesy

- When you meet someone and have a professionally meaningful conversation, before you leave, tell the person how much you appreciated the conversation and meeting.

- After you meet someone and have a professionally meaningful conversation, send them an email within 24 hours with a brief comment telling them how much you appreciated meeting them the day before. This is courteous; it will also help them to remember you later on.

- When someone helps you get an interview with a professional contact, complete a project, or learn about an internship or position, send them a "thank you" email the next day. This takes practice, but after a while, it will become automatic for you.

- When you work in groups (whether in class, on the job, or in other extracurricular activities), remember to be a team player. Be gracious. Praise others when they do good work. Pull your weight on the team and do it very well. Be willing to help others, but in moderation. Do not take over too much of the work. Demonstrate your willingness to work hard and your appreciation of others' efforts. If a team member appears to be having difficulty getting his or her work done, offer your help. Don't just do it yourself; find out what the challenges are, and then ask if there is anything that you can do to help. Down the road, that person may be able to help you out in some way.

Social Media

- Make strategic use of your social media sites: Facebook, LinkedIn, Twitter, and so on. When you meet people, add them to your contacts in the appropriate "friends" or associates list. LinkedIn is an excellent vehicle for maintaining a listing of your professional contacts, but it does not provide the more personal contact that solidifies connections in the ways that are possible via Twitter (through frequency) and Facebook (through greater detail and flexibility). Also take advantage of other social media outlets that offer group membership. Online like-minded groups provide excellent opportunities for networking.

- Facebook is an excellent vehicle for maintaining professional contacts and moving them into a more informal friendship category. If you want to make strategic use of Facebook, then remember to scrutinize closely whatever you post—your posts should be appropriate for a wide range of friends, relatives, and professional associates. Only post photos that you would be comfortable having a prospective employer see.

- Consider keeping different Facebook groups, with one that is more professionally oriented and a bit more formal. Many people do this successfully. The challenge is to be sure that you never send one of your informal posts to the professional group. It is much easier to err on the side of decorum, propriety, and circumspection, and to simply post only that which you consider appropriate for anyone to read.

- Some find it helpful to set up a schedule for checking social media sites. Decide how much time you want to spend on social media each day or each week, and then

stick with that schedule. I have found that 15 to 20 minutes a day is sufficient to quickly check the newsfeed, keep up with everyone, note a few posts that I like, respond to one or two specific posts, check friend requests and messages, and occasionally have a short chat with someone who is online. Find a reasonable and satisfying schedule that works for you. Remember that Facebook is not a popularity contest; maintain a reasonable number of contacts so that your social media time does not become a time sinkhole.

In-Class Networking

■ Students regularly complain about doing group work in their classes. A strategic student will perceive group work as an opportunity to get to know other students better and as an opportunity to practice networking skills. Working on a task with others is one of the best ways to get to know them. Suggest comfortable and effective meeting locales such as your school's student center or a local café. As people begin to feel comfortable with each other, they also begin to take their mutual responsibilities more seriously. Remember that how you perform as a group member communicates much to your fellow students about the sort of person you are and about your quality of effort and work. Ten years down the road, a former team member might be just the person you need to help you with a project or employment change. You want her to remember you as one of the most impressive individuals she ever worked with on a team: remarkable, hard-working, creative, gracious, and a disciplined team player.

■ In the professional world, people learn how to "work a room" at social events as individuals try to meet and get to know new and important people. Networking is not just about connecting with important and powerful people. A network that is diverse both vertically and laterally will be much more robust than a smaller network with just a few key people. Add to your circle of contacts throughout college by learning to work the room in your classes! Get to know your fellow students, your course T.A., and your professor as you explore additions to your developing professional network.

■ Become a top student in your classes so that your fellow students will perceive and remember you in a very positive light. Ask helpful questions in class. Provide thoughtful answers and comments without taking too much class time. Be gracious and provide space for other students to answers questions even when you know the answer. And refer to your fellow students' comments and questions to show your attentiveness to what they say. This communicates that you have valued their contributions in class. It also demonstrates your critical thinking as you build on others' ideas.

Contact Information

■ Start your contact list with those you meet in your dormitory, classes, and campus organizations. Also think about family members, friends, and instructors. Now is the time to begin your professional network. Do not wait until you are out of college.

■ An easy way to stay in contact with your growing network of professional contacts is simply to add or "friend" them on your social media sites. But remember to be strategic about whom you add to which site. If you use Facebook informally, then keep your professional network on LinkedIn or another such site. If you choose to use Facebook both informally and professionally, then feel free to add your contacts there. Just be careful and strategic about how you are using your social media sites.

■ Many now use blogs in interesting ways to communicate professional thoughts and activities. This is an effective way to share occasional or scheduled thoughts and learning with your professional network.

■ When you meet professional people, remember to ask for their business cards. You want their contact information. Then send an email the next day to thank them; you may even formally ask them whether you may add them to your professional network.

Classes, Lectures, Arts Events, Conferences, and Professional Meetings

■ Take advantage of your scholastic learning environment and make valuable connections with your fellow students in class and at extracurricular lectures, arts events, service activities, and at professional conferences. Get to know your peers, and make note of those you think you might want to include in your growing professional network.

■ Get to know other people who are attending public lectures, arts events, and conferences. You never know what valuable connections you might make. Wherever you go, be open to meeting new people.

■ In class and at extracurricular lectures, arts events, conferences, and professional meetings, be one of the most attentive audience members. Ask thoughtful questions and engage in interested conversations. Go up to the presenters at the end and thank them. If you think you would like to add them to your professional network, feel free to ask whether they would consider a follow-up question via email. If they say yes, then ask for their professional cards or email addresses; follow through on that the next day.

Faculty Office Hours

■ Visit your professors', teaching assistants', and other instructors' offices. If you have questions about course work, bring your questions to office hours. One-on-one contact is the most important connection that you can make with anyone. Email, Facebook, Twitter, and phone time can never replace the value of in-person contact. Take advantage of the time your faculty set aside for students during office hours.

■ If you do not have any specific questions about the course work, think about what you are currently studying. Find some element of it that interests you and stop by during office hours to chat with your instructor about what you are learning.

■ Feel free to stop by during office hours simply to talk with your professor, teaching assistant, or instructor about your studies, study habits, grades, major, career plans, summer plans, and so on. If your instructor cannot help you directly about any of these, he or she can certainly point to others who can help. This will expand your network further.

Beginning Networking and Professional Contacts Worksheet

List 20 people you know who are important to include in your developing professional network—now and into the future. These can include students, professors, relatives, family friends, coworkers, volunteers, supervisors, and bosses. For each name, note the person's relationship to you and the distinctive assets he or she brings to your network: specific knowledge base or skill set, experiences, position, etc.

1. _____
   _____
2. _____
   _____
3. _____
   _____
4. _____
   _____
5. _____
   _____
6. _____
   _____
7. _____
   _____
8. _____
   _____
9. _____
   _____
10. _____
   _____
11. _____
   _____
12. _____
   _____
13. _____
   _____

14. _____
_____

15. _____
_____

16. _____
_____

17. _____
_____

18. _____
_____

19. _____
_____

20. _____
_____

Mentoring Relationships in College

Mentors are those individuals who are more experienced than you in certain areas, more knowledgeable than you in a specific field, and willing and able to assist you as you move forward along your respective career and life paths. Throughout time and in all cultures, people have learned from and leaned on others as they progress through their lives. In earlier times, apprentices would work with and learn their crafts from master craftsmen and women. In your own life, you have already had many mentors who have helped you along the way.

In college, some mentors will be provided, as in the case of your professors in your classes or the faculty and staff advisors for campus organizations.

What is different in college is that you have the responsibility to seek out your mentors.

- Drafts of your essays will often be reviewed by peers, tutors, friends, and faculty; and you will rewrite those essays based on their helpful tutelage. The result of such assistance will be more polished, focused, and developed writing.
- When you join a fraternity or sorority or other student organization and are involved in specific projects, there will be those who are more senior who will help guide you and other new members.
- When you volunteer (on campus or off), there will be supervisors and more experienced volunteers who will oversee and provide assistance.
- When you receive assignments in your classes, your professors and other instructors will provide the necessary information for students to accomplish the work and will provide their expertise to guide the process.
- If you run into a technological problem, there will be technical specialists, a help desk, instructional technology experts, graduate teaching assistants, and administrative staff to provide you with the needed help.

In each of these examples, you did not need to seek out and discover these guides on your own. Just as when you were a child and teenager, you did not need to strategically develop your relationships with them in order to receive their help.

But as an adult, you need to step up to the plate on your own and seek out your own professional mentors and professional mentoring relationships. College provides you with the opportunity to begin and practice your mentoring relationships. You have ready access to many additional professionals as well as more advanced students whom you can meet, get to know, and consider as potential mentors. Now is the time to start selecting key professionals at your college and elsewhere for possible long-term relationships, beginning to nurture those relationships, seeking assistance (references, academic advice, professional advice, contacts, professional leads, etc.) during your transitions beyond college, and beginning to mentor others in return.

The benefits of strong and successful mentoring relationships are paramount for your education and development as a college student and for your development and accomplishments in the workplace. One widely regarded expert on mentoring is Lois J. Zachary, president of Leadership Development Services, director of its Center for Mentoring Excellence, and author of *The Mentee's Guide: Make Mentoring Work for You*. Regarding the diverse benefits to protégés/mentees, Zachary relates, "Some mentees say that mentoring gives them exposure to people and ideas they would never have encountered on their own. Others find that their mentor's belief in them gives them strength and bolsters their courage in taking risks. Some report that mentoring helps demystify their profession, organization, or job. Still others find the benefit of mentoring a way to jump-start their learning process in new and unfamiliar areas" (Zachary & Fischler, 2009, p. 6). There is no question that smart and strategic mentoring is key to any person's continued and directed learning and growth—both in college and beyond.

Seven Key Elements of Successful Mentoring Relationships

It is important to learn how to initiate a potentially valuable mentoring relationship, how to develop the strong and enduring connections that are crucial to effective mentoring relationships, and how to work with and utilize your mentors in strategically successful ways. In order to get a clear view of what constitutes a successful and effective mentoring relationship, it helps to examine seven key elements of productive mentoring relationships: honesty, trustworthiness, respect, appreciation, availability, professional boundaries, and realism.

Honesty

Your relationship with your mentor may be one of the most important that you will have in your life. Ideally, your primary mentors are experienced, hard-working, successful people who are sincerely concerned about your well-being and success. They are willing to spend additional time to help you along your way in life. Whether someone is a protégé or mentor, the first principle of mentoring relationships (and indeed of *all* relationships) is that truth is the foundation. Be honest with *yourself* about what you are doing, about what sort of assistance you want and need from your mentor, and about what you can do *for* your mentor. Be honest with your mentor.

- Ask your professors for advice. If you are having trouble with grades and you want to begin approaching your studies more strategically and successfully, ask your professors or advisor for guidance. Seek out your college's or university's tutoring service. Talk with the people in your school's student affairs or dean of students office. Colleges are filled with personnel ready and waiting to assist your academic success in college.

- Seek advice from your advisor or department chair. If you are having trouble procuring an internship, ask your advisor or department chair or career center staff member for assistance to help make that possible.

- Meet with the people in the career center at your college. If you are having trouble with a major and questioning your chosen career path, meet with people in your career center and with your professors and other professionals to get as much information to help you make the right decisions that will *work for you*.

- Seek guidance from your instructor regarding teamwork. If you are having trouble with another student assigned to your group or team, feel free to talk with your professor for guidance in dealing with that student and other teamwork challenges. This also communicates to your professor your commitment to your group's success.

- Bring challenges to supervisors or advisors for their advice. If you are having trouble in an internship or with an organization where you are a volunteer or in a student organization, bring your situation to the attention of your supervisor or group advisor, but do so professionally. You do not want to be a complainer—rather you are a person who is committed to success and excellence and who is simply seeking out experienced guidance to help with a personnel or communications challenge.

- You should always be comfortable going to your mentors, advisors, supervisors, and other superiors for assistance, but there are two caveats here:

1. Present challenging situations with which you are seeking advice calmly, rationally, empathically, and kindly—in short, professionally. Do not present yourself to your mentor as continually in need.

2. Perhaps the most important lesson in your mentoring relationships is to *listen to your mentors*. Ask them about their experiences. Ask them for their recommendations about your current work and your career trajectory. Ask them for their suggestions about how you can improve, grow, and develop in your desired profession.

- Remember to share your successes with your mentors. Let them see the positive results of your work and their efforts on your behalf.

Trustworthiness

Keep your word. Fulfill your promises. Be timely. And respect the boundaries of your mentoring relationships. What is private should be kept private.

- If you are asked to accomplish a particular task prior to your next contact with your mentor, make sure that you get it done, and do so on time. If you have any trouble meeting that deadline, contact your mentor well ahead of time and share the challenges you are facing. Give your mentor the opportunity to help you out with the difficulty and/or to reschedule your meeting.

- Be clear to identify any areas of confidentiality that are not to be shared outside of the mentoring relationship. For example, your mentor might be willing to give you his or her cell phone number; do not give that to others without prior approval. Do not share communications with others without first deliberating about whether it would be appropriate to do so; when in doubt, ask your mentor's permission. In other words, be a trustworthy protégé.

Respect

- When you have contact with a mentor, remember that you are seeking guidance and assistance from him or her. When your mentor is speaking, listen carefully and take notes. If there is anything with which you disagree, avoid that immediate gut reaction. Definitely do not argue back in an emotional manner. Hold those thoughts. Think through them later, after your conversation or meeting. Take the time necessary to give those items due thought and consideration so that you will gain the needed perspective to see them more clearly. You just may decide that you *agree* with one or more of those points that you had disagreed with before!

- You can always seek additional information from others. Just as you would go to several doctors for their thoughts regarding a major medical procedure, you should meet with multiple professionals (instructors, staff members, supervisors, more senior students, etc.) to get a variety of thoughts on big decisions so that you can make the best and most strategic choices for you.

- Maintain proper professional courtesy and decorum when you are interacting with your superiors. You should be courteous with everyone, but it is especially important for protégés and mentors to be courteous and respectful with each other. In this way, you are learning and practicing your professional decorum.

Appreciation

- Always remember to be thankful for that which you receive. At the end of any meeting, thank your mentor for his or her time. If it is an extended meeting, send a follow-up email within two days with a short thank you and a brief comment about how you are following up on the advice. In this way, you have demonstrated your responsibility, work ethic, time-management skills, and reciprocal efforts as a protégé.

- In the majority of cases, a simple email is sufficient. But depending on the extent of the help you received and how ongoing your relationship has been, another gesture of thanks may be in order. Even in this new era of omnipresent digital communications, hard-copy thank you notes are still appreciated. A greeting card of thanks is always nice to receive, and it is a symbol of your mentor's efforts that he or she can display and share with others. For major contributions to your education and career, you could also put together a digital portfolio of images that displays the fruit of your mentor's guidance and assistance. Such a gift provides your mentor with a graphic presentation of his or her help and your accomplishments.

- If your mentor assists you in a big way, thank him or her accordingly. If your mentor helps you procure a prize internship, a thank you gift is in order. A gift basket of cheese and crackers or specialty chocolates, coffees, or teas are good choices. As you get to know your mentor better over time, you will have a good idea of the appropriate ways to thank him or her. Generally it is best to avoid personal gifts such as clothing; however, clothing and other items with your school's logo are definitely suitable.

Availability

- Be as flexible as possible to accommodate your mentor's busy schedule. Also make sure that you select key mentors who have sufficient availability to work with you. If one mentor is especially busy, develop additional mentors who will guide and assist you in different ways. Therefore, if one mentor is not available, there will be someone else to whom you can go for the assistance you need.

- Everyone seems to be very busy these days, but never think that your schedule is set in stone. Review it to see where you have flexibility. For example, getting up an hour or two earlier . . . yes, YIKES! . . . then you can be up, perhaps exercised, breakfasted, caffeinated, cleaned, dressed respectfully, and prepared and on time for an early meeting with your mentor.

- Your availability is really a function of your time-management skills. Use your college years to develop good habits of time management.

Time-Management Tips

If you are struggling with time management, remember these tips:

- Talk with successful students about their strategies.
- Go to your college's counseling or tutoring center or website.
- Meet with your instructors and advisors.
- Ask your own parents and other relatives about their time-management struggles and successes in college and in the workplace.
- Search online for information about improving time-management skills.

Professional Boundaries

Appropriateness in relationships may be the most sensitive area regarding mentoring, and it is the one that is least discussed. You need to think about this, and make sure that you proceed accordingly.

- Mentoring relationships are professional relationships. A mentoring relationship is an informal contractual relationship. You want to make sure that the parameters of the contractual framework are clear to each of you (e.g., time frame, responsibilities, expectations). Revisit those boundaries periodically to ensure that they continue to be clear and are upheld on both sides. Know the ground rules and abide by them.

- If you want your relationship with your mentor to be successful for you over time, it is recommended that you do not step over the boundaries of professional propriety. In most mentoring relationships, the protégé will *only* have in-person contact with the mentor in his or her office; in public cafés, student centers, and restaurants (usually over lunch); and at professional meetings and conferences. It is appropriate to go to your mentor's home *only* when there are others there for a gathering: a dinner party where you can network, an afternoon barbecue where you can meet others, or a family meal with his or her spouse and children. Err on the side of caution: do not go to your mentor's office in the evening when you two would be alone.

- Mentoring relationships, as with all relationships, can be complicated. All relationships have their difficulties and can be confusing at times. Expect that there will be times when you look at your mentor and feel gratitude and affection. Be careful not to confuse feelings of admiration and appreciation with romantic desire or love.

- If you begin to have romantic feelings for your mentor, you will have to make some choices: (1) If your mentor is married or in a relationship, minimize your contact, look for a different mentor, or figure out how to change your perceptions. (2) If your mentor is neither married nor in a relationship, and you are certain that your feelings are returned, then decide whether you want this person as a valuable professional mentor or as a significant other. Take some time to think through the relationship and its ramifications. For example, will a personal relationship risk your mentor's professional reputation and yours? If the relationship ends bitterly, what harm could your former mentor do to your college career or professional future?

- Approach your mentoring relationships as opportunities to not only move your career and life forward, but also to practice and develop your professional behaviors, interactions, and decorum.

Realism

- Approach your mentoring relationships with a clear sense of realism. All relationships require work. All relationships have rocky moments. When there are difficulties, first see what you can do to change *your* perceptions and behaviors. Work on your side of the mentoring relationship first. If you still have concerns, you have a number of choices: (1) Simply accept the problem and work around it. (2) Bring the concern up directly with your mentor. (3) If the problem is too complicated, shift gears and work with other mentors instead.

■ Remember that your relationship with a mentor is not a marriage for life. You will have many different mentors over the course of your life as your mentoring needs change and evolve. Some mentors will be lifelong guides; others will not.

■ Truly successful mentoring relationships are two-way streets with a flow of information and guidance going in both directions. While the majority of the information and guidance comes from the mentor, a smart, dedicated, active, and strategic protégé will contribute to her or his mentor's work as well. Remember that mentoring should be mutually beneficial. Do not expect more of your mentor than is realistic. Appreciate the ways in which your mentors can assist you, but do not expect any one mentor to solve all your career problems.

Recommended Mentoring Practices

Now that you have a good understanding of the importance of mentoring relationships, let's drill down to specific practices involved in developing and maintaining successful mentoring relationships in college and beyond. Remember that you want to be strategic in whom you choose to approach as potential mentors, in how you nurture and develop these relationships, and in how you evaluate their success.

There are specific practices and logistics involved in mentoring relationships that contribute to their effective and successful execution: selection of the right mentors, initial contact, meetings, follow-up, and ending or redefining a mentoring relationship.

Selecting the Right Mentors

This involves strategic thinking from the get-go. It used to be that protégés were selected by mentors, but now it is understood that protégés can and should initiate. A leading expert on mentoring is Dr. Susan Canfield, director of the MBA Mentor Program at the Foster School of Business at the University of Washington. Canfield explains that "mentees are in the best position to choose their mentors because they often know what they want to learn and from whom they want to learn it. This more widely accepted practice is supported by research on mentor matching, which shows mentees have more 'skin in the game' when choosing their own mentors" (Quast, 2013, n.p.). So take an active role in seeking out strategic mentoring relationships.

There are innumerable people who could potentially serve as mentors for you. Many of these people may be important to you throughout your life. Some will assist you just once; others will work with you more extensively over time. As a college student, you want to begin thinking strategically about potential mentors for your success in college and your success in transitioning from college to the workplace. Mentors range from those whom you know personally as friends and relatives to those with whom you have more formal and distant relationships. According to the United States Office of Personnel Management in Washington, D.C., there are four types of mentoring roles:

■ Career Guide—promotes development through career guidance, counseling, and visibility

■ Information Source—provides information about formal and informal expectations

■ Friend—interacts with the protégé socially and provides information about people

- Intellectual Guide—promotes an equal relationship, collaborates on research projects, and provides constructive feedback and criticism (United States Office of Personnel Management, 2008, p. 4).

Professors, lecturers, teaching assistants, tutors, advisors, and career center consultants can help you in college and beyond. By the end of your college years, these individuals will number in the dozens. Other strategic mentors at college include professional staff members and college administrators whom you have gotten to know well. There will also be the many people who provide oversight to you in your internships, volunteer activities, student organizations, and jobs. Faculty, graduate students, peer undergraduates, and alumni will be available as intellectual guides. Family members and friends will round out your prospective mentors.

Look around you for plum mentoring opportunities.

- If you are your school's student council president, you will have the opportunity to get to know your college president well; he or she would be a valuable mentor. But you do not need to be your student body's president to develop strategic relationships with various other professional staff at your college or university.

- If you have a work-study job on campus, you will get to know various staff members in your office or division. Feel free to seek out a supervisor (or even your supervisor's boss) as a mentor.

- If you are involved with a fraternity, sorority, honor society, or other campus organization, there will be senior members and alums in the organizations who could serve as valuable mentors.

- If you have a part-time or full-time job, your boss could be an important mentor. Even if your academic major is not directly related to what you do at your job, your boss might be a valuable asset to you as a mentor. For example, if he or she is a people person, you can draw on his or her experience to develop people skills. He or she may also be able to point you towards other valuable contacts through his or her own network.

- If you have the opportunity to participate in a research project or creative production with one of your professors, that faculty member can serve as both an intellectual/ creative guide and a career guide. Your work with that faculty member may lead to a presentation at an important conference or even to a highly respected publication.

Potential Mentors Worksheet

List 15 people whom you already know and who could become valuable mentors for you now and into the future. Much like the beginning networking list you did previously, these could include more senior students, graduate students, professors, relatives, family friends, people with whom you have worked, people with whom you have volunteered, supervisors and bosses, other professionals you have recently met, and friends' relatives. Unlike the networking list, this list does not include your peers or those junior to you.

Include their names, relationships to you, and what you perceive as their distinctive mentoring assets: knowledge base, skill set, experiences, position, etc.

1. _____
   _____
2. _____
   _____
3. _____
   _____
4. _____
   _____

5. _____

6. _____

7. _____

8. _____

9. _____

10. _____

11. _____

12. _____

13. _____

14. _____

15. _____

Dream Team Mentors Worksheet

Now you will dream big. List 10 people whom you may not even have met, but whom you would consider your *A-list "dream team" mentors*. These could include the student senate president, endowed professors, department chairs, deans, your university's provost or president, distant relatives or acquaintances who are leaders in their fields, leading professors in your major who are at other universities, government officials, department heads, and professionals in your specific career trajectory.

Include their names (or titles if you don't know know their names) and why you've listed them on your "dream team." Include the name of anyone you know who might help you make contact with them.

1. _____

2. _____

3. _____

4. _____

5. _____

6. _____

7. _____

8. _____
_____
9. _____
_____
10. _____
_____

Now that you have a couple of lists with current and potential mentors, think about how to initiate, develop, and nurture valuable mentoring relationships. This is vitally important for success in any field. The interconnections between people are the underlying network or grid that holds families, communities, organizations, and nations together. The relationship-building skills you develop while you are a college student will be of great benefit to you throughout your work life.

Initial Contact

In selecting mentors, begin by establishing professional relationships with them. In some cases, you will already know the individuals well, but you have not yet developed the relationship into an explicit mentoring one. In other cases, you will not know the individuals well or even at all. In these cases, you need to make your first contact and then proceed forward to develop the relationship in a mentored direction.

If you already have a developed relationship with a particular individual and would like to develop it into a mentoring relationship, meet with the individual and make this explicit. Communicate that you value the individual's knowledge, expertise, and experience and that you would like to have him or her as a mentor. Your relationship with such potential mentors may arise from course work, volunteerism, student organization activities, your part-time or full-time work, or your family and friend networks. These mentors will already know many of your strengths: your hard work, your positive attitude, and your commitment to excellence. The down side is that they may also be familiar with your deficits. Remember to choose your mentors strategically and play to your strengths.

If you have not yet met your potential mentor or, already having some degree of acquaintance, you do not know him or her well, you may make the initial contact via email, but it is best to have an in-person meeting. Express your interest and hope in having the individual as a mentor. You will need to help the individual get to know you and your strengths. Provide him or her with a courtesy copy of your résumé or vita.

Once you are certain regarding your mentoring choice, contact the selected individual and request a meeting to talk about your mentor's position and experience and your career progress forward into the future. It is best to request beginning mentoring assistance in person. If this is not possible, you could arrange a video or audio meeting. If necessary, communicate via email, LinkedIn, or other digital means. See what your mentor prefers.

Meetings with Your Mentor

- **Welcome meetings in a variety of places.** Your meetings will take different forms and occur in different venues. They may take place in person, in an office, at a café or restaurant, or even on the golf course. In many cases, your in-person meetings will be via Skype, Webex, or other digital formats. These can be time efficient, but you also want to have the occasional informal meeting over a meal or cup of coffee, if possible. Try to maintain a regularity of contact with your primary mentors (and, later in life, with your own protégés).

- **Schedule informal, yet professionally acceptable, meetings.** Occasional informal meetings help to deepen the mentoring relationship. But they should be done in a public place to maintain professional boundaries.

- **Be prepared.** Read what your mentor has previously recommended. Review your current and potential mentors' professional vitas and look over some of their work. Bring print copies of specific material that you have prepared for the meeting (your résumé/ vita, information relevant for the letter of recommendation you are seeking, etc.).

- **Ask questions.** Bring previously prepared questions to your meeting. Also ask thoughtful questions in response to what your mentor says. You want to show that you are listening carefully and that you have thoughtful, intelligent, and relevant questions and ideas.

- **Accept suggestions and criticism.** Listen thoughtfully to your mentor's suggestions and criticism. Be open to new and different ideas and information. In most cases, accept your mentor's criticisms and recommendations for change. If you really do not agree with a specific critique or need clarification, seek more input. Then reconsider the suggestions. You may still disagree, but you will have greater understanding upon which to base your decisions.

- **Take notes.** Write down the suggestions and information that your mentor offers. This shows (1) that you value your mentor's knowledge and experience, (2) that you are responsible and will keep a record of important suggestions and information, (3) that you are an active and respectful listener, and (4) that you are interested in what you are learning.

- **Be honest and open.** Honestly present who you are, what you have done, and what you do and do not know. If you are asked if you are familiar with someone, something, or some company, and you are not, honestly admit that fact and ask for more information. This shows that you are willing and interested in learning, and that you value your mentor's knowledge and experience.

- **Be positive.** No matter what, stay positive. Try to avoid saying anything negative about any person, class, department, or company—unless it is relevant to the specifics of your discussion. If you have specific critiques that you need to mention, try to do that in an empathetic and understanding manner so that your criticisms do not come across as harsh. It is not a bad idea to preface any negative concerns you have with a positive comment. For example, if you are asking advice about a co-worker you are having trouble with, say something positive: "John is such a friendly person, but I'm often distracted by his constant conversation." This is invaluable practice for your future.

- **Show appreciation.** Be appreciative and show it. Begin each meeting by thanking your mentor for scheduling you in. Mention your mentor's knowledge and experience and how much you appreciate his or her help with your project, initiative, education, or career. Conclude your meeting with a reiteration of your thanks.

Follow Through

After your meetings with your mentors, follow through. As discussed previously, you should immediately email your thanks. You should also follow up by acting on suggestions and sending updates.

- **Accept recommendations and act on them.** This is the largest area of response to your mentoring meetings. Make sure that you follow through with any tasks you have been given. If you are given the name of a valuable contact, make sure that you reach out shortly after your meeting.

- **Provide brief informational updates.** As you go forward with your mentor's recommendations, when you have achieved a significant milestone (e.g., added that second major, received a research assistantship, been selected for an internship, gained a second interview at a company to which you were referred), send your mentor a note informing him or her of what you have done and your continued appreciation of his or her help.

■ **Have a reasonable regularity of contact.** Remember that long-term mentoring relationships require regular contact if they are to be strategically effective.

Ending or Redefining a Mentoring Relationship

There are cases in which you will need to stop working with a particular mentor. In your life, you will have multiple mentors of different ilk and for different ends. Some you will work closely with throughout your adult lives; others will be there for briefer periods and for specific ends. There is nothing wrong with changing gears and working more or less closely with different individuals over time. This reflects the natural ebbs and flows of a person's life. You will be changing and maturing throughout your adult life, and your relationships will also grow, change, and evolve as needed.

■ **Natural beginning and ending points.** Many of your mentoring relationships will encompass a specific time period, such as collaborative work on one specific project, or mentoring assistance at one specific stage in your career. This means that there will be natural points in the process when the mentoring relationship will need to be redefined or ended. When possible, it is best to schedule a meeting for formal closure and your final thanks.

■ **Problematic mentoring relationships.** There are also those times when a mentoring relationship becomes problematic, unhelpful, or possibly even destructive. The problem may be as simple as conflicting time constraints that prevent a more involved mentoring relationship. However, there may be more serious difficulties such as a lack of responsibility on either side, disagreements that are not resolved effectively nor with mutual satisfaction, or even discomfort and distrust (e.g., undue pressure or even threatening language or behavior). In these cases, it is best to minimize or altogether end the relationship. Depending on the situation, you can either work to achieve a formal and mutually comfortable closure of the relationship or, when necessary, avoid the person outside of ordinary, public events.

Reciprocity with Mentors

Remember to find opportunities to help others.

Be strategic in your requests. Appreciate your mentors' time and efforts. Seek help when you really need help, but accomplish on your own what you can reasonably do yourself. If you've sought the help of one mentor recently and need some additional assistance, you might want to consider seeking out another. Everyone is busy, so don't take too much of anyone's time. Mentors have other responsibilities and work to do. Respect their time constraints.

One way to show appreciation for the help you have received is to pay it forward. As you near the final stages of your college years, there will be opportunities for you to step up and mentor beginning students. Do not wait for people to ask for your help. Offer your assistance when it is possible and reasonable. You could assist one new student majoring in your field. You could give snippets of advice on occasion when appropriate. Or you could give a formal presentation to a gathering of new majors.

Do not minimize the importance of your mentoring relationships. Relationships are valuable to the world. As noted above in this chapter, remember that what you do is never just about you. No man is an island. We are all interconnected in so many ways that we will never even know. Your mentoring relationships—when done honorably, reciprocally, collaboratively, respectfully, and graciously—really do help knit together the world.

Epilogue

> Think of yourself as on the threshold of unparalleled success. A whole, clear, glorious life lies before you. Achieve! Achieve!
>
> — *Andrew Carnegie (1835—1919)*

We are the music makers,
And we are the dreamers of dreams,
Wandering by lone sea-breakers,
And sitting by desolate streams;—
World-losers and world-forsakers,
On whom the pale moon gleams;
Yet we are the movers and shakers
Of the world for ever, it seems.

With wonderful deathless ditties
We build up the world's great cities,
And out of a fabulous story
We fashion an empire's glory:
One man with a dream, at pleasure,
Shall go forth and conquer a crown;
And three with a new song's measure
Can trample a kingdom down.

We, in the ages lying
In the buried past of the earth,
Built Nineveh with our sighing,
And Babel itself in our mirth;
And o'erthrew them with prophesying
To the old of the new world's worth;
For each age is a dream that is dying,
Or one that is coming to birth.

—*William Edgar O'Shaughnessy (1874), "Ode"*＊

＊During the 20th century, this poem was usually included in poetry anthologies in its shortened three-stanza version, which has been described as a perfect poem on its own. I love the full nine-stanza version, having first discovered it as a teenager. You can find both versions online.

We are indeed the music makers and the dreamers of dreams. We dream our dreams and sing our songs, and out of this, we become "the movers and shakers/Of the world for ever, it seems." As a professor who has taught literally thousands of students over the course of my teaching years, I want you and every student to have a great life and do wonderful things in the world, to follow your abilities, dreams, and passions so that you will contribute in big ways to this age "that is coming to birth." I want each of you to build on your innate talents and develop valuable skill sets for the forward progress of our technologically driven and globally rich information age.

But in order to do this, you must step up to the plate and work to make this happen. "At a moment when the number of students currently enrolled in [higher education] institutions across the globe is several times larger than was the case only a generation ago, there is unprecedented skepticism about the benefits (both intellectual and material) of a university education" (Collini, 2013, p. 1). Employers are assessing the job-ready abilities of college graduates and, in many cases, are rejecting job applicants as underprepared with weak critical- and creative-thinking abilities, poor writing skills, a mediocre work ethic, undistinguished teamwork and leadership experience, inadequate problem-solving skills, and a lack of entrepreneurial initiative.

Too many college students have already slipped through our fingers without making their college education work for them in big ways. Make *your* college education work for you and for what you can accomplish in the world. Work hard and develop the tools for your postgraduate life.

This book is a guidebook, a roadmap, a primer [pronounced primmer], or introductory/primary book to help you maximize the return on your college investment so that you can fulfill your dreams to become a most valuable player throughout your life. Remember that it is *you* who are the key player who must make this happen in your life. You are the one who must step up and develop the self-discipline needed for success in your classes, extracurriculars, and jobs.

Like the development of your writing skills, your development as an involved student, both in and out of the classroom, is a process. Continue to rethink what you are doing and how you are prioritizing and organizing your time. See where you can increase or decrease time for greater success. Revise your schedule when needed and add, modify, and delete activities. When mistakes are made, learn from them. Then step up and do better the next time. Don't stress too much: just enough for you to get

moving, but not so much that you are immobilized. Take time to look back at what you have already accomplished and learned. College is a great time! Make the most of it to have an absolutely wonderful and rich time in college and throughout your future.

O'Shaughnessy's beautiful "Ode" speaks very much to the transformational times of today. The world that we live in is changing very quickly, and there is demand for people with both a depth and a quickness of thought. Critical thinking, creativity, global perspectives, and a strong work ethic are all essential. Seek out opportunities to develop, expand, and practice your learning and various skill sets. Step up to do this throughout your remaining college years and life—a life that, thereby, will be a life rich in learning. In this way, your college life serves as the foundation and model for your life thereafter with high caliber performance on the job, committed community involvement, and continued growth and learning.

Take your classes and experiential learning opportunities seriously. But please remember that studying is your #1 job in college! Everything else is important, but how you study and how well you study are what are most important. It is not just the degree. It is not just the G.P.A. It is all about what you have learned and developed during your college years:

- Your creativity
- Your strong work ethic
- Your communication skills
- Your problem-solving skills
- Your time-management skills
- Your engaged interest in learning
- Your teamwork and leadership skills
- Your critical- and creative-thinking skills
- Your knowledge and developed skill sets
- Your commitment to excellence and success
- Your community involvement and "giving back"

The primary reason you are in college is not just to get your degree. The credentialing is important, but it is only a small part of your overall accomplishments as a college student. Prospective employers and graduate/professional school admissions officials understand this and take it very seriously. When they evaluate you for a job, a graduate school, or professional school, they look for evidence that demonstrates what you have learned, what you have accomplished, how you have performed, and at what level of accomplishment.

Did you receive As, but at the bottom end of the A grading scale—just good enough to maintain your high G.P.A. and to get letters of recommendation from your professors? Note that there is a world of difference between "good" letters of reference for the B+/A– students and the impressively stellar and distinctive A+ level letters of reference.

John was one of the top students in my Argumentative Writing class. He performed strongly in his debates and was a solid team player. His papers and assignments are consistently in the B+ to A grade range. His paper on marriage equality was especially strong. He is very bright, does his work very well, and maintains a perfect 4.0 G.P.A. through all of his classes.

This is good, but pretty generic. Virtually every letter of recommendation says these sorts of things. Note that nothing really stands out as terribly distinctive about John. Wouldn't you rather have the following written about you?

John was without a doubt one of the most impressive students that I have ever known in my 25 years of teaching. John's commitment to excellence is such that even as he worked on an otherwise "A" paper, he would come to my office hours to talk about his ideas and writing in order to improve his work to the highest of levels. This was especially true in his final research paper on marriage equality in which he demonstrated first-rate research skills, balanced reasoning, and sensitivity to issues of justice. His intelligence and critical-thinking skills stand out among his peers, even beyond that of the other "A" students. Regardless of the assignment, John always strives towards excellence in the best of ways.

If you work at the highest of levels, your reference letters will, in turn, be written with the highest levels of recommendation. Make sure that your performance in class, in extracurriculars, and on the job is exemplary and exceptional. These are the letters that will set you apart from the many other candidates for the jobs or graduate programming you seek. You want to be a go-getter in class as well as in your organizational involvement, and you want your professors to perceive you accordingly: as a go-getter who works hard, is committed to excellence, and finds passion in learning.

You want to walk out the door of your college with a great education and a great return on your investment. You want this, and employers want this. Robert J. Sternberg reports in *The Chronicle of Higher Education* that "employers want the knowledge and skills that will be crucial not only to a student's first job, but also to his or her second, third, and fourth jobs. They want a student who has learned how to learn and how to adapt flexibly to rapidly changing demands" (2013, n.p.).

Martha Nussbaum, the Ernst Freund Distinguished Service Professor of Law and Ethics at the University of Chicago, argues the importance of college in helping to develop students' abilities in creative thinking, creative production, and creative innovation—especially through humanities and arts classes. Pointing to nations that are raising the bar for education in their own countries, Nussbaum (2010) writes in *The New York Times* that "nations such as China and Singapore, which previously ignored the humanities, are now aggressively promoting them, because they have concluded that the cultivation of the imagination through the study of literature, film, and the other arts is essential to fostering creativity and innovation." The appreciation for the importance of creativity and innovation are extremely valued in today's workplace.

The most recent report of the state of secondary education around the world (Programme for International Student Assessment of 2012) documents that American students are falling behind their peers in many other nations. In a *U.S. News & World Report* news story about the PISA test results, the U.S. Secretary of Education Arne Duncan is quoted, "In a knowledge-based, global economy, where education is more important than ever before, both to individual success and collective prosperity, our students are basically losing ground. . . . The hard truth is that the US is not among the top performing OECD nations in any subject tested by PISA" (Allie Bidwell, Dec. 3, 2013). Commenting on the United States's scores, Angel Gurria, secretary-general of the OECD (Organisation of Economic Development) that administers the PISA test says, "This is not only a great loss to the American economy, it's obviously

a very great consequence to people's future . . . Poor educational performance limits access to employment and widens social inequality" (Bidwell, 2013). While student preparation in mathematics, science, and reading is less strong in the United States than in many other countries, college students who approach their college years in smart and strategic ways can achieve a college education at the highest of levels. In many cases, this may mean taking more time, more years, and more credits prior to graduation, but if this means graduating with strong grades, significant learning and skill development, great experiential learning opportunities, and a terrific job upon graduation, then the extra time will be well worth it.

You want to walk out the door of college with a great education that demonstrates that you value learning and will be an active learner throughout your life. Highly successful and creative people around the world demonstrate lifelong commitments to continued learning and growth and improvement. Ken Bain's study of such individuals discovered that central to their success is their openness to new and different ideas and change: "The deep learners we've discussed here learned to make wise judgments by making decisions and getting feedback on their thinking. . . . They engaged in a deep conversation with friends, professors, and themselves, imagining what no one else would consider and testing their own thinking against rigorous standards. Yet the progress they made depended on more than that experience or those conversations. . . . You don't learn from experience; you learn from reflecting on experience" (Bain, 2012, p. 163).

Reflection, thought, reconsideration, re-evaluation, reinterpretation, and new and evolving understanding: This is the learning process that reflects a maturation of thought freed from the limiting biases of rigidity and stasis. Utilize your college years strategically to develop your skills in creative, analytical, and critical thinking, for use both in your personal life and on the job.

Ask yourself some tough questions. What kind of life do you really want? Do you want to make a difference in the world? Do you want a life in which you gain the respect and esteem of those around you? Do you want to look back on your college years with great pride and satisfaction in your accomplishments? You can achieve this. Every student can achieve this. No matter what your major is, no matter what type of job you have, no matter what direction the trajectory of your life and career takes you, you can live your life in deeply meaningful and contributory ways to the world, your community, your family, and yourself. This is what I would like to see for you, for every student, and for every person: consciously working each day to make the world a better place, even just a little bit. It would make for a very different world, wouldn't it?

It all comes back to discipline, moderation, and balance. Maintain a victorious "can-do" attitude with a commitment to service, a continued development of talent, an intensity of effort, and the direction of passion. And remember the three S's for SucceSS in college: your Smart credentialing, Strategic skill set development, and Significant accomplishments that together will lead to your Successful college trajectory through college and eventually into the workplace.

So if you are interested in making college work for you, if you are interested in using college to develop and perfect your skills and behavior for excellence at school and on the job, and if you are interested in being a strategic student, then roll up your sleeves and get to work. Be prepared to take advantage of the different opportunities made available to you on campus, including serious studying, prepared and active class attendance, and valuable extracurricular involvement.

Like a solid and impressive building, your college foundation will be strong so that you can continue to build on it throughout your life. Like the foundation of a skyscraper or a tall oak tree, a strong and broad undergraduate college foundation will enable you to achieve great heights of accomplishment throughout your life. Have a great time in college, and make it work for you! Have a wonderful life and do many meaningful things! Forward and onward!

References

Frontmatter

Pace, C. Robert. "Recollections and Reflections." In John C. Smart, ed. *Higher Education: Handbook of Theory and Research*, volume xiii. (New York: Agathon Press, 1998). 1–34.

Introduction: Make the Most of Your College Experience

Alter, D. (2013, January 31). Why the January 2013 U.S. Jobs Report May Surprise You. *Money Morning*. Retrieved from http://moneymorning.com/2013/01/31/why-the-january-2013-u-s-jobs-report-may-surprise-you.

Bain, K. (2012). *What the Best College Students Do*. Cambridge, MA: Harvard University.

Bosanquet, B. (1901). *The Education of the Young in The Republic of Plato*. Cambridge, MA: Harvard University Press.

Brill de Ramírez, S. (2013, August 16). Interview with Henry C. Duquès. Unpub.

Carlson, S. (2013, April 26). How to Assess the Real Payoff of a College Degree. *The Chronicle of Higher Education*, A26–A32.

Cobb, S. (1921). A New Movement in Education. *The Atlantic Monthly*, 127, 227–234.

Cobb, S. (1932). *Discovering the Genius within You*. New York, NY: John Day.

Commission on the Humanities and Social Sciences. (2013). *The Heart of the Matter: Humanities and Social Sciences for a Vibrant, Competitive, and Secure Nation*. Cambridge, MA: The Academy of Arts and Sciences. Retrieved from www.humanitiescommission.org/_pdf/hss_report.pdf.

Coughlan, S. (2012, December 3). Downward Mobility Haunts US Education. *British Broadcasting Corporation News*. Retrieved from www.bbc.co.uk/news/business-20154358.

CSEQ. (n.d.) College Student Experiences Questionnaire Assessment Program. Retrieved from http://cseq.iub.edu/index.cfm.

Duckworth, A. L. & M. E. P. Seligman. (2005, December). Self-Discipline Outdoes IQ in Predicting Academic Performance of Adolescents. *Psychological Science*, 16, 939–944. Retrieved from http://pss.sagepub.com/content/16/12/939.

Farrell, J. J. (2010). *The Nature of College: How a New Understanding of Campus Life Can Change the World*. Minneapolis, MN: Milkweed Editions.

Gee, J. P. (2013). *The Anti-Education Era: Creating Smarter Students through Digital Learning*. New York, NY: Palgrave Macmillan.

Hansen, E. T. (2013, March 15). Top Students, Too, Aren't Always Ready for College. *The Chronicle of Higher Education*, A33.

Lewin, T. (2011). Record Level of Stress Found in College Freshmen. *The New York Times*. Retrieved from www.nytimes.com/2011/01/27/education/27colleges.html.

Nonis, S. & G. Hudson. (2006, January/February). Academic Performance of College Students: Influence of Time Spent Studying and Working. *Journal of Education for Business*, 151–159. Retrieved from http://web.ebscohost.com/ehost/detail?sid=5450ecc6-fe2c-4024-ba35-de1ab7c65d46%40sessionmgr114&vid=1&hid=123&bdata=JnNpdGU9ZWhvc3QtbGl2ZQ%3d%3d#db=tfh&AN=19949456.

Siemens, G. (2004). Connectivism: A Learning Theory for the Digital Space. Retrieved from www.elearnspace.org/Articles/connectivism.htm.

Thucydides. (2009). *The History of the Peloponnesian War* Trans. P. J. Rhodes & Martin Hammond. Oxford, UK: Oxford University Press.

Woellert, L. (2012, July 24). Companies Say 3 Million Unfilled Positions in Skill Crisis: Jobs. Retrieved from www.bloomberg.com/news/2012-07-25/companies-say-3-million-unfilled-positions-in-skill-crisis-jobs.html.

Zeiler, D. (2013, July 30). How We Can Fix Education and the U.S. Economy, Too. *Money Morning*. Retrieved from http://moneymorning.com/2013/07/30/how-we-can-fix-education-and-the-u-s-economy-too.

Chapter 1: Daily Habits: Fitness and Wellness

Ambrose, S. A., M. W. Bridges, M. DiPietro, M. C. Lovett, & M. K. Norman. (2010). *How Learning Works: Seven Research-Based Principles for Smart Teaching*. San Francisco, CA: Jossey-Bass.

Bain, K. (2012). *What the Best College Students Do*. Cambridge, MA: Harvard University.

Berman, A. & S. J. Snyder. (2012). *Kozier & Erb's Fundamentals of Nursing*. Upper Saddle River, NJ: Pearson Education.

Blake, J. (2011). *Life after College: The Complete Guide to Getting What You Want*. Philadelphia, PA: Running Press.

Cobb, S. (1932). *Discovering the Genius within You*. New York, NY: John Day.

LaFountaine, J., M. Neisen, & R. Larsen. (2012). Wellness Factors in First-Year College Students. *Headwaters: The Faculty Journal of the College of Saint Benedict and Saint John's University*, 24, 60–65.

Lewin, T. (2011). Record Level of Stress Found in College Freshmen. *The New York Times*. Retrieved from www.nytimes.com/2011/01/27/education/27colleges.html?_r=1&.

Linden, W. (2005). *Stress Management: From Basic Science to Better Practice*. Thousand Oaks, CA: Sage Publications.

Lyubomirsky, S. (2007). *The How of Happiness: A Scientific Approach to Getting the Life You Want*. New York, NY: Penguin.

Lyubomirsky, S. (2013). *The Myths of Happiness: What Should Make You Happy, but Doesn't, What Shouldn't Make You Happy, but Does*. New York, NY: Penguin.

Massoni, E. (2011). Positive Effects of Extra Curricular Activities on Students. *ESSAI, 9*(1), 27. Retrieved from http://dc.cod.edu/essai/vol9/iss1/27.

Parker-Pope, T. (2010, June 3). "Vigorous Exercise Linked with Better Grades" [Web log comments]. Retrieved from http//:well.blogs.nytimes.com:2010:06:03:vigorous-exercise-linked-with-better-grades.

Pascarella, E., & Terenzini, P. T. (2005). *How College Affects Students: Findings and Insights from Twenty Years of Research.* San Francisco, CA: Jossey-Bass.

Sander, L. (2013, April 26). Campus Counseling Centers See Rising Numbers of Severe Problems. *The Chronicle of Higher Education,* A18.

Selye, H. (1956). *The Stress of Life.* New York, NY: McGraw Hill.

Chapter 2: Class Performance: Preparation and Participation

Berrett, D. (2013, May 10). Students May Be Reading Plenty, but Much of It Is Not for Class. *The Chronicle of Higher Education,* A6.

McGraw Center for Teaching and Learning. (2012). Understanding and Overcoming Procrastination. Retrieved from www.princeton.edu/mcgraw/library/for-students/avoiding-procrastination.

Wei, F. F., Y. K. Wang, & M. Klausner. (2012). Rethinking College Students' Self-Regulation and Sustained Attention: Does Text Messaging during Class Influence Cognitive Learning? *Communication Education,* 61(3), 185–204.

Chapter 3: Academic Skills: Commitment, Time Management, Study Habits

Chickering, A. W. & Z. F. Gamson. (1987, March). Seven Principles for Good Practice in Undergraduate Education. Retrieved from www.temp.lonestar.edu/multimedia/SevenPrinciples.pdf.

Crede, M. & N. R. Kuncel. (2008). Study Habits, Skills, and Attitudes: The Third Pillar Supporting Collegiate Academic Performance. *Perspectives on Psychological Science,* 3, 425–453.

Drumheller, K., T. L. Hanson, J. Mallard, C. Mckee, & P. Schlegel. (2010). Cell Phones, Text Messaging, and Facebook: Competing Time Demands of Today's College Students. *College Teaching,* 59(1), 23–30. Retrieved from www.tandfonline.com/doi/full/10.1080/87567555.2010.489078#.UYV0OrWTghV.

Entwistle, N., J. Thompson, & J. D. Wilson. (2004). Motivation and Study Habits. *Higher Education,* 3(4), 379–395.

Gaither, C. (2006, August 11). They Do It All While Studying. *Los Angeles Times,* 11A. Retrieved from http://articles.latimes.com/2006/aug/11/business/fi-pollhomework11.

Kantor, J. (2012, September 6). Obama Girls' Role: Not to Speak, but to Be Spoken Of. *The New York Times.* Retrieved from www.nytimes.com/2012/09/07/us/politics/obama-girls-though-unheard-figure-prominently-in-race.html.

Lucier, K. L. (2011, October 5). Learn to Manage Your Time in College: The College Experience. *US News & World Report.* Retrieved from www.usnews.com/education/blogs/the-college-experience/2011/10/05/learn-to-manage-your-time-in-college.

Maes, N. (1986, August 3). Time Management Can Mean College Success. *Chicago Tribune.* Retrieved from http://articles.chicagotribune.com/1986-08-03/news/8602260008_1_time-management-college-students-college-success.

Nonis, S. & G. Hudson. (2006, January/February). Academic Performance of College Students: Influence of Time Spent Studying and Working. *Journal of Education for Business,* 151–159. Retrieved from http://web.ebscohost.com/ehost/detail?sid=5450ecc6-fe2c-4024-ba35-de1ab7c65d46%40sessionmgr114&vid=1&hid=123&bdata=JnNpdGU9ZWhvc3QtbGl2ZQ%3d%3d#db=tfh&AN=19949456.

Chapter 4: Strategic Credentialing: Majors, Minors, Skill Sets

Berrett, D. (2013, March 29). Double Majors Produce Dynamic Thinkers, Study Finds. *The Chronicle of Higher Education,* A20.

Blake, J. (2011). *Life after College: The Complete Guide to Getting What You Want.* Philadelphia, PA: Running Press.

Carlson, S. (2013, April 26). How to Assess the Real Payoff of a College Degree. *The Chronicle of Higher Education,* A26–A32.

Wagner, T. (2013). Tony Wagner's Seven Survival Skills. *Change Leadership Transforming Education for the 21st Century.* Retrieved from: www.tonywagner.com/7-survival-skills.

Chapter 5: Communication Skills: Oral, Written, Digital

Baron, N. S. (2013). Redefining Reading: The Impact of Digital Communication Media. The Changing Profession. *PMLA,* 128(1), 193–200.

Bean, J. C. (2011). *Engaging Ideas: The Professor's Guide to Integrating Writing, Critical Thinking, and Active Learning in the Classroom.* San Francisco, CA: Jossey-Bass.

Berrett, D. (2012, March 30). Freshman Composition Is Not Teaching Key Skills in Analysis, Researcher Argue. *The Chronicle of Higher Education,* A29.

Collins, J. (2013). "Reading, in a Digital Archive of One's Own." The Changing Profession. *PMLA: Publications of the Modern Language Association,* 128(1), 207–212.

Curzan, A. (2013, August 14). Dinging for "Grammatical Errors." *Lingua Franca: Language and Writing in Academe.* Retrieved from http://chronicle.com/blogs/linguafranca/2013/08/14/dinging-for-grammatical-errors/?cid=at&utm_source=at&utm_medium=en.

Elbow, P. (1981). *Writing with Power: Techniques for Mastering the Writing Process.* New York, NY: Oxford University Press.

Janzow, F. & J. Eisen. (1990). Grades: Their Influence on Students and Faculty. In M. D. Svinicki (Ed.), *The Changing Face of College Teaching.* New Directions for Teaching and Learning, no. 42. San Francisco, CA: Jossey-Bass.

Pearson Education. (2011). Pearson Writing.com: Writing Resources for Students. Retrieved from http://media.pearsoncmg.com/long/pearsonwriting/.

Shaughnessy, M. P. (1977). *Errors and Expectations: A Guide for the Teacher of Basic Writing.* New York, NY: Oxford University Press.

Silko, L. M. (1981). Language and Literature from a Pueblo Indian Perspective. In Leslie A. Fiedler & Houston A. Baker, Jr. (Eds.), *English Literature: Opening Up the Canon*. Baltimore, MD: Johns Hopkins University Press, 54–72.

Sternberg, R. J. (2013, June 17). Giving Employers What They Don't Really Want. *The Chronicle of Higher Education*. Retrieved from http://chronicle.com/article/Giving-Employers-What-They/139877.

Wagner, T. (2013). Creating Innovators: A Lecture with Tony Wagner. Retrieved from www.youtube.com/watch?v=jYTwLysgx5w&feature=colike.

Wiseman, P. (2013, June 23). Firms Seek Grads Who Can Think Fast, Work In Teams. *The Big Story*. Retrieved from http://bigstory.ap.org/article/firms-seek-grads-who-can-think-fast-work-teams.

Chapter 6: Campus Activity: Clubs, the Arts, Athletics

Astin, A. W. (1993). *What Matters in College? Four Critical Years Revisited*. Jossey-Bass Higher and Adult Education Series. San Francisco, CA: Jossey-Bass.

Caldwell, L., N. Darling, & R. Smith. (2005). Participation in School-Based Extracurricular Activities and Adolescent Adjustment. *Journal of Leisure Research*, 37(1), 51–76.

Carlson, S. (2013, April 26). How to Assess the Real Payoff of a College Degree. *The Chronicle of Higher Education*, A28.

Dana Foundation. (2008). Learning, Arts, and the Brain: The Dana Consortium Report on Arts and Cognition. Eds. Carolyn Asbury & Barbara Rich. New York, NY: Dana Press. Retrieved from www.wjh.harvard.edu/~lds/pdfs/DanaSpelke.pdf.

Hounsell, J., H. Christie, V. Cree, V. McCune, & L. Tett. (2008). "A Real Rollercoaster of Confidence and Emotions": Learning to Be a University Student. *Studies in Higher Education*, 33(5), 567–581.

Wang, J. & J. Shiveley. (2009). *The Impact of Extracurricular Activity on Student Academic Performance*. Retrieved from www.csus.edu/oir/Assessment/Nonacademic_Program_Assessment/Student_Activities/Student_Activity_Report_2009.

Chapter 7: Off-Campus Endeavors: Internships, Jobs, Volunteerism

Dingle, S. H., M. A. Eppler, M. A. Errickson, & M. Ironsmith. (2011, December). Benefits of Service-Learning for Freshmen College Students and Elementary School Children. *Journal of the Scholarship of Teaching and Learning*, 11(4), 102–111.

Khan, S. (2012). *The One World School House: Education Reimagined*. New York, NY: Twelve/Hatchette Book Group.

Light, J. (2011, May 16). Interns Get a Head Start in Competition for Jobs. Retrieved from http://online.wsj.com/article/SB10001424052748704681904576321543988841626.html.

Schnoebelen, A. (2013, March 29). Many Professors Say Their Students Lack Professional Qualities for Future Jobs. *The Chronicle of Higher Education*, A21.

Chapter 8: Networking and Mentoring: Teamwork, Leadership, Strategic Relationships

Carlson, S. (2013, April 26). How to Assess the Real Payoff of a College Degree. *The Chronicle of Higher Education*, A28.

Collins, J. C. (2001). *Good to Great: Why Some Companies Make the Leap . . . and Others Don't*. New York, NY: HarperCollins.

Quast, L. (2013). Debunking Common Mentoring Myths. Retrieved from www.forbes.com/sites/lisaquast/2013/01/14/debunking-common-mentoring-myths.

United States Office of Personnel Management. (2008). *Best Practices: Mentoring*. Retrieved from www.opm.gov/policy-data-oversight/training-and-development/career-development/bestpractices-mentoring.pdf.

Weiss, T. (2008, October 7). In Depth: How to Network Your Way up the Corporate Ladder. *Forbes*. Retrieved from www.forbes.com/2008/07/10/network-building-careers-lead-cx_tw_0710bizbasics.html.

Wittgenstein, L. (1980). *Culture and Value*. Trans. P. Winch. Chicago, IL: University of Chicago Press.

Zachary, L. J., & Fischler, L. A. (2009). *The Mentee's Guide: Make Mentoring Work for You*. San Francisco, CA: Jossey-Bass.

Epilogue

Bain, K. (2012). *What the Best College Students Do*. Cambridge, MA: Belknap Press.

Bidwell, A. (2013, December 3). American Students Fall in International Academic Tests, Chinese Lead the Pack. *U. S. News & World Report*. Retrieved from www.usnews.com/news/articles/2013/12/03/american-students-fall-in-international-academic-tests-chinese-lead-the-pack.

Collini, S. (2013). *What Are Universities For?* New York, NY: Penguin Books.

Nussbaum, M. (2010, October 17). Cultivating the Imagination. *The New York Times*. Retrieved from www.nytimes.com/roomfordebate/2010/10/17/do-colleges-need-french-departments/cultivating-the-imagination.

Sternberg, R. J. (2013, June 17). Giving Employers What They Don't Really Want. *The Chronicle of Higher Education*. Retrieved from http://chronicle.com/article/Giving-Employers-What-They/139877/?cid=at&utm_source=at&utm_medium=en.

Index